THE COCK MACHINE

and Other Plays

P L A Y S
T O
O R D E R

A Plays to Order collection
Published by Plays To Order
5724 Hollywood Blvd., Suite 109
Los Angeles, CA 90028
www.playstoorder.com

First Edition: April 2018

ISBN –13: 978-0-9984173-3-2
ISBN –10: 0-9984173-3-5

THE COCK MACHINE

and Other Plays

By Ross MacLean

HERO OF THE JUNGLE
DECEMBER WEDGE
NELSON AMERICANA
FOUR PLAY
EAST MONROE
FOOD
DELUSIONS REVEALED
HYAENA
THE COCK MACHINE
AN IVAR MEMOIR

PLAYS TO ORDER

Susan Barnes and Frances Bay in *Delusions Revealed* at the Odyssey Theatre, Los Angeles (1980)

TABLE OF CONTENTS

INTRODUCTION

By Sean Abley

I met Robert Patrick many years ago at an International Thespian Society convention. He'd decided, after spending years as one of the driving forces behind the creation and ongoing sustenance of the Off-Off Broadway theater scene, to spend time conducting workshops for high school students across the country. He convinced me I could be a playwright that day.

Upon my return home, I researched Mr. Patrick, beginning in the Capital High School library (in Helena, MT), which inexplicably had a copy of his play, *Kennedy's Children*, on the shelves. From there I discovered Off-Off Broadway at the local public library, and fell in love. To this day, three-plus decades later, I still consider myself a student of that DIY scene, and hold Mr. Patrick and his contemporaries, Sam Shepard and Charles Ludlam, in the highest regard as influences on my own playwriting.

And now I can add Ross MacLean to that list. I met Ross in early-2017 and at some point during our first conversation he mentioned he was a playwright. At that moment my brain pulled a very old memory to the front of the queue--somehow, someway (I still can't remember the exact situation), at some point over the years of being a working theater professional, I'd come across a copy of Ross's play *The Cock Machine*. He told me he'd had work mounted at La Mama Hollywood and at some theaters in NYC and Actors Theatre of Louisville and he knew Robert Patrick and holy shit I'd just met my second Off-Off Broadway playwright!

When I asked Ross where I could get my hands on his work, he told me he'd remained unpublished save for one play in an anthology years before. As luck would have it, my OOB DIY aesthetic had extended to the creation of a micro-publishing company as an outgrowth of my commission-based playwriting services. At that point I'd only published my own work, but on impulse I asked, "Would you be interested in having your work published?" He said yes, and now here we are.

I'm thrilled to publish this collection. Ross's plays are fun, funny, nostalgic, perfect artifacts of a time in American theater that also transcend the era to feel fresh today. I hope you enjoy discovering Ross's work as much as I did.

Sean Abley
Publisher, Plays to Order

FOREWORD

By Robert Patrick

I met Ross MacLean in the early 1970s when he was a stage-struck teenager hanging around an L.A. theatre group called La Mama Hollywood, doing any tech– or dreck–work which needed doing, just so he might be allowed to be there. Among the work he wound up doing was writing plays to be done by that theatre and then by many others–though never enough.

Looking back at Ross' plays, it seems to me that what they basically express is shock, sometimes stylishly teetering over into rage. He has had in the last half–century plenty to be shocked by, enraged about. I remember thinking, when I read his first plays, in which the characters talked about awful social and personal predicaments in a ticky–tocky dialect rather like Muppets, "This is the first playwright I've known who comes to us from TV." But Ross just this moment, in a chat (not knowing that I am writing this introduction), said that Thornton Wilder's *Our Town* is "absolutely one of my favorite plays." So perhaps his initial shock was that the world was so very different than an image of itself (*Our Town*) which it claimed to adore?

Ross once took me on a bright, chipper, daffily–detailed tour of Hollywood's Western Avenue, with a perky anecdote about every cigarette butt and candy wrapper, long before anyone had coined the concept of "performance art" or "environmental solo work," and was later endlessly informative and entertaining when describing the antics of the working girls and the paying–guest guys at a Hollywood strip–club on Ivar where he happened to be because there was tech–dreck work (running the follow–spot) to be done. Perhaps only Ross and his fortunate audience of friends remember that that building, now The Los Angeles Film School, was once where local secretaries went at lunch to earn "all the money they could wash."

As you may have begun to surmise on your own, Ross could have written *South Park, Married with Children, 30 Rock*. But they may someday be remembered, if at all, as far–flung offspring of the kind of original work Ross created. He is still with us to write down yet more of his unique observations. It seems that there is, and is likely to continue to be, still more to shock and madden him.

Robert Patrick
2018

ACKNOWLEDGEMENTS

Special thanks to Sean Abley, Tricia Stevens, James Dybas, Mark Finley, Rocky Heck, Richard Martin Hirsch, Ellen Nickles, ManuelaTheiss, James Shepard, Paul Silliman and Doric Wilson for their help and support.

DEDICATED TO

Robert Patrick

Smitty

William M. Hoffman

THE COCK MACHINE

and Other Plays

HERO

OF THE

JUNGLE

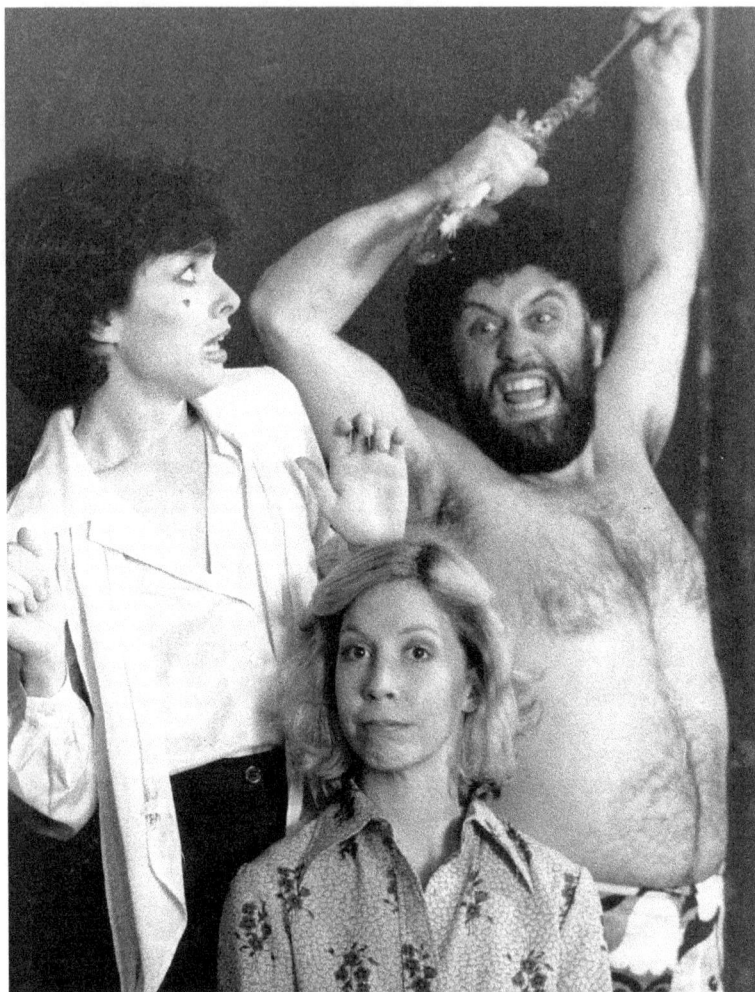

Anya Cronin, Karl Honaker and Kristine Callahan from the 1978 cast of *Hero of the Jungle* at the Deja Vu Coffeehouse, Los Angeles CA, (1974)

"Hero of the Jungle" was first produced by La Mama Hollywood at Theater Vanguard, Los Angeles CA, July 5, 1974 as a curtain–raiser to Robert Patrick's *I Came To New York To Write.* Scenery and costumes by Mystic Knights of the Oingo Boingo. The cast was as follows:

Katy	Lesley Sue Ferguson
Lucille	Jessica Miller
Suicide Man	Michael Dare
Bongo, Zumbo, Mugsy....	Roger Cruz

SYNOPSIS

Two women lost in the wild find a most unusual protector.

CHARACTERS

KATY

LUCILLE

SUICIDE MAN

BONGO

ZUMBO

MUGSY

SETTING

A jungle clearing.

HERO OF THE JUNGLE

By Ross MacLean

(*The scene is a jungle clearing; we see two beautiful ladies in semi–distress.*)

LUCILLE. Wait Katie, I can't go another step.
KATIE. Again?
LUCILLE. I have a rock in my shoe.
KATIE. We've got to keep moving Lucille. I think we're lost and I'm starting to get frightened.
LUCILLE. It's nice you work yourself up to things. Do you remember which way back to camp?
KATIE. Do you think we'd be lost if I did?
LUCILLE. You're right.
KATIE. Oh, we should never have left Chicago!

(*A GIANT GORILLA appears and harasses them.*)

KATIE. Lucille, look! What are we going to do?
LUCILLE. Help! Get away from me you big monkey– help!
KATIE. Don't hurt us.
LUCILLE. Oh, I wish I were at home in bed.
KATIE. Lucille, this is no time to be playing visions of leisure— help me be scared!
LUCILLE. Yes! Let's scream our little heads off, as if we were both city girls out for the first time in the real world and are about to suffer consequences for it.
KATIE. Yes! Help, Help!
LUCILLE. Get away from me– don't come near me!
KATIE. OOOooo!

(*The GORILLA begins to carry off LUCILLE.*)

LUCILLE. Put me down, put me down!
KATIE. I haven't seen such horrible things in movies. If only there was someone here to rescue us...
LUCILLE. Help!

(With the cry of the jungle hero, SUICIDE MAN swings in on a noose to save the day. He pulls a knife from his loincloth.)

SUICIDE MAN. Stop that: If you don't put her down and leave them alone, I'll slash my wrists!

(LUCILLE is released.)

LUCILLE. My Hero!

KATIE. Help– now he's coming after me!

SUICIDE MAN. Don't scream. Bongo just like to frighten people, not hurt them.

KATIE. Don't you think fear is harmful?

SUICIDE MAN. I'm here to provide safety, not discuss philosophy. Bongo, Go– be off!

(Exit GORILLA.)

LUCILLE. What is your name, strange hero?

SUICIDE MAN. I am Suicide Man, and I work to make the jungle a happy place to live.

KATIE. You have indeed brightened a portion of our lives.

SUICIDE MAN. Gosh ma'am, you make me blush.

LUCILLE. Oh, such boyishness provides much charm. What may I do to thank you, my strong man?

SUICIDE MAN. I have never accepted reward before, but a woman as pretty as yourself does make my spirit rise.

LUCILLE. Let me kiss you.

SUICIDE MAN. Heaven!

KATIE. Lucille, behave yourself!

SUICIDE MAN. A woman should not be left alone in the jungle, you world only provoke trouble. Why don't you come live with me?

LUCILLE. Could I do it? I was going to go back to the states, but I've never lived in the jungle before. It would be different.

KATIE. Lucille, I understand the temptation, but this man has only saved our lives. Now we must go home and continue them.

LUCILLE. Nonsense. He deserves a prize like myself.

KATIE. What is to become of me?

LUCILLE. You may go back home, like you wanted.

SUICIDE MAN. Or you can stay with us.

LUCILLE. Suicide Man!

SUICIDE MAN. (*Holds his knife menacingly across his throat.*) Don't be selfish– I love everyone, and they should all be given the same opportunities, when possible.

LUCILLE. Yes! Yes, you are a wonderful man. I haven't heard words more generous and true.

SUICIDE MAN. And they are spoken, I trust, for women of the same values.

KATIE. Who would have thought this to happen? Two delicate beauties taken under wing by a handsome jungle victor– and I had been working towards a business career!

LUCILLE. That was quite an ordeal we've been through, and it's gotten me excited. You'll excuse me while I retire to the powder room behind this bush to freshen up?

SUICIDE MAN. I'll go away for a minute, in case I should hear any strange sounds. (*He does.*)

KATIE. Since everyone is busy and I'm alone, I'll sit here on this tree stump, and file my nails. (*She does.*)

(*Enter ZUMBO, a wild jungle native who behaves accordingly.*)

ZUMBO. Omma Omma Omma! Omma Omma Omma!

KATIE. Goodness! The things that happen to a woman the moment she is left alone...

ZUMBO. Omma Omma Omma!

KATIE. Oh my... Nothing but a nail file to defend myself with. And I doubt this wild native has enough nails to make it a genuine threat. What can I do?

ZUMBO. Omma Omma!

KATIE. No, get away! Get your fingers away from my gorgeous and wonderful body.

ZUMBO. Omma Omma!

KATIE. Don't touch me! Put me down! First a gorilla and now a funny man: how much can go on in a day?

(*SUICIDE MAN appears with a book of matches.*)

SUICIDE MAN. Zumbo! What are you doing?

ZUMBO. Omma Omma Omma!

SUICIDE MAN. Release her— unhand her I say, or— Or I'll set my hair on fire!

(*KATIE is freed.*)

KATIE. Safe, thanks to you, Suicide Man.

SUICIDE MAN. What possessed you to attempt theft of my beauty?

ZUMBO. Omma Omma Omma.

KATIE. What flattery– What poetry!

SUICIDE MAN. No, just truth. Zumbo, this lady is under my protection. She is not to be harmed.

KATIE. —Or fingered.

SUICIDE MAN. This is another: (*Enter LUCILLE.*)

LUCILLE. Hello Zumbo.

SUICIDE MAN. Remember– Touch one of these ladies, and my head goes up in flames.

ZUMBO. Omma!

SUICIDE MAN. And then I would be overcome– I would fall to the ground and set a tree on fire. The tree would burn and fall, setting the flames to travel on their own, and then a rhinoceros would catch on fire, and he would run and carry the flames everywhere he passed until he dropped. The entire jungle would burn, but you wouldn't. You'd escape and have to live, always tormented knowing you had hurt so many living things.

LUCILLE. Poor Zumbo, don't cry.

SUICIDE MAN. It is all right. Go, and be happy to everything.

KATIE. Good bye, short native. (*And ZUMBO, humbled, leaves.*)

LUCILLE. Suicide Man, you are an ideal.

KATIE. What did he want me for?

SUICIDE MAN. A volcano.

KATIE. Oh, then he wanted to warn us, didn't he? He was going to carry me away.

SUICIDE MAN. Yes, to the volcano. He would have thrown you in.

KATIE. I feel weak.

SUICIDE MAN. No, feel strong and alive! Don't let a missed adventure ruin your day!

KATIE. You make me feel so good!

LUCILLE. Now what about this volcano? Are we safe here?

SUICIDE MAN. Yes. That volcano hasn't erupted. Zumbo, like so many of us, just hopes to satisfy an overpowering greatness that he cannot understand. He wants to give to an urge what would be most valuable to him, were it his to give.

LUCILLE. All that, and wisdom too.

KATIE. We do have a prize.

SUICIDE MAN. Ladies, I can't tell if I am embarrassed or ashamed. Sometimes I think I am like this only to win your flattery.

LUCILLE. No indeed– we love you.

KATIE. Life in the city is so different. It is precarious, but... here in the wilds of the jungle I've had my life threatened twice in the last fifteen minutes, without an automobile in sight. It's exhilarating– and all thanks to you.

SUICIDE MAN. Yes. Let's go away now, to our house. Do you want to go and see your new home?

LUCILLE. Yes!

KATIE. Lucille, what about the camp? I want to stay here as much as you do, but we can't just disappear.

LUCILLE. Why not?

KATIE. It doesn't seem right. We'll be declared dead and our belongings will be willed to all the wrong people.

KATIE. So?

KATIE. The men will worry over us. We should go tell them.

LUCILLE. They can hang.

SUICIDE MAN. That is fierce talk. Be nice.

(*Enter MUGSY.*)

MUGSY. Katie! Lucille! I've been so worried. (*He pulls a gun.*) You're safe. Get over here, are you all right?

LUCILLE. Mugsy, this is a friend of ours. This is Mugsy. Mugsy, this is Suicide Man.

SUICIDE MAN. Hello.

MUGSY. Get away. Come on, we've got to get back to the states.

LUCILLE. Mugsy, I am not coming. I'm staying here to live with Suicide Man.

MUGSY. What?

KATIE. (*Reluctant.*) I am too.

MUGSY. What is this, I'll blow his brains out.

KATIE. What for?

LUCILLE. Mugsy, I love this man. I want to stay here with him. Don't shoot. (*She stands in front of SUICIDE MAN.*)

SUICIDE MAN. Get out of the way Lucille. You could get hurt.

LUCILLE. Drop the gun Mugsy. We're not going.

SUICIDE MAN. I'm so afraid...

KATIE. Suicide Man, what's wrong with you? Why don't you defend yourself?

(*Now comes the exciting action section. Try this: MUGSY aims his gun. KATIE, who isn't watching him, runs angrily at SUICIDE MAN. SUICIDE MAN sees KATIE could be in danger, so he knocks the gun out of MUGSY's hand and grabs it. He stands holding it, and regains his heroic and harmless manner.*)

SUICIDE MAN. Don't you think I deserve the same protection I provide for others? It would have been nice to have someone do it for me. (*He puts the gun to his own head.*) Now go away. (*MUGSY stares.*) Go, or I'll shoot. I'm not kidding.

MUGSY. Katie... Lucille... (*He runs off, defeated. SUICIDE MAN lowers the gun from his head, relieved.*)

LUCILLE. My champion.

SUICIDE MAN. Now we are together, and we can all be happy.

LUCILLE. We can start our new life of adventure in the jungle.

(*Suddenly, a rumble is heard.*)

SUICIDE MAN. Look– That noise! The volcano is erupting!

LUCILLE. Is there anywhere we can go to be safe?

SUICIDE MAN. Yes. Let's go to our new home, high in a tree.

LUCILLE. Let's go!

KATIE. I feel self–conscious.

LUCILLE. No time to be prim when our lives are in danger and our hearts are a–throb.

SUICIDE MAN. I'll keep us safe.

KATIE. I can't go.

SUICIDE MAN. I'll cut off my foot.

KATIE. I won't take a step.

SUICIDE MAN. I'll give you mine.

KATIE. (*Grabs SUICIDE MAN's knife and threatens herself.*) Suicide Man!

LUCILLE. Katie! (*Points the gun to herself, threatening KATIE.*)

SUICIDE MAN. Girls! (*He is astonished.*)

(*BLACKOUT.*)

END OF PLAY

DECEMBER
WEDGE

Debora Klose and Dave Nicholson in *December Wedge* at the Deja Vu Coffeehouse, Hollywood, CA. (1978) Photo credit: Meredith Tovatt

December Wedge was first performed at the Deja Vu Coffeehouse, Hollywood, CA on Dec. 19, 1975 and again on November 26, 1978.

1975 - Directed by Foxxe Marshall

Frank.............　　Foxxe Marshall
Joy................　　Linde Smith
Mexican Lady...　Carmen Ruggiero

1978 - Directed by Foxxe Marshall

Frank............　Dave Nicholson
Joy...............　Deborah Klose
Mexican Lady...　Rene Avery

SYNOPSIS

It's Christmas Eve in Hollywood, and two homeless people struggle to find some comfort in survival.

CHARACTERS

FRANK (m)   Homeless alcoholic. Whatever age he is, life's difficulties have made him look at least ten years older. Thin coat and torn shoes.

JOY (f)   Similar in age to Frank, and same life description. Long ragged coat, has managed to find some scrap of Christmas decoration to stick on herself.

MEXICAN LADY (f)   Age range consistent with the others. Adequately dressed for a minimum-wage job.

SETTING

The main playing area is a small, tight corner in the back alley of the Citizen News building in Hollywood. There is a single caged light on the cinder block wall. Not a spec of comfort about it. Bits of garbage here and there, but otherwise stark.

DECEMBER WEDGE

By Ross MacLean

SCENE ONE

(*The scene is the back alley of the Citizen News Building in Hollywood, CA. Filthy beyond repair. It is a cold dark afternoon, December 24. Seated among the scum and wrapped in newspaper is FRANK. He is trying to get warm. He throws the newspapers from himself.*)

FRANK. Aaah. They don't keep fish warm either.

(*He takes the papers and begins stuffing then into his shoes and sleeves. He hears someone coming; reacts. An invasive sound of some one banging hubcaps together.*)

JOY. (*Calling.*) Deck the halls! Do you hear me? It's the holiday, are you back here?
FRANK. Oh Christ...

(*He shoves all the papers and whatever personal belongings he may have behind a board, and squeezes himself against the wall holding a piece of the newspaper over him as if he were reading it. JOY makes her entrance with a sprig of tinsel in her hair. We may suspect that she is slightly tipsy.*)

JOY. I am the ghost of December Twenty-Four! Don't you do anything but hide?
FRANK. What are you here for?
JOY. I am Joy, the holiday spirit. Merry Christmas.
FRANK. Get out of here with that.
JOY. (*Relaxing her posture.*) This is not the real me you're seeing.
FRANK. Wish it was true. You can go back the way you came.
JOY. Already? I just got here.

(*She throws down her hubcaps, making a loud crash.*)

FRANK. No mistake about that.

JOY. You aren't kidding. Frank, it's Christmas.

FRANK. What's that got to do with anything?

JOY. I thought I'd come see you. See how you been.

FRANK. (*Not impressed at all.*) Thanks a lot.

JOY. How you been?

FRANK. Cold.

JOY. It's not so cold if you go out. You want to come with me?

FRANK. I don't want to go anywhere.

JOY. The Salvation Army Band's playing at the corner of Hollywood and Vine. They're not too bad.

FRANK. Then go listen to 'em. I'm staying.

JOY. Do I have to drag you out to get you to do anything? (*She starts to do that.*) Come on, Frank!

FRANK. Goddamit, get your hands off me!

JOY. You're frozen

FRANK. Don't you ever touch me!

(*She takes off a sweater and gives it to him to wear.*)

JOY. Here. Warm yourself up.

FRANK. I don't want your god-ugly sweater.

JOY. Your fingers are stiff enough to break. Don't you ever leave this alley?

FRANK. Don't worry about it.

JOY. Why don't you take care of yourself?

FRANK. I'm living aren't I?

JOY. You could be doing better.

FRANK. So what?

JOY. Here, do you want a cigarette? Put something warm in you.

FRANK. Thanks. Thanks a lot.

JOY. They're my best friend.

FRANK. I said thanks.

JOY. Have you been out at all? The streets decorated up so pretty. And all the people with their bags of boxes. You'd really think they were doing something.

FRANK. I was up a couple nights ago, real late. There was just the street lights. Looked like a lot of junk.

JOY. Of course it looks like that if it's not lit up. That's all it is anyway. Do you feel all right?

FRANK. No. I want a drink. I haven't had anything for three days. My stomach's burning like one big hole.

JOY. I'm sorry, I don't know what I can do.

FRANK. You could get me something.

JOY. I don't have any money. If I did—

FRANK. Yeah, if I did I would too. Why don't you go and get some then, you're so hot for going out.

JOY. Just smoke. That's something at least. Breathe deep so it gets in your stomach.

FRANK. Won't you get me anything?

JOY. Get it yourself it means so much.

FRANK. You know what it's like.

JOY. Sorry. Sure you don't want to come hear the band? They're playing our music.

FRANK. Too cold to go out. Where's all the Hollywood sunshine? Summer all year long, it's a lot of crap. It's freezing.

JOY. It's winter.

FRANK. Tell me. And it might rain tonight.

JOY. It won't rain. Can't rain on a holiday.

FRANK. Might as well.

JOY. If you came out, people will give you money. They'll take care of you this time of year.

FRANK. They don't care.

JOY. So what? They give you the money.

FRANK. I don't like the way they look at me.

JOY. Oh! Aren't you the proud one—

FRANK. Shut up—

JOY. Can't stand to support yourself and I should do it for you?

FRANK. Get out if you're going to bother me.

JOY. People spend all year building up to this holiday and now's when they're about to let it all go. You should be there to catch what you can. That's the Christmas Way!

FRANK. No it's not, it's not right. I don't believe in it anyway. They might think they're doing something, but they just do it. They don't mean it.

JOY. What do you want Frank, sentiment? Some of that Holiday Love?

FRANK. Don't make fun of me.

JOY. People have gone on about that for years Frank, give it up. If spirit is cash, take it, it can't hurt you.

FRANK. (*A short gasp from his stomach pain.*) Aah. It burns.

JOY. Have you eaten anything?

FRANK. Why? What do you have on you?

JOY. Nothing. If I did—

FRANK. Yeah, if you did, I know. It's easy to be generous when you got nothing. And you don't seem to mind keeping it that way either.

JOY. What am I supposed to do? You want me to go out and get it for you?

FRANK. Gosh, that's real nice of you, Joy—

JOY. You crack me up! I'll go if you will. Fair?

FRANK. Uh, can't go. That's OK.

JOY. Sure come on while it's still daylight. Down at the Max Factors they have the prettiest display of a perfume bottle sitting in some snow, with a mirror in the back and plastic icicles hanging all around the top. The whole boulevard's done up like that.

FRANK. You mean you take time to stop and look in windows?

JOY. Sure. What else can I do with them?

FRANK. You stand outside at windows where people can— look at you?

JOY. They don't look. Get up, you can lean on me and we'll go out and see the people.

FRANK. Yeah, you and me hobbling down the street. People would get a kick out of that.

JOY. They would not. (*She is not sure if that is true.*) You've been back here so long you don't know what it's like.

 FRANK. I told you. I was out.

JOY. Yeah, but you wait till there's no people.

FRANK. I know what they're like.

JOY. Is there something wrong with you you're not telling me about?

FRANK. I told you what I want.

JOY. Yeah, but what else? You don't look good.

FRANK. Hell woman, I'm living in the trash. I don't care how I look. And what did you eat today you're so hopped up?

JOY. Nothing. Not much I mean, I... It's Christmas and so I was paying more attention to everything around me than how I felt...

FRANK. Ass.

JOY. Is that what's wrong? You haven't eaten have you? For how long?

FRANK. Why do you want to know?

JOY. Well, you're in fine shape. Alkie with your gut rotting out and no food in you either for— how long?

FRANK. Three days.

JOY. Three days! That's a riot, and you sit back here with coins walking the street? What do you think this is, Lent?

FRANK. Stop.

JOY. Stop? Like you? You ought to get out where there's life going on. How do you expect to stay alive, there's no food back here, and sure no people come by.

FRANK. You did.

JOY. Someone has to.

FRANK. I've had enough of you. You drive me up a wall.

JOY. Good luck you could make it.

FRANK. Get out of here.

JOY. What?

FRANK. Go away. You bothered me long enough.

JOY. Wait— I didn't mean to bug you, I just got carried away.

FRANK. Well carry on! –that way, with the rest of those jerks.

JOY. No, you don't want me to leave do you? Not for good. It's Christmas Eve.

FRANK. What does that have to do with anything?

JOY. People should be together.

FRANK. Yeah, well you said there was a lot of 'em out on the street. Go get together with them.

JOY. I'd rather stay with you.

FRANK. Go to hell. (*Pause.*)

JOY. I better go. (*No reaction.*) Yes, I better go.

(*FRANK gasps again from his stomach pain. He tries to stifle it and ignores the lady.*)

JOY. Frank, I don't want to be by myself.

(*He doesn't stir. She turns to leave.*)

FRANK. Joy— let me have a cigarette.

JOY. What's wrong with the one you got?

FRANK. For later on. Thanks.

JOY. You can't stay like this Frank. Not tonight. It's going to be very cold.

FRANK. It's going to rain.

JOY. Let me stay with you.

FRANK. If you get me something.

JOY. Sure, if that's the way you want it.

FRANK. No really Joy, this is serious. I haven't had a thing in three days. Not even a drink. I had some water; it hurts.

JOY. Yeah, I'm hungry too, it's kind of a permanent state, isn't it. I'll go see what I can get up. You know, I might even be able to get a tree.

FRANK. A what?

JOY. A tree. You know, a Christmas tree. If there's leftovers at the lot I'm sure I could grab one.

FRANK. What do you want with a tree?

JOY. It's Christmas. We can have a celebration, do you think?

FRANK. Forget the celebration, just get some food.

JOY. Sure! That's part of it too. And... I bet I could find some decorations. Yeah. It would be just like I had a house of my own, sort of, only...

FRANK. Don't be ridiculous.

JOY. Why not? If I can't do much I want to do as much as I can at least.

FRANK. Just try for some substance woman. I don't have a thing in me and it's tearing me up.

JOY. I know. I'll take care of you. People will help me out. I want it to be just like when I was little. A candle. Some lights, a Nativity. There must be someone around who doesn't need those things.

FRANK. I don't.

JOY. Then I'll have to find someone who is very much like you. And I'll take theirs.

FRANK. You're going to spend your time looking for that?

JOY. Sure! That's what it used to be like, I remember.

FRANK. It's not like it used to be.

JOY. Few things are.

FRANK. When I was a kid we didn't believe in anything, but Santa brought us lots of fruit and nuts, and some meat, real meat, and cigarettes if we were really good, and wine too...

JOY. How nice. Things sure have changed, haven't they. We can do it though. We can make some happiness for ourselves. It's those extra things that make it a holiday, you know, things like the tinsel and the Salvation Army and the plastic snow.

FRANK. I don't know if I can stand any more.

JOY. Sure you can. You just haven't had enough that's all. I'll have to do all the setting up, but that's OK. Once I put all those lights in front of you you won't remember a thing about how you feel.

FRANK. Bring back whatever you want long as it goes inside me. None of that paper and tinsel, it makes me sick.

JOY. But I want it for the holiday! What do you want?

FRANK. Huh?

JOY. I told you what I want. If you could have anything you wanted to make you happy, what would it be?

FRANK. Another life.

JOY. No, really.

FRANK. Will you get the hell out of here? I'm starving—

JOY. Of course you are! Look at where you live. But don't worry when I go out, I'll bring back some real food. I don't mean scraps and diggings, but real food! I have a friend at a restaurant who's good to me. I won't tell you where it is.

FRANK. Anything, anything.

JOY. I haven 't had a Christmas in so long.

FRANK. This is not Christmas, Joy, this is survival! Poor people don't have holidays.

JOY. Holidays were made for poor people. Come out with me. If we don't have fun, at least it will be something different.

FRANK. I can't go out there. There's people out there.

JOY. You don't want to come look in the windows?

FRANK. No!

JOY. I'll go by myself then. You'll be surprised at what I can dig up. It'll be a Christmas like you haven't seen in years!

FRANK. I don't care for your Christmas.

JOY. Humbug! You remember that story? Well I'm going to show you just what humbug means!

(*BLACKOUT as she exits determinedly.*)

SCENE TWO

(*A back alley of among other things, a restaurant. There are three trashcans. JOY has been wandering for some time now.*)

JOY. Huh... It seemed a lot more hopeful when I started out... I know they would have stopped. I guess they didn't have the time. And pickings are miserable. What's the use? People who move that fast don't have time to drop anything... Still... I ought to find some scraps somewhere. There's got to be. Frank's starving and I'm not doing so well either.

(*She approaches the back door of the restaurant.*)

JOY. I hope the manager doesn't answer. He sure is a son of a bitch. Oh please be in...

(*She knocks at the door and calls.*)

JOY. Mitch? Mitch, are you in there? It's Joy! Is anyone there? Come on, answer the door, dammit Mitch!

(*She retreats and looks at the door.*)

JOY. Gone. They must have closed early. And all gone home to their...

(*Her eyes drift across the ground. She finds a pop bottle.*)

JOY. Five cents! There's a start.

(*She sees the trash, eyes it wearily: "Am I doing this again?"*)

JOY. I can't go back empty handed.

(*She goes directly to the can, takes the lid off and lets it fall. The crash annoys her. When she looks inside she is shocked.*)

JOY. Empty!

(*Entire confusion and dismay. She tears off the lid of the next can.*)

JOY. Empty... (*Just stares.*) What has happened. What's wrong, I don't understand...

(*She looks back at the restaurant door and back at the cans, reaching inside to convince herself.*)

JOY. How can this be, what— where did the— Trash collection! They took it away. What day is this? It is, it's— Christmas Eve! You can't collect trash today, why did you do this to me?

(*To the third can. She tears the lid off. It is full. She is slightly relieved.*)

JOY. Garbage. And I'm going on like this over a can of garbage. Please Mitch, you didn't forget, not tonight.

(*She digs through. There is just crap, and then she finds a hunk of aluminum foil. It looks like it has possibilities.*)

JOY. Mitch, did you! Bless you let's see. Cake?

(*She begins unwrapping layer upon layer of foil. That's all there is right through to the center.*)

JOY. Shall I ever give up hope? What else have I got to bang my head on? On Mitch...

(*Back in the trash again. She finds a couple slices of bread and a plastic bag of wilted lettuce.*)

JOY. Oh good. Is this any good? (*She tastes it.*) God I'm hungry.

(*She makes the bread and lettuce into a sandwich and nibbles on it while she talks, eating half of it by the time she is finished.*)

JOY. Should take this back to Frank. He needs it. This is awful. He must be wondering where I am by now. This isn't enough for a party. What was I thinking of? But there's nothing left anywhere! There must be, I've got to get it from someone. I'll have to keep looking.

(*She goes off. LIGHTS UP on FRANK in his corner.*

FRANK'S MIME: He has been sitting in the alley waiting for JOY to return. It has been so long he doesn't think she will, but he still waits, hoping. He is smoking the cigarette she gave him, and playing with the newspapers, making paper dolls out of them. His movements are careless but automatic, as his mind is miles away. He fashions a lady doll, and also one we can accept as a man doll. He holds them both, considers them. With the hand holding the lady doll, he takes the cigarette from his mouth and burns the face of the man doll with it. He stops, notices what he has done, and rubs the face with his fingers, trying to brush off the burn.

He notices that JOY has not returned.

Again he burns the face of the man doll with the cigarette, this time as if he has discovered a wicked thrill in doing it, but again he feels bad and tries to soothe the burn. He listens to see if he can hear JOY coming, he looks all about him as if he were in a great cathedral and was disgusted by it all.

He puts the cigarette in the hand holding the man doll and sends it over to scorch the lady, but he stops before it touches her face. He doesn't know why, but he is not curious over it either; his mind is miles away. He is aggravated that JOY said she'd come back and hasn't yet, and he has lost interest in playing with the dolls. The lady doll is stuffed in his shirt to keep warm, and he grinds the cigarette out on the floor, saving the butt if there is one left. He holds the man doll in front of him, looking at it; then he loosens his grip on it and it comes apart, looking like mangled paper bones. He looks once more to see if JOY is coming; then he throws the paper down before him, staring in wonder at the twisted pile.

LIGHTS OUT on FRANK.

Our attention is brought to the MEXICAN LADY who is standing at a bus stop. She carries a bright piñata, a medium sized shopping bag, and a purse.)

MEXICAN LADY. Where is that darned bus? They should have been here ten minutes ago. The kids will be driving Carlos nuts. I shouldn't have had to work so late on Christmas Eve, I missed family dinner. Well, I'll be home in a while, if that bus ever comes. Wait till they see what I bring them. Their eyes will light up when they see this. As long as I'm waiting, why don't I…

(She takes from her bag a small bag of Brach's candies which she pours into the piñata. She also puts in a dollar.)

MEXICAN LADY. For the lucky winner! I can't wait to get home— It's freezing out here. Why don't I call Carlos and have him come get me? He usually gets mad, but it's different tonight. He couldn't leave the kids alone though. They'll all come then! But that might spoil the surprise. Maybe I'll wait. Well, where's a dime?

(She searches her purse. She must put the bag and the piñata down to do this.)

MEXICAN LADY. Here's one. Is it coming? Maybe I should wait just a minute more. (*She looks.*) Let me call.

(She leaves the bus stop to go to the payphone off stage leaving her piñata and her bag. JOY has been standing in the shadows watching the MEXICAN LADY, and now that she has gone off leaving her wealth unguarded, JOY knows what she must do. Still holding close to her own bag of scrappings, she dives in to steal the goods.)

MEXICAN LADY. No! No!

(Obviously, she has seen JOY. She runs back on, grabbing at her things, tries to beat JOY with her purse, which is still open so some of the contents fall out. JOY also drops her bag, which tears

and spills. It is a messy scene. The MEXICAN LADY is screaming things like:)

MEXICAN LADY. Filthy woman! What are you doing? Get out of here— My poor children, you ruin the Christmas! Ugly, ugly lady!

(…while JOY is cowering and trying to scrape up as much as she can take with her. After she gets what she can and must get out fast she grabs the piñata and tries to make her escape. The MEXICAN LADY screams some more and grabs at the piñata. There would be a tug of war over it, except it is only paper-maché and it breaks, spilling candy and toys, which they both scramble for. Pathetic. JOY has everything she will get by now, and runs to leave.)

MEXICAN LADY. Filthy, filthy lady!

(And she throws a handful of candy at JOY. LIGHTS OFF on her very angry.

JOY stands alone, very heavy, and miserably bends down to pick up a few pieces of candy. She turns and walks quietly to FRANK's alley. It is night and only lit by a single light bulb on the wall. She stands before him in the cold.)

SCENE THREE

JOY. Did you think I'd be back sooner? (*No reply.*) I did too. Walked all over. I've been walking the whole time I was gone. It's been getting colder, and colder, and well… so I came back. Not that I wasn't going to, you know that, but… after I started looking for what I could find… There wasn't much.
FRANK. What did you bring me?
JOY. First I walked up on the boulevard. It was nice, like I told you. The band had gone home though. I didn't try and stop any people because I was so busy watching. They all looked so busy and just seemed to… walk on by. I started out all charged up, it

was almost like I was one of them, I... (*She trails off.*) It was all there, the excitement was all there, it just wasn't...Well, they kept it inside them, like it was all in their heads or something. But *I* felt it, somewhere I saw it. Are you listening to any of this?

FRANK. No. Go away.

JOY. I did, I'm telling you about it. So I went to the restaurant I told you about, where I have a friend? It's way down past Western, halfway to Vermont. I walked on Sunset. He wasn't there. I looked all over, I guess I was looking in the wrong places, that's all. There'll be a lot more tomorrow anyway. People will throw out more, waste a lot. I feel silly the way I marched out of here like that.

FRANK. You could have kept marching. You're no good to me here.

JOY. Look— are you hungry?

(*He gives her a look.*)

JOY. I got this Frank, it isn't much....

(*She holds out the sandwich. Frank stares at it.*)

JOY. There should have been more, but there was only one piece of bread so I tore it in half. I shouldn't have come back so soon, I'm sorry. Please take it. (*She would like to cry, but she doesn't because JOY is not the type to cry.*) Let me sit down with you, please Frank.

(*She puts the sandwich in his hand. He holds it. She sits down beside him, but not too close.*)

FRANK. (*Not looking at her.*) Thanks.

JOY. This is all I want.

FRANK. Don't stay. I don't want you to stay.

JOY. It's cold.

FRANK. I've lived through colder nights than this.

JOY. You shouldn't have to... tonight.

FRANK. Why did you come back here? Why don't you leave me alone?

JOY. Man's hardest enemy is the cold. I came back here for... some protection.

FRANK. There's nothing here that isn't anywhere else, so I don't see why you bothered.

JOY. It's not going to rain.

FRANK. I'm sorry if I'm rude to you, but I—

JOY. I understand.

FRANK. I appreciate what you did for me, but I like to be alone, so I wish you would—

JOY. Frank—

FRANK. Not right now, but in a few minutes, if you could go.

JOY. Please.

FRANK. I don't want to be seen like this.

JOY. It's all right, I understand.

FRANK. I don't want you to understand, I want—I like to be left alone. And you here makes me feel worse.

JOY. Why?

FRANK. Don't ask questions like that.

JOY. I'd think someone who spent so much time in such an ungodly place would appreciate a few signs of life.

FRANK. I don't belong anywhere else. This is where I live.

JOY. You belong to the world! You're alive Frank, and you should remember that. Don't hide back here all by yourself.

FRANK. It's warm for me. It's dark and I'm forgotten. No one knows the difference.

JOY. When I was out wandering around, I passed a TV store. They had a whole line of TVs in the window, there must have been twenty of the them. They were all on the same channel. I couldn't hear the sound, but the picture was a... poor... well a person like you are— he didn't look the same, but the kind of person that you— we— are... and he was locking up and smiling while a man in uniform asked him questions. People remember you. They know who you are. Only on TV you were handsome because he was only made up to look like that, and the sets cost a million dollars. We're famous on TV. People like to see us there.

(*FRANK makes some vocal reply and takes the first bite of his sandwich.*)

JOY. I have... well, here. Let me give you this.

(*It is a small wine bottle in a bag.*)

JOY. Don't look at what it is. Just drink it.
FRANK. How did you get this?
JOY. A few pop bottles here and there. And some coins I already had. It came up to enough.
FRANK. Here, take some of this.
JOY. No I couldn't...
FRANK. Take some!

(*She lets herself be forced into it.*)

JOY. I 'm sorry. (*Pause.*) It's past twelve. It's Christmas.
FRANK. I hate Christmas.
JOY. So many people do.

(*She takes a candle from her bag and begins to light it.*)

FRANK. I... I'm sick Joy. I don't like it anymore.
JOY. It's just cold. Nothing's going to happen to you. Just let me stay here tonight.
FRANK. I'm burning up so bad, and there's nothing there. How can I feel it when there's nothing there?
JOY. (*The candle is lit by now.*) It will get better. I'll take care of you.
FRANK. I don't want that.

(*JOY sits down close to FRANK. She takes out two cigarettes and lights them, giving one to FRANK, also handing him the candle in the same hand.*)

JOY. Here. Merry Christmas.
FRANK. Don't tell me that. Please.

(The only light now is from the candle, FRANK is staring into the flame. JOY takes a drag on her cigarette, looks at FRANK. She holds her hit, then blows the smoke so that the candle is blown out.)

<u>END OF PLAY</u>

NELSON
AMERICANA

Judy Kerr and Lupre Autajay in *Nelson Americana* at Smitty's Deja Vu Coffeehouse, Hollywood CA (1976) Photo credit: Loretta Ayeroff

Nelson Americana was first produced at Smitty's Deja Vu Coffeehouse, Hollywood CA on May 26, 1976, directed by the playwright. The cast was as follows:

Ricky…..	Bob Gossett
Dave…...	Ned VanZandt
Ozzie…..	Brian Tomlinson
Harriet…	Judy Kerr
Managua Joe	Lupre Autajay

Nelson Americana was subsequently produced once again at the Deja Vu in November 1978, with the following cast:

Ricky…..	Harry Hart-Browne
Dave…...	Brian Tomlinson
Ozzie…..	David Christmas
Harriet…	Deborah Klose
Managua Joe	Wayne Woodson

SYNOPSIS

A 70s update of "Ozzie and Harriet," the all-American TV family of the 60s.

CHARACTERS

OZZIE (m)	Awkward Father
HARRIET (f)	Cheerful In-charge Mother
DAVE (m)	Responsible Son
RICK (m)	Creative Son
MANAGUA JOE (m)	South American

SETTING

The simple living room of a 60s TV family. Sofa, chair, and simple furnishings.

NELSON AMERICANA

By Ross MacLean

(*OZZIE enters, approaches what he thinks is his loving wife from the rear.*)

OZZIE. How ya doing honey?

(*He kisses her.*)

RICK. It's me pop

OZZIE. Ricky! What are you doing dressed like that? It's still daytime!

RICK. Gee I know pop, but I didn't want to mess up my school clothes.

OZZIE. Harriet? Harriet!

(*DAVE enters.*)

DAVE. Hi pop.

RICK. That's not mom either. Watch out Dave, dad's getting jumpy.

DAVE. I thought I heard someone come in, was it only you? I was expecting someone else.

OZZIE. No, it's me. Hi Dave.

DAVE. Hi.

OZZIE. Where is your mother?

DAVE. She's not home.

RICK. She went to play golf with her club.

DAVE. Gosh Rick, what do you think she'd go with, a bat?

RICK. Sort of Dave, a few of 'em. She went with her Women's Club.

OZZIE. And you meant they were all bats, huh Rick?

RICK. Yeah.

OZZIE. Huh huh… little joke. Look boys. We have something to deal with here. Your mother is not home.

RICK. We can swing it.

OZZIE. But this is a very special problem. You see boys, I've been working on a little something down in the basement and I wanted to show it to you all today. But your mother suggested last night that I wait till we're all home and make it an event of family pride.

DAVE. Yeah?

OZZIE. And she's not here! I can't show my surprise!

RICK. Do you want me to show you a surprise? (*Lifting his skirt.*)

DAVE. We've seen it.

OZZIE. So tell me boys, how do we get through this big family problem?

RICK. I guess we wait for mom to get home.

OZZIE. All that time?

DAVE. But was that mom's car I just heard in the driveway? As a matter of fact, she should be coming in just about now.

(*HARRIET enters on cue.*)

HARRIET. Howdy boys. Hello Ozzie. I'm back from my golf game.

DAVE. How did it go?

HARRIET. I whipped the pants off 'em.

RICK. Sore loser, huh?

HARRIET. How have you been getting on while I was out? Everything OK?

RICK. Pop made a funny mistake.

HARRIET. Oh?

OZZIE. Yeah well, huh. huh huh... We ought to do something about Ricky you know. I came home and I thought he was you.

HARRIET. Do I look that good to you dear? And I thought I was getting old.

OZZIE. But he shouldn't be doing that in the daytime.

HARRIET. Ozzie, Ricky can do what he wants with my clothes when I'm not in then. You just make sure he goes into show business so we can be proud.

OZZIE. Speaking of pride Harriet I'd like to… you know…

HARRIET. Oh, now? All right. Boys your father has been up to some tricks and he's made something he would like to show us all. Isn't that right?

DAVE. Yeah, he already told us.

HARRIET. (*Glaring.*) Oh did he?

OZZIE. I'm pretty excited with it.

RICK. Come on pop, tell us about it.

OZZIE. Well, with all the American excitement over the big election, I got down and did a little work on *my* part, on *my* contribution to the citizen's effort.

DAVE. Then let's see pop, show it to us all.

OZZIE. Gee, do you think so? Hold on, I'll get it.

(*He goes out.*)

HARRIET. Now boys, be kind to your father. I don't know what it is, but Oswald is a naïve, simple man. In fact, he probably has no idea what he's made, so let's all act surprised to make him feel good.

DAVID / RICK. Sure!

(*OZZIE enters.*)

OZZIE. Here it is!

RICK. Gee pop, what is it? A little blimp?

OZZIE. No Rick, it's a hydrogen bomb.

HARRIET. That's wonderful Ozzie. Do you think the fire department will allow it?

OZZIE. Well gosh I don't know. You're the law student Dave, what do you say?

DAVE. I say we should call and ask.

RICK. I'll do it!

(*He does.*)

HARRIET. That was a nice treat for you to think up Ozzie. Won't the neighbors be pleased.

OZZIE. Do you think they'll like it?

HARRIET. Let's wait before we find out.

RICK. (*On phone.*) We got an H-bomb. What do you say to that? - They hung up.

DAVE. They're only civil service men Rick. They don't know much about accomplishment.

OZZIE. (*Bouncing the bomb in the air.*) It floats too!

ALL. My!

DAVE. Imagine: An H-bomb in my own house. I wish the guys were around to see this!

HARRIET. Well Ozzie, now that we've all seen it I think you should put it away til the fourth.

OZZIE. Sure, I think I—

HARRIET. Don't stall Ozzie.

OZZIE. But I have an important question. As you see, this is pretty lightweight, and I've got to make it heavier, but I don't know how much. So tell me this so I can get an idea: If an Italian, a Puerto Rican or a Jew fell out of an airplane, which do you think would hit the ground first?

HARRIET. Who cares! Get that down to the basement!

(*OZZIE exits.*)

HARRIET. Boys, your father has obviously flipped his lid. We ought to get rid of that thing, but I don't know where.

RICK. How about a Good Will collection box?

(*The doorbell rings.*)

HARRIET. Who can that be? Can things get more complex than this?

(*She opens the door. It is MANAGUA JOE, a friend of DAVID's.*)

HARRIET. Who are you? Oh, obviously you're a door-to-door salesman, must be the Fuller Brush.

DAVE. Gee mom, this is Managua Joe. He goes to law school with me.

HARRIET. Oh. Forgive me Managua. I'm sure you're used to little mistakes like that by now.

DAVE. Managua is from Nicaragua. That's in South America.

RICK. Gee! Do you live near Disney World?

HARRIET. David, I want you to know how pleased I am that you're expanding to inter-racial companions. Not like Ricky there, who limits himself to the strangest types.

RICK. Aw mom, I sit with my legs apart. I have to.

DAVE. Managua's not only a law student, but a member of a minority as well.

HARRIET. I spotted that right off. Tell me Managua, are you an Official Minority as recognized by the manipulative and brainlessly obsequious white masses, or is it something you were born with?

DAVE. What mom wants to know is, do you have your own college fund?

MANAGUA JOE. No at this time we do not, but I feel it is time for my people to stand up and stop being discriminated against. For too long my people have been oppressed and humiliated, simply because they are human beings like anyone else. Many of my people have been denied good paying jobs and positions only for the simple reason that they cannot speak English in America! Isn't that pure foolishness? The time has come for my people to rise and be treated equally, and since there is an imbalance in power, I demand that the gut-stinking supremacist white ninnys *hand it over!*

HARRIET. That's wonderful Managua. I'm glad you feel that way and I wish you the best of luck.

(*Enter OZZIE.*)

OZZIE. Oh hi kids, am I interrupting anything?

RICK. Dave's brought home a new friend.

OZZIE. I thought you looked familiar.

DAVE. This is Managua Joe.

RICK. That's my pop! I'm Rick.

HARRIET. What's surprising about Managua Joe here is first off he's a minority, that you can tell; but he also goes to law school with David.

OZZIE. That's nice. Tell me Managua, are you a genuine minority, or do you just think of yourselves as insignificant?

MANAGUA JOE. Yes to both questions Mr. Nelson.

OZZIE. How interesting.

MANAGUA JOE. And that's not all! Our race happens to be credited as the BEST LOVERS IN THE ENTRE WORLD! No one can make love as skillfully as my people can; therefore, our solution to this oppression is to BREED, and we will all have giant families and eventually not leave room for any human to stand on the face of the earth.

OZZIE. That's quite an ambition. We just have our two boys, David and Rick. That's enough for us.

RICK. My dad's a whiz! Pop, show Managua your latest!

OZZIE. Latest what? Oh, that!

HARRIET. (*Aside.*) It might be better if you didn't right now Ozzie. We don't know this boy. He might steal it.

OZZIE. OK.

HARRIET. Well Managua, now that we've had a taste of your background, why don't you sit here on the davenport with me and I'll show you what white families are like.

(*She gets out her pocketbook, the section with the photos.*)

HARRIET. Now I never keep more than a dollar in here so you don't need to look any farther than what I show you. These are my photos of the pets and our furniture. See this one here? This is Tennyal, our pet water buffalo.

RICK. The Bison-Tennyal!

HARRIET. Once the actual bicentennial was over we had little Tennyal put to sleep. Ricky has never forgiven us.

MANAGUA JOE. Speaking of water buffalos, may I use your bathroom?

OZZIE. Sure, go right ahead. There's towels on the rack.

RICK. I'll show you where.

(*He follows him out. HARRIET immediately opens MANAGUA's wallet, which she has lifted from him and pulls out the driver's license.*)

HARRIET. Fake ID. I know he can't be a day of twenty-three, look at this. David, what are you doing hanging around friends like that?

DAVE. It's a cover mom. The guys on campus see me with someone like that and they'll automatically assume I'm a liberal.

HARRIET. Are false impressions that important to you Dave?

OZZIE. Come on Harriet, Managua seems like a fine citizen.

HARRIET. Don't get me wrong. I agree that Managua has a certain degree of ethnic charm.

OZZIE. But Harriet, there's more to it than that. He's just as good as you and me. We've got to make adjustments so that, someday, we can all be equal. Think of it— Blacks, reds, yellows, whites, and Chicanos, queers and women all working together in social unity.

DAVE. Well pop, that sounds altruistic, but you can't assume that just because people are all people that they can work together.

OZZIE. Why not?

DAVE. This is how we figured it in sociology class. Look at it this way: You have a carburetor, an electric fan, a gooseneck lamp, a mix master and a vacuum cleaner. Put that all together and what can you make out of it?

OZZIE. Nothing.

DAVE. But they're all appliances. Now let's put that in human terms. You have a genius, a twerp, an ignoramus, a fool, an idiot and an asshole. What are you going to do with that?

OZZIE. But I'm a moralist!

DAVE. It's all right to want to even things out pop, I've felt that way myself. But it's the same old story. You give a guy an inch, and you loose the inch.

HARRIET. Speaking of inches, look over there. Sometimes I get quite a kick out of little Ricky. His eye couldn't be tighter to that keyhole if it were fastened with epoxy glue.

OZZIE. Yow! A family problem! Is that any way for my son to behave?

HARRIET. What's wrong Ozzie? You just said how you liked Managua Joe. Well, Ricky likes him too.

OZZIE. That's not right.

HARRIET. Ozzie, relax. I'm sure if Managua comes around enough we'll all be acting differently. Ricky there is just setting an example.

OZZIE. Gosh.

HARRIET. I'll take care of things from here.

(*MANAGUA enters, RICK, too.*)

HARRIET. Hello Managua. Enjoy yourself?

MANAGUA JOE. Yes. I find your American family a pleasure.

OZZIE. (*Aside to Dave.*) Did he say "pleasure" or "treasure?"

HARRIET. Ricky, it's time for dinner so you better wash up. Managua, it's been wonderful meeting you, but you'll have to go now. We don't like strangers around our table when we eat.

MANAGUA JOE. Certainly Mrs. Nelson. Goodbye.

(*He leaves, dropping a spoon or fork on his way.*)

OZZIE. (*Seeing the spoon.*) Hey!

(*He exits to the bathroom.*)

DAVE. What do you know…

RICK. What about dinner?

HARRIET. At three in the afternoon? That was an excuse to get Managua Joe out of here.

RICK. Hey, I think Managua's a swell guy.

HARRIET. So do I Rick, but we've got to take care of your father and that hydrogen bomb before we're all blown sky high.

RICK. Sounds like heaven.

OZZIE. Harriet! Did you put out clean towels?

HARRIET. Sure I did dear, why?

OZZIE. There doesn't seem to be any in the bathroom.

HARRIET. I know I put them in there, fresh today.

OZZIE. They're gone.

ALL. Hmmm.

OZZIE. Excuse me, I have some very important things I want to check on in the basement.

(*He goes out.*)

HARRIET. Well! It looks like we have a lot on our hands here boys, and I assure you that the quicker we clear this up, the happier we will all be. The best way to clean up is to get to work. David, you go and draw up a lawsuit, just in case that darned explosive goes off before its time, and Ricky, you run upstairs and write a hit song about world peace.

DAVID / RICK. Aw mom…

HARRIET. David, you could make a lot of money in a flash, and Ricky if you don't become a star, you will not only be a personal failure, but a disgrace to the family as well. So hop to it, *pronto!*

DAVID / RICK. Right!

(*They go.*)

HARRIET. Now I'm alone and I can think. My, life sure can get complex, can't it? That Ozzie— When I married a simple man I had no idea how literal that was. He comes up with an H-bomb and doesn't even realize. And for David to deliberately invite a guest over, and now our house is fraught with scandal. I'll just tidy up while I solve this problem. (*She gets out her dishpan and sponge, and washes a plate, thinking.*) Now what can I do about Ozzie and that ol' HB? If I plainly took it away from him, it may ruin his sense of accomplishment. But we can't keep it; if it went off, kaput goes the neighborhood. I couldn't let that happen. Mmm as I wash the grime off this plate, I know just how to solve this little family dilemma.

(*She puts away the dishes and gets out her wig.*)

Bob Gossett, Ned VanZandt, Brian Tomlinson, Judy Kerr and Lupre Autajay in *Nelson Americana* at Smitty's Deja Vu Coffeehouse, Hollywood CA. (1976) Photo credit: Loretta Ayeroff

Judy Kerr in *Nelson Americana* at Smitty's Deja Vu Coffeehouse, Hollywood CA. (1976) Photo credit: Loretta Ayeroff

HARRIET. This way I'll rid the house of the nuisance and give a boost to the family's spirit as well. And I'll do it all with this—

(*She puts on an enormous wig.*)

HARRIET. *Bouffant*!

(*Enter OZZIE. HARRIET has her back to him at the time.*)

OZZIE. Harriet?
HARRIET. ("*Freeze!*") *Ozzie* –Get a load of *this*!

(*She wheels around, hands on hips, immediately becoming an even greater sex goddess than Mamie Van Doren or Zsa Zsa Gabor. OZZIE is stunned by the beauty of her fresh new hairstyle.*)

HARRIET. What is it Ozzie?
OZZIE. Oooh, ohh I...
HARRIET. Come on Ozzie, speak up.
OZZIE. Harriet, you're— enchanting. I see a new beauty in you, what could it possibly be? Do I remember you like you were in college, or could it be— could it be...
HARRIET. Yes?
OZZIE. Or could it be your hairstyle???
HARRIET. Ozzie dear, I don't know what you're talking about. Now sit down here and tell Harriet all about that hydrogen bomb.
OZZIE. Yes. Anything. What did you want to know about it? Did you want to buy it?
HARRIET. Ozzie dear, I'm your *wife*, I already own half of it.
OZZIE. Oh, I see. Which half did you want, my dearest, my sweet, my pet, my love, my my my...
HARRIET. There there, I only want the half that doesn't blow up.
OZZIE. Why?
HARRIET. Oz, I can't lie to you. I want it for safety reasons.
OZZIE. Safe from what?
HARRIET. Why us of course. Do you know what happens when those things go off? Mushroom soup. Where do you think we'd be then?
OZZIE. Smithereens!

HARRIET. Indeed. Why did you make something so destructive?

OZZIE. Gosh Harriet, I, I, (*He is becoming further entranced and can only speak the truth.*) I never thought of it as something I had made, but rather, something that was always in me.

HARRIET. I see. Did you even consider your little spree might wipe out the neighborhood?

OZZIE. Harriet, there's even more to it than that. There was in me, a feeling so intense, that this monument was... an extension of myself, and what I feel. It's big, it's broad. It's something I can share with a great many people. Something I want to do, something I want to say!

HARRIET. Emotional fireworks, huh?

OZZIE. Love of country

HARRIET. You poor dear, let other people take care of grandeur. Keep our home life nice.

OZZIE. I do, I do.

HARRIET. This— "extending yourself"— you already have one and a half fine sons, and a fine wife to boot. Should you need more than that? You shouldn't have a care in the world, so just go about your life. Little people with big ideas just get in the way, understand?

OZZIE. Harriet, you're so beautiful you must be right. Who else could put it so honestly, and curtly? I know it is the truth because you are such an attractive person, and that assures pure thought. That kind of thinking is best, I think.

HARRIET. Right. Now stop your prattle and bring me that bomb.

OZZIE. OK.

HARRIET. All right. Now to keep things rolling: David!

DAVE. Yes mom?

HARRIET. How are you coming with that report?

DAVE. Swell. I got one that should send pop up the river for good.

HARRIET. David, you get so ahead of yourself. For shame you'd do such a thing to your own father.

DAVE. All you said was to "make a lot of money."

HARRIET. I'm afraid it didn't make myself clear. We don't want the blame to fall on your father. See that it falls on someone else instead.

DAVE. Like Ricky?

HARRIET. David, settle down! Come here and look at me.

(*He does. He too is mesmerized by HARRIET's bouffant.*)

DAVE. Gosh!
HARRIET. I know. Dave, I meant someone entirely outside the family, do you understand that?
DAVE. Oooh...
HARRIET. Uh huh. Now think hard Dave, think of all the different people you have come in contact with during, let's say... the last fifteen minutes. Can you think of anyone, possibly, that you would like to see behind bars?
DAVE. Um um um... !
HARRIET. Good. Go to your room and bring me back a box and some postage stamps.

(*He goes.*)

HARRIET. Two down and one to go: Ricky!
RICK. Hi mom!
HARRIET. Ricky, come in here a minute.
RICK. Sure!
HARRIET. Now look at me.

(*He does. He too is stunned.*)

HARRIET. Notice anything different?
RICK. Beauty! Faith! Trust! Oh lord lord.
HARRIET. Of course. Now Ricky, what I called you in for is I need a little help with a small practical joke I want to play. So I'm going to need a very important piece of information that I'm sure you have. Would you give it to me?
RICK. What is it?
HARRIET. I want Managua Joe's address and phone number.
RICK. (*On guard through trance.*) Whatever for?
HARRIET. (*Forcing the power of the bouffant.*) I need it.
RICK. What makes you so sure I have it?
HARRIET. I saw you follow him to the bathroom, now fess up.
RICK. Gosh!
HARRIET. Well?
RICK. But mom, but mom, you're not going to— you don't want it for him; you're not going to steal him from me are you?

HARRIET. Why would I want to do a thing like that?

RICK. I don't know, and—

HARRIET. And what makes you think you'd have anything to do with him anyway?

RICK. I won't mom, I couldn't... But, you know, just that it could ever possibly happen in my imagination makes it worthwhile. And if you— and he— or anyone else for that matter were to spoil my fantasy then— then—

HARRIET. Ricky stop! Act like a man! Don't panic, I said "Act." What are you doing harboring fantasies when you are one? Be a hero, not a fool. Give me that address! (*He does.*) Thank you. Now go and don't come back until you can fulfill your purpose: Write that song!

RICK. I promise.

(*He is subdued under the power, and exits.*)

HARRIET. (*Takes stance and sings:*)
IT'S TRUE WHEN WE HAVE A GOAL AT HEART
THAT'S BEAUTIFUL AND PURE,
SUCCESS WILL STRIDE THE GOLDEN PATH FROM
YEAR TO YEAR TO YEAR.

AND IF WE DO AS WE BELIEVE
(NOT AS WE THINK WE MUST,)
THEN TRUTH WILL CROWN OUR GLORY
AS LAURELS ON A BUST.

BUT IF OUR HEARTS GET OUT OF HAND
AND WANT TO CHANGE THE WORLD
THEN THAT IS WHEN TO SETTLE DOWN
AND RE-EVALUATE RENOWN
CONSIDERING EACH HUMAN LIFE
AS SOMETHING LIKE A TIC OR MITE—

THEN SIMPLIFY OUR COMPLEX LIVES
BY PERPETRATING PETTY CRIMES.

IF MORALS EVER HELD US BACK,
THEN WERE THEY ANY GOOD?

OR DID THEY ONLY SAVE US FROM ACHIEVING
WHAT WE SHOULD?
I KNOW THAT FROM THE START OF BIRTH
IF WE'RE TO MOUNT TO ANY WORTH
CRUSADE WITH VALOR AND WITH MIGHT
TOWARDS DOING WHAT IS BEST
AND RIGHT!

(*OZZIE enters, with bomb.*)

OZZIE. Here you go, Harriet. Careful with it, like you said, it's a little touchy. I don't know what's come over me. I wish I could put my finger on what has suddenly made you so captivating.

HARRIET. Don't try dear, I couldn't guess myself. Ozzie, I want you to know I'm more than a little impressed that you could make something this— dynamic.

OZZIE. Do you mean it?

HARRIET. Oh yes. It's a lovely bomb Ozzie, just lovely. But I want to give it away to someone who I think would have a bigger need for it, OK?

OZZIE. What? What do you mean give it away? For free? Just like that?

HARRIET. Of course for free. That's the traditional way of giving explosives.

OZZIE. But my baby! My project! Do you know how much of me, of my own personal life has been invested in this? I was hoping to sell it.

HARRIET. You're such a sweetheart. I'm doing this to protect our cozy home. This is hot property! And we do want a cool life don't we? Easy? Carefree? Of course. So we've got to keep the house rid of all perverse elements, understand?

OZZIE. Well, if you say so.

HARRIET. And this will be quite a surprise for some poor, deserving citizen who only wants his due.

OZZIE. Consideration from a golden heart, my pet. Gosh, you know it makes me feel good to know that there are still people...

HARRIET. Yes?

OZZIE. ??? That's all I guess. It just makes me feel good to know that there are still people.

HARRIET. Wonderful, I'll bring out a few more of 'em then. David, Ricky! You want to come out now?
DAVID / RICK. All *right!*
HARRIET. That's the spirit.
OZZIE. Are we all going to sit in here?
HARRIET. Sure. This is an event the whole family can participate in. Why don't you go in and get some paper cups and soda?
OZZIE. A nutritional suggestion.

(*He goes out. HARRIET takes off her wig, and everything returns to a normal family atmosphere.*)

HARRIET. Ooo, that's cooler; makes me feel nice again. Ricky! Would you please bring some brown paper and string with you?
RICK. OK!

(*DAVE enters.*)

DAVE. Here I am mom. Look (*He means the report.*) All typed, double spaced, and in triplicate with removable carbon between each sheet.
HARRIET. That's a wonderful job honey, I can tell you're going to be quite a success. Let me check and make sure the name's right, not up to any tricks…
DAVE. Here it is!
HARRIET. My, but it's written big and clear. That's very good Dave, I'm proud of you.
DAVE. And not only that, but I brought the box and stamps like you said.
HARRIET. Superb! You know, I've cleared it all up, and we're going to pack off that bomb through the post to you-know-who!
RICK. Here it is. The brown paper you wanted. And the string too.
HARRIET. Thanks Ricky, you're a dear.
RICK. Uh huh.
DAVE. Hey Rick, what's wrong?
RICK. Oh nothing. Just a little disappointment.
DAVE. Cheer up, that's what life's all about.

HARRIET. I'm sorry if I was a little sharp with you Ricky, but everything's clear. The family's going to sit down and do some mail work, that should interest you. –See? Perked him right up. I have persuaded your father to hand over the bomb, and we can all live in peace.

DAVE. Hooray!

HARRIET. Oh, one more thing. Not a word about this to the neighbors, OK? It would make a laughing stock out of your father, and if that happened do you know what I'd do? I'd die. You don't want that to happen do you?

(*OZZIE enters with a tray of soda crackers and a jumbo bottle of cola.*)

OZZIE. Hi boys! Care for some soda pop? Diet!

DAVE. Sure.

OZZIE. And I brought a nice baloney sandwich.

RICK. Aw pop, you only brought one.

OZZIE. You can *share.*

HARRIET. Here we all are in our pleasant family get-together. And boys, your father has something special he wants to tell us.

OZZIE. Already? Oh, uh um. I just wanted to say that I have the greatest family around, and I wanted you to know that. I may have gone a little overboard by making a hydrogen bomb, but I only did it to demonstrate what I feel, for my family, and other things as well. But your mother, who is always on the watch for us, pointed out that this is a strength that we should share. Now that we've had our fun, your mother and I have decided— (*Reproving glance from HARRIET.*) I have decided that we should give it away to a needy family across town.

HARRIET. Charity is the spice of daily survival. And what spice-cake is this gift going to? Tell us Dave.

DAVE. My good pal, Managua Joe!

RICK / OZZIE. What? –

OZZIE. (*Fast to RICK.*) You stay out of this!

HARRIET. That's right. I can't think of anyone who deserves it more.

OZZIE. Harriet, should it go to that boy? Is that someone we should award? He was crooked! He stole our towels, and silverware! Shouldn't we give it to someone nice?

HARRIET. Ozzie, I realize there are a lot of people you think this should go to, but it's not being sent as a cordial gift. In fact, if all goes well, it should blow his face off.

OZZIE. That's terrible too!

HARRIET. More than that Ozzie, it's necessary. This is a problem we ought to nip in the bud. Otherwise, well... Do you remember just a while ago, your son on his knees before a closed door, straining to catch a glimpse while that foreigner was in there living it up? Is that how the future should be?

OZZIE. No!!!

HARRIET. All right. (*The matter is closed.*) Well, fellas, how's it going?

DAVID / RICK. Swell!

HARRIET. That's good. Rick, you about ready with that song?

RICK. I'll give you a song!

HARRIET. Then you sing it while we all wrap up this delightful gift.

RICK. (*He sings.*)
WE'RE PACKIN' UP OUR CARES
DIVIDIN' UP THE SHARES
TO RID OURSELVES OF EXCESS WEIGHT,
I HOPE IT AIN'T TOO LATE.

THE LIGHT IN HEART CAN SING
WHEN WORRY'S ON THE WING
AND WE CAN HOLD A BROADER SMILE
WHEN UGLINESS IS OFF A MILE
SO:

WE'RE HACKIN' UP AFFAIRS
A STERILIZING PRAYER
THAT WE COULD LOVE AND STILL FEEL SAFE
I HOPE IT AIN'T TOO LATE
I HOPE IT AIN'T TOO LATE
I HOPE IT AIN'T TOO LATE

HARRIET. Well isn't that a refreshing, spritely ditty. A real hoot, Rick.

DAVE. And so is this box, I might add.

OZZIE. You're right there Dave. If this is doing what I think it is, I'll hope to send out more of them.

HARRIET. (*Reminding.*) Ozzie— simplicity.

DAVE. Rick, come here and be part of this. Here, you write the address.

OZZIE. No, let me! I'll print it big. That was a great song Rick, you keep up the talent and you'll slay 'em! And stay away from strangers.

(*A knock at the door, RICK goes to answer.*)

HARRIET. That's right Rick. Keep your life simple and free of warped influences and you'll be a happy success.

DAVE. Who was that at the door?

(*RICK has returned with a wrapped package.*)

RICK. Special delivery. A Mission-Pac.

DAVE. What?

RICK. –From Managua Joe. Five pounds of dates! And I only wanted one…

HARRIET. Why that conniving little snipe! Let me at that report; I'll run off *six copies*!

DAVE. Hey, what happened to it?

OZZIE. I don't see it.

HARRIET. Where did you lose it? You know, I bet I packed it in the box. I get so anxious.

RICK. I bet you did. What are you going to do about it?

OZZIE. I guess we'll have to open it.

(*OZZIE, HARRIET and DAVE go to the box and tear it open. Of course it goes off, and so they must perish. RICK, the only survivor, takes the law paper from under his shirt and lays it on the table. He walks off strumming his guitar and singing.*)

RICK. (*Singing.*)
    THAT'S HOW WE LOVE AND STILL FEEL SAFE
    I HOPE IT AIN'T TOO LATE
    I HOPE IT AIN'T TOO LATE
    I HOPE IT AIN'T TOO LATE

<u>**END OF PLAY**</u>

FOUR
PLAY

Four Play was first performed at the Los Angeles Actors Theater on September 12, 1977. Directed by Bruce French, with the following cast:

Jim.........	Barry Michlin
Arlene......	Marion Scherer
Fred.........	Philip Charles MacKenzie
Molly......	Christina Callahan

The New York Production opened on October 4, 1979, produced by the Fourth E Company at the New York Theater Ensemble, directed by Bonnie Young, with the following cast:

Jim.........	Steve Nelson
Arlene......	Denise Galonsky
Fred.........	Kip Savage
Molly......	Carol Nelson

SYNOPSIS

Two married couples practice infidelity in every possible combination. But in this situation, practice does not make perfect.

CHARACTERS

JIM (m)

ARLENE (f)

FRED (m)

MOLLY (f)

SETTING

The playing area is divided into two halves: initially, the left half of the stage is the house of Jim and Arlene, and the right half, Fred and Molly's. Very basic furnishings, couch, bed, chair, etc. For the last scene, the full stage becomes the home of Jim and Arlene. The furniture pieces should be lightweight and easily movable to be re-positioned quickly when needed. A low wall along the back can help define the portions of the action taking place outside the house.

FOUR PLAY

By Ross MacLean

SCENE ONE

Jim and Arlene

(The play opens at the house of JIM and ARLENE. JIM is receiving a phone call.)

JIM. Hello, Molly? You called at just the right time. Yes, I can come over, but I won't be there right away. I want you to have plenty of time to get your husband out of the house. I can't stand sneaking in the front door while you're kissing me in the rear door. I don't want to meet him as long as he's married to you. No, I'm not suggesting divorce, that would ruin everything. I'll be there shortly.

(ARLENE has overheard a part of the conversation. She enters, and behaves as if she has heard nothing.)

ARLENE. Who were you talking to?
JIM. It was a prank call.
ARLENE. You talked a long time for a trick.
JIM. I've got to show some spirit. I won't be victimized.
ARLENE. Are you going out? You said you'd spend the day with me.
JIM. Oh? I did. But something's come up.
ARLENE. Uh huh.
JIM. How about tonight?
ARLENE. Where are you going?
JIM. It's a personal affair, you don't need to know the details.
ARLENE. It's cruel the way you leave yourself open to suspicion— Don't I deserve to be lied to?
JIM. Arlene, I'm not going out on you. I'm just going out.
ARLENE. I wish I could believe you.
JIM. There's nothing I can do to make you trust me. That's something you'll have to take a chance on.
ARLENE. You're impossible.

JIM. Will you save me tonight?

ARLENE. Are you getting out of here or not?

JIM. Yes. Don't be angry, OK?

ARLENE. If I seem mistrustful dear, that's just my little way of showing how I care for you.

JIM. Thank you dear. Thanks a lot.

SCENE TWO

Fred and Molly

(*At their house. FRED is on his way out, when he spots a scrap of paper, glances quickly at it.*)

FRED. Who does this phone number belong to?

MOLLY. I couldn't say.

FRED. It looks suspicious to me.

MOLLY. Why? There's no name attached.

FRED. Is this who you were just talking to?

MOLLY. I wasn't on the phone.

FRED. You were, I just heard you.

MOLLY. I can't account for it.

FRED. I think you're up to something.

MOLLY. What do you know? Why should it be any concern of yours if I was?

FRED. Don't use that flippant attitude with me— I think you may be having an affair.

MOLLY. Nonsense. What would you do if I was?

FRED. I'd beat the man to a pulp— and then I'd start in on you.

MOLLY. You talk tough.

FRED. It's not idle talk, it's promise.

MOLLY. You also promised I'd be the happiest woman alive as your wife. Your convictions are invalid.

FRED. I'll have no more of your trouble, hear? Tell me who this phone number belongs to.

MOLLY. (*Takes a casual glance.*) That looks like your handwriting.

FRED. (*Looks at it, is caught.*) That's enough! I don't need you for abuse. There are other places I could go.

MOLLY. What? Leave me?

FRED. Not permanently, don't get excited.

MOLLY. Fred, please don't go— I need you.

FRED. I don't believe you.

MOLLY. I didn't mean to insult you so effectively. Please reconsider.

FRED. I'm sorry Molly, the damage has been done.

MOLLY. You'll come right back won't you? Right away, so I won't be left all alone?

FRED. I'm afraid I'll be gone a while.

MOLLY. No, no! You're only doing this to punish me!

FRED. I've had enough. Your behavior is disgraceful.

(*He turns and exits through the front door.*)

MOLLY. No! Please come back— Fred!

(*He is gone. MOLLY drops the despair and turns to greet JIM, who has immediately entered.*)

JIM. You let it happen again.

MOLLY. What's wrong as long as you don't see each other? A wife can't throw a man out of his own house can she?

JIM. If she can't, who can? It's degrading for me to sneak about like this.

MOLLY. A little degradation is good for you. It should remind you who you are.

SCENE THREE

At the house of Jim and Arlene

(*FRED surprises ARLENE at her house.*)

FRED. Guess who!

ARLENE. What are you doing here? I told you before I didn't want to see you again.

FRED. You didn't mean it.

ARLENE. No, but please understand that I can't carry on with you. I have a husband to care for, and that's misery enough.

FRED. You don't still claim that you love him do you?

ARLENE. I never said any such thing. I said I had to accept the responsibility of marriage; love has nothing to do with security.

FRED. You know you want me. Why do you punish yourself?

ARLENE. I want to live a decent, upright life. Why do you insist on corrupting it?

FRED. When I held you in my arms that night, and you said you loved me— me, a lonely bachelor... It put a new dimension to my wretched life.

ARLENE. It was a toss-off remark that seemed right at the time. You shouldn't have taken me so seriously.

FRED. I don't believe you. Is your married life so ideal?

ARLENE. No. My husband is cheating on me.

FRED. Is he! Do you know who with?

ARLENE. Only that it's a woman. I overheard him on the phone.

FRED. Are you sure you heard right?

ARLENE. Yes. I don't want to let him get away with it.

FRED. Then give yourself to me.

ARLENE. But I don't like you.

FRED. That doesn't matter, as long as I get what I want. And this way you'll have your revenge.

ARLENE. I couldn't enjoy it.

FRED. You're not supposed to. Punish him by indulging yourself.

ARLENE. Maybe I could... are you free this evening?

FRED. I could be.

ARLENE. Plan on coming over. I do have plans with my husband, but I'm sure he'll break them.

FRED. All right. I'll call before I come, to make sure it's ok.

ARLENE. I'm always afraid I won't answer first. I wish you'd get a phone.

FRED. Don't worry. No one will find out through any fault of mine.

(*He starts to go.*)

FRED. 'Til tonight!

ARLENE. Yes: 'til tonight!

SCENE FOUR

At Molly's house, finishing up in bed.

JIM. (*As he blows out a cigarette.*) Is your husband suspicious?

MOLLY. He loves me too much to think of it.

JIM. Naive jerk. That leaves us free to do as we please.

MOLLY. Go on, you're just jealous that you don't have a wife as trusting with you.

JIM. If I ever need a wife I'll want one smarter than your husband.

MOLLY. Until you get one, I'll be glad to train you as to what a good wife is like.

JIM. Do you love me Molly?

MOLLY. (*Horrified, indignant.*) What do you take me for!

JIM. Don't get upset, I didn't mean anything.

MOLLY. See that you don't! There's nothing between us, it's just for play.

JIM. You have got to know what a security that is for me.

MOLLY. I have my own to consider as well. So don't worry Jim, we'll stay exactly as we are: the best of friends.

JIM. And hope no one finds out.

(*There is a knock at the door.*)

MOLLY. It's locked. (*Calls.*) Just a minute!

JIM. Your husband?

MOLLY. It might as well be—

JIM. I thought you said you were going to keep our times free together!

MOLLY. Next time I'm free we'll be together. How about tonight?

JIM. That's short notice.

MOLLY. Please do— I'll prepare a nice dinner. By candlelight.

JIM. Nothing intensifies romance like a sleazy atmosphere.

MOLLY. Get out will you— the back way.

JIM. 'Til later!

(*He leaves.*)

MOLLY. ...or nothing intensifies atmosphere like a sleazy romance!

(*She opens the door, ARLENE is standing there.*)

MOLLY. Darling!

ARLENE. Don't "darling" me, who did you have in here?

MOLLY. No one.

ARLENE. Honestly, I come to you for shelter from my awful husband, and you're carrying on with some other woman. You were, weren't you!

MOLLY. Between you and my husband, I haven't the time.

ARLENE. Then who left this cigarette?

MOLLY. There's no lipstick on that.

ARLENE. Of course not, that's not your type.

MOLLY. It belonged to my husband. Why are you so upset?

ARLENE. I think my husband is cheating on me.

MOLLY. I thought you couldn't stand him.

ARLENE. That doesn't mean I don't care what he does with my life.

MOLLY. You should never have married in the first place. Deception takes too much skill for your nerves.

ARLENE. I'm not deceiving anyone, I'm lying outright. I took a husband for appearances only. Somehow I get emotionally involved and the relationship deteriorated.

MOLLY. Aren't you cheating on him?

ARLENE. Yes, thank god, it's my last grasp on sanity. But you're no threat to a marriage.

MOLLY. I could be.

ARLENE. Don't. You're the only person I don't have to care about.

MOLLY. There's no cause for you to be upset over your husband's behavior. I'd be delighted if my husband was smart enough to cheat on me. At any rate, you're keeping the score even, being guilty of the same offense.

ARLENE. Guilty? I suppose I am. But I need to be, it makes me happy.

MOLLY. It is possible to have love without guilt.

ARLENE. Then how would I know it's genuine?

MOLLY. By giving little tests. My husband, for instance, is an amusing source of devotion. Just the other night, I sent him out for some ice cream, said I couldn't possibly live without it. It was late, and I knew he'd have to go out of his way to get it. But he brought it back: four hours later, and he apologized for having me wait. That was Tuesday.

ARLENE. The night I came to visit.

MOLLY. Not only did I play a trick, but I was rewarded for it as well. If you had any concept of management, you could handle your married life and still have everything else.

ARLENE. I have everything else, it's the marriage I don't want! Having that man around, constant support and affection. He doesn't pass five minutes without telling me he loves me.

MOLLY. I don't understand. Then what's the problem?

ARLENE. I don't believe him!

SCENE FIVE

Fred and Jim at Jim's house.

FRED. There's no reason you should believe her. Women are inherently deceitful. That's why I chose to stay single, Jim. I can't stand liars.

JIM. It's no excuse for her to carry on with some other man.

FRED. Why not? You are.

JIM. Men are supposed to have affairs, on women it's cheap.

FRED. Generally it's acceptable when the man is seeing another woman. An arrangement like ours is completely off the wall.

JIM. So I'm seeing a man. Now I'm cheap, big deal. Does she need to run out and even the score?

FRED. Don't ask me. I wouldn't trust a woman farther than I could throw one.

JIM. I've been seeing you for idle amusement. But what if she leaves me? We might be forced into a real relationship.

FRED. And would that be so bad? You know how I feel about you. If you could believe that, you could dump your wife completely.

JIM. I won't dump her, I love her. More than anything in the world. Except myself. If I catch her with the man she's seeing, I'll kill him!

FRED. Literally?

JIM. I'll mess him up good, believe me.

FRED. Come on, is she worth all this?

JIM. No! That's why I'm so angry.

FRED. Do you know if she plans to see him tonight?

JIM. It's likely. She'll make up some phony excuse. Like the ones I use, but not as good. Well I'll fix her: I'll go away, just long enough to let them get started. Then I'll burst in and ruin their smutty little antics. Oooh, I tell you, when I catch him, is he in for it!

FRED. What! You'd take it out on the man? It's your wife deserves the beating!

JIM. I want to scare him from the house, not entertain him.

FRED. Settle down, settle down! Forget about her and take what you can for yourself. Me for instance. Boot her out for a night, and we'll spend it together. You'll be getting the same thing she would, and no one will get hurt.

JIM. That's an idea... but I have ... well. I've made other plans.

FRED. Change them. Break them, and you can spend the night with me.

JIM. I won't be like Tuesday, when you had to rush off?

FRED. On my honor, my closest friend.

SCENE SIX

Jim and Arlene, at home.

ARLENE. Bad news dear, I'm afraid I won't be able to keep our little date.

JIM. What little date?

ARLENE. We were going to spend the evening together. It was your suggestion.

JIM. I forgot all about that hon, I thought you said no from the start. I've made other plans.

ARLENE. Did you? That's just as well. I had planned on going out too.

JIM. Oh? Out to where?

ARLENE. I thought I'd do a little shopping, if you don't mind.

JIM. No, I think it's great, really.

ARLENE. And where are you going?

JIM. I have to visit a sick friend. No one you know.

ARLENE. Gee, that's too bad. Will you be gone long?

JIM. I think so. It's a lingering illness.

ARLENE. Oh dear. You will be late then.

JIM. I expect so.

ARLENE. I just want to be sure when you'll be home so… so I won't think you're a burglar or something.

JIM. Don't worry for me, Arlene, stay out as long as you like.

ARLENE. Well… As long as you're going out too….

JIM. You're sure you don't mind? You're not upset with me are you?

ARLENE. Not at all.

JIM. I can't believe that.

ARLENE. You'd better.

JIM. Of course. Excuse me, I'll get ready to go.

ARLENE. You do that, dear.

SCENE SEVEN

Molly and Fred

(*At home, in the midst of a fierce argument.*)

MOLLY. I had to wait till after we were married to find out how stupid you are!

FRED. You should have known that when I asked you!

MOLLY. I can't stand having you around any more. I used to think you were the best man alive!

FRED. I am!

MOLLY. I know. The disappointment is enormous.

FRED. You have none of the delicate sensitivities of a woman.

MOLLY. But you have, there's no loss.

FRED. You never cared for me!

MOLLY. Of course not. How can I, when you have always hated me!

FRED. No, I never did. You've misunderstood.

MOLLY. Liar! I'm going out for the evening.

FRED. You're having an affair with another man, aren't you!

MOLLY. I would never repeat such a stupid action!

FRED. You can't have all the credit. That I ever believed a word you said makes me a bigger ass than you.

MOLLY. Have it your way. I'm leaving!

FRED. Good! Get out!

(*They each go out to make phone calls.*)

SCENE EIGHT

Telephone Scene

(*Everyone is at their own homes.*)

FRED. Arlene? This is Fred. Listen, about our date tonight—

ARLENE. I'm afraid I have to cancel, Fred. I intend to begin living like a respectable woman.

FRED. Oh. –Some other time?

(*She hangs up.*)

MOLLY. Jim, this is Molly. I need you over as soon as possible. I've just had a row with my husband and I need a shoulder to cry on.

JIM. You've got two of your own, kid. I can't make it.

(*He hangs up.*)

ARLENE. Now that Jim's going out, there's no reason for the house to be left unused. Or me to be left alone!

MOLLY. Men ruin enough women's lives— I'm not going to put up with it any longer.

FRED. Lucky I made alternative plans— I can't depend on women for anything.

JIM. So what Fred said was true: Arlene is lying on me. Well, I'll be lying on someone else tonight, at any rate.

(*And more calls.*)

ARLENE. Hello, Molly? I hate every man in the world. You've got to come over right away!

MOLLY. Certainly dear, just give me your address!

FRED. Jim— is everything clear?

JIM. Yes unfortunately. She's going out, determined to ruin the marriage. Come on over, and do your part.

(*All head for their destinations. BLACKOUT.*)

SCENE NINE

Arlene, Jim, Molly and Fred

(*At Jim and Arlene's.*)

ARLENE. Jim dear, I thought you were going out.

JIM. I decided to stay home after all. Someone should keep the home fires burning.

ARLENE. That's just what I had planned to do, so you go on your way. I decided to stay home tonight after all.

JIM. What?! You can't stay home tonight, you already told me you'd be gone.

ARLENE. I can change my mind can't I?

JIM. You can change your mind easily. It's holding it still that gives you all the trouble. Put on your coat and get going.

ARLENE. I wouldn't think of it. You go out, a man deserves a night to howl.

JIM. I intend to howl here tonight.

ARLENE. You can't!

JIM. I will! Have a pleasant evening. And take care in the parking lots, they're getting dangerous.

ARLENE. Yes, maybe I should stay home after all, for safety's sake.

JIM. Nonsense. More accidents happen in the home than anywhere; I intend to avoid all mishaps tonight.

ARLENE. So do I. So I think I'll just...

(*She sits down. JIM grabs her by the arm and ushers her to the door.*)

JIM. Get something nice for yourself, will you? I want you to have lots of fun, and uh... Here's five: Splurge!

(*And he shoves her out the door.*)

ARLENE. Why that—Not even the subtlest courtesy. I've got to get to a phone and call Molly.

(*She runs off. MOLLY enters and knocks at JIM's door.*)

JIM. One moment!

(*He flits about, making final adjustments on hair and clothes. All set—he flings open the door and embraces the guest.*)

JIM. Darling! (*Immediately too late, sees it's the wrong person.*) What are *you* doing here?

MOLLY. I'm not sure I know. Is that how you greet anyone who knocks?

JIM. Yes, get in here right away.

(*He pulls her in, closes the door.*)

MOLLY. What are you doing here?

JIM. It's where I live, how did you find out?

MOLLY. It was an accident, I swear.

JIM. You've done your accident at the worst possible time. I am expecting a person I would not like you to meet.

MOLLY. I would like some explanation.

JIM. There isn't time. Wait in the bedroom, and I'll get you out as soon as possible.

MOLLY. Why can't I just go out the door?

(*There is a knock at the door.*)

MOLLY. OK.

(*And she goes into the bedroom. JIM prepares himself and opens the door again, with similar but strained flourish.*)

JIM. Darling!

(*ARLENE enters.*)

JIM. You!

ARLENE. Of course me you fool. You threw me out before I was ready, I had to come back for my key.

JIM. Is that all? I would have been here to let you in.

ARLENE. Alright. I'd best be honest with you. I was expecting a friend to come and keep me company. Has anyone come by?

JIM. No one. I'll tell whoever it is that you've gone out.

ARLENE. I'll try and call to see if I can catch them.

JIM. And then you'll both be off shopping?

ARLENE. Don't be a smart ass.

(*He goes into the kitchen, tries to phone. There is a knock at the door, JIM answers.*)

FRED. Darling!

JIM. Get away you fool— my wife is home. Wait here for me. She'll be leaving through the back door, and I'll get you when it's clear.

FRED. I'll come back in a minute.

JIM. No, wait here like I told you.

(*The door closes, FRED waits. JIM goes into the bedroom. ARLENE comes out of the kitchen and starts out the front door.*)

ARLENE. What are you doing here?

FRED. I—I guess I just had to see you.

ARLENE. You've come at a bad time, come in anyway, quick.

FRED. No!

ARLENE. I'm so upset. I was expecting a guest who didn't show. But you're here. Now I know who cares for me.

FRED. That's not true.

ARLENE. I have some good news: my husband is a lout: I've decided that I do love you.

FRED. I'm not glad to hear that.

ARLENE. What do you mean? —My husband is in the bedroom. Come in here and I'll keep you hidden. He'll leave in a minute, and then we can discuss this.

(*They go into the kitchen.*)

ARLENE. Jim, are you finished in there?

JIM. Just a minute dear! (*To MOLLY.*) That was my wife. I know I told you I was single, but I lied.

MOLLY. She can't see us together— if she saw me with you she'd never forgive me.

JIM. For the next few minutes I don't want to be associated with you. Please step into the closet.

MOLLY. That's an indecent suggestion.

JIM. It's essential.

(*She is in, and JIM leaves the bedroom, closing the door behind him. Once the door is closed, MOLLY immediately comes out of the closet. She paces the room, looking for escape.*)

JIM. I'm out.

ARLENE. Don't make a sound. I'll get my husband out of here and we can explore real passion.

(*She goes to the bedroom.*)

JIM. What did you want?

ARLENE. To check the bedroom.

JIM. For what?

ARLENE. My own peace of mind.

JIM. I'm free from guilt.

ARLENE. You're ignorant of guilt. That's not the same thing.

(*ARLENE opens the door. MOLLY does not have time to get to the closet so she ducks behind the bed and crawls under it. JIM has gone to the front door where he told FRED to wait for him. FRED is not there— JIM looks outside, and circles to the back door. He goes in, meeting JIM in the kitchen.*)

JIM. There you are!

FRED. Yes. Jim, I've got to tell you here and now that you're the only one I care about.

JIM. Don't talk foolishness to me now. There is serious business going on here.

FRED. Let's leave.

JIM. I can't. There is another lady here who I must get rid of first.

FRED. I've just seen her. She said she was in love with me.

JIM. Was it a traumatic experience?

FRED. It may get to be. I hear her coming.

JIM. We can't be seen together. Go out here and wait for me in the front like I told you in the first place.

FRED. But she knows I'm here.

(*He is thrown out. ARLENE enters.*)

ARLENE. Jim! What are you doing in here?

JIM. Is the sight of me that disappointing?

ARLENE. Yes.

JIM. Who were you expecting?

ARLENE. I thought you would have left.

JIM. I haven't. But I will. Was the bedroom to your satisfaction? Oh. Excuse me.

(*He exits the kitchen and goes directly to the bedroom to check the closet, which is empty.*)

ARLENE. What has happened to Fred? Did I scare him off with my forward approach? And why hasn't Molly shown up yet? She may come in at the worst possible moment. I better look to see if she's coming.

(*ARLENE goes to the front door while JIM is still in the bedroom. She opens the door, FRED is waiting.*)

ARLENE. Fred! Get in here, you're like a stray cat, loitering on the doorstep.
FRED. Are you putting me in the kitchen again?
ARLENE. No. Keep quiet for a minute and we'll go where we can be intimate.

(*She leads him to the bedroom.*)

FRED. The kitchen was fine.
ARLENE. It's no place for romance. Come this way.
JIM. She made her escape, must have gone out the window. Good thinking, and all the better for my pleasure.

(*JIM leaves the bedroom, walking a determinedly straight line to the front door. FRED and ARLENE are standing out of his path, so they are covered by the open door while he passes. ARLENE immediately pulls FRED around and into the bedroom, closing the door behind her.*)

JIM. He's disappeared again. I'll try the kitchen.

(*ARLENE opens the closet.*)

ARLENE. Get in here until I'm sure he's left.
FRED. That's a closet!

ARLENE. Of course it is you fool! We can't take a chance of being seen together.

FRED. You said you'd take me to an intimate place.

ARLENE. It's an extreme, I know, but it's necessary.

(*She pushes him in and closes the door.*)

ARLENE. And don't make a sound if you value your life.

(*MOLLY peeks out from under the bed.*)

MOLLY. Arlene?

ARLENE. Molly! Oh, this is a nightmare.

MOLLY. My opinion exactly.

ARLENE. I'm surprised to see you. Why did you wait for me under the bed instead of on top where I could have seen you?

MOLLY. That was a whim of your husband's. We've met.

ARLENE. He's found out about us! You don't need to explain any further. Instead of punishing me, like a normal man would, he's decided to get his revenge by humiliating you. It won't work Molly. He can disgrace you all he likes. I've always liked you for what you are.

MOLLY. You've go everything wrong, as usual, but you've got to get me out of here. No one can see us together.

ARLENE. Right. You go out the window. It's the only way. Wait for me in front of the house, I'll be there directly.

(*MOLLY climbs out the window and heads in the direction of the kitchen. JIM has been looking outside for FRED, and can't find him. He comes around to the back door just in time to intercept MOLLY.*)

JIM. There you are, I thought you had escaped.

MOLLY. I've been doing my best.

JIM. Everyone has deserted me. Come inside, I'm willing to love you with all my heart.

MOLLY. You can't. Your wife is in there.

JIM. No, I'm sure she's left by now. She's trying to trace down some illicit lover who stood her up.

MOLLY. Then you definitely can't take me in there!

JIM. Why not?
MOLLY. I'm the lover.

(*Pause as JIM stands, holding MOLLY by the arm. His lips curl in distaste.*)

JIM. Eeeew…
MOLLY. Let me go, please!
JIM. Nothing doing! This mess is your fault. I'm not going to take the blame.

(*He pulls her back into the house.*

Shift focus to FRED and ARLENE in bedroom. ARLENE at closet door.)

ARLENE. Fred, please come out. (*No reply.*) I was lying when I said I loved you. If you'll get out of here, I promise never to lie to you again.
FRED. I'm not coming out, I like it in here.
ARLENE. If my husband finds you he'll kill you.
FRED. Not if I know him he won't.
ARLENE. He'll kill me then.
FRED. I can't care for your troubles. This is the only safe place a man has in the world.
ARLENE. Your cowardice is classic. –I hear someone coming. I don't care who it is, I don't want to be seen by anyone!

(*She scrambles out the window, closing it behind her. JIM hauls MOLLY through the house.*)

JIM. My wife is probably combing the streets for you. Until I'm sure where she is, you get back in the closet where you belong.

(*MOLLY is put back in the bedroom, and the door is closed. She tries the window, but can't get it open. She tries the closet, and FRED is holding it tightly shut. She must hide under the bed. ARLENE comes around the front of the house.*)

ARLENE. I can't stand this any longer. I'm going to fall in love with the very first person I see.

(*JIM comes out the front door.*)

ARLENE. Unless it's him.
JIM. Honey! What are you doing out here in the cold night air? Do you want to catch your death? Come in, I have a surprise for you.
ARLENE. Where are you taking me, you hateful idiot.
JIM. Just in here, to the bedroom.

(*They go in.*)

ARLENE. There, it's completely empty. What's so unusual about that?
JIM. I have serious reason to believe that you wanted me out of here to carry on a sordid affair.
ARLENE. That shows what a dunce you are. I know for a fact that's what you've been up to.
JIM. In this room is a person who claims to be a lover of yours.
ARLENE. Please, let me see who it is.
JIM. Come out, the jig's up.
ARLENE. Yes, come out.

(*FRED comes out of the closet, MOLLY comes out from under the bed.*)

MOLLY. Fred!
FRED. Molly!
JIM. Arlene?
ARLENE. Fred?
FRED. Molly?
JIM. Fred?
ARLENE. Jim?
MOLLY. Arlene!
JIM. So! You have been having an affair with my wife? Excuse us ladies, we have a score to settle here.

(*The men go into the living room, the women stay.*)

ARLENE. What a couple of assholes.

MOLLY. I swear I'll never wear another pair of pants again.

ARLENE. So you have been carrying on with my husband?

MOLLY. I'm afraid so.

ARLENE. Somehow I thought he was better than that.

(*Shift to FRED and JIM.*)

JIM. What do you mean, you're having an affair with my wife! You're supposed to be having an affair with me!

FRED. Does it make much of a difference?

JIM. Molly told me she was having an affair with Arlene.

FRED. Then let's get even: you tell them about your devotion to me.

JIM. If only that were true.

(*Shift to the women.*)

ARLENE. I am condemned. It's not bad enough to be a deviate, but I have to imagine that I am loved by three others as well.

MOLLY. What can I say. It's a clear case of "like attracts like."

ARLENE. Doesn't any of this embarrass you?

MOLLY. Yes. The fact that I actually married that fool. Call them out of there, I want this settled.

(*ARLENE opens the door; she sees FRED and JIM in an incriminating pose.*)

ARLENE. Oh my god: Jim, when you said you had to visit a sick friend, I had no idea...!

(*She goes back with MOLLY.*)

MOLLY. What is it?

ARLENE. First us, now them. My whole world is broken, both my husband and lover are queer.

MOLLY. There is no truth anywhere.

JIM. We've been caught. The situation is hopeless.

FRED. What can we do?

JIM. We've got to confess. It's time to take responsibility for our actions.

(*They all join in the bedroom. JIM shouts at ARLENE.*)

JIM. YOU are responsible for tearing my life to shreds.
ARLENE. I'm sorry I haven't been more complete.
FRED. Molly, I've got to tell you, I'm in love with you.
MOLLY. Tell your lies to some other gullible idiot.
FRED. (*Turns to JIM.*) I love my wife.
JIM. I don't want to hear your problems.
ARLENE. Don't let them bother you Molly, I still care.
JIM. What a thing to hear from my own wife.
MOLLY. How are you so perfect? You've violated even the respectable aspects of adultery. (*To FRED.*) Your cavorting with this man has reduced our marriage to a shambles.
FRED. But Molly, I thought of you the whole time I was doing it.
ARLENE. I don't mind you loving another person. But you make me out such a fool for letting me think you cared for me.
JIM. But I told you I loved you.
ARLENE. So did he, and so did she.
JIM. But I'm your husband!
ARLENE. Don't confuse me with irrelevant facts.
FRED. Let's face reality—
MOLLY. I can't bear to.
FRED. We all love each other very much.
ARLENE. Speak for yourself.
FRED. I was. You all love me, don't you? (*No reply.*)
MOLLY. I think Fred may have a point. Let me rephrase that— You all love ME, don't you?
FRED. I do.
MOLLY. You're already my husband, you don't count.
JIM. I confess, it's true.
ARLENE. What!
MOLLY. How about you Arlene?
ARLENE. I love myself. Past that I will make no commitments.
FRED. Despite your reluctance, I think everything's become clear.
JIM. I don't see how this lessens our predicament.
FRED. Well, we know how we all stand. Why don't we... Why don't we all just... do it together?

ARLENE. That's disgusting!

JIM. How repulsive!

MOLLY. I'm ashamed!

FRED. (*Angry.*) Look here, I'm offering a feasible solution.

JIM. You're reintroducing the original problem.

MOLLY. Then let's go back to our first arrangement. (*To JIM.*) I won't like you if you promise not to like me. –It works, we got along very well.

ARLENE. This one kept insisting that he loved me. No wonder we couldn't get anywhere.

FRED. OK, I was lying. Now will you have me?

ARLENE. Now I don't want you. If it was possible that anyone could love me at all, this never would have happened.

MOLLY. Well it's not, so it did.

FRED. Is frustration the ultimate romance has to offer?

JIM. My friends— and I use that term with caution—I am afraid we are destined to be discontent.

MOLLY. Is there no alternative?

FRED. We've tried absolutely every combination. Unless someone here is willing to make some concessions, we're stuck.

ARLENE. We have only one solution, our one last resort.

MOLLY. And what is that?

ARLENE. That we return to the person we love.

FRED. ??? And who is that?

MOLLY. Husbands and wives, you jerk! Wives return to husbands, and husbands return to wives.

JIM. Whose husband or whose wife?

FRED. I don't care anymore. I'll share my wife with you, Jim.

JIM. What sacrifice.

MOLLY. You dog!

JIM. I'm not going to just hand over my wife to you.

ARLENE. You can't barter me like a piece of property: what if I *want* to be with Fred?

MOLLY. Lay off my husband, Arlene. You're staying with me.

JIM. No she's not, she's mine.

FRED. Let her go, Jim— You can have me.

MOLLY. No he cannot: you're mine!

FRED. I refuse to be owned by anyone!

(*LIGHTS BEGIN TO FADE.*)

ARLENE. Who do you think would want you?

(*MOLLY and FRED's, and JIM and ARLENE's conversations play out simultaneously.*)

MOLLY. (*To FRED.*) I would!
FRED. (*To MOLLY.*) But we're married!
MOLLY. (*To FRED.*) I'm willing to defy convention!
FRED. (*To MOLLY.*) That's what got this started in the first place!
JIM. (*To ARLENE.*) Arlene, I love you, will you believe me this time?
ARLENE. (*To JIM.*) You're just saying that to make me feel good.
JIM. (*To ARLENE.*) No, I'm saying that to make *me* feel good.
ARLENE. (*To JIM.*) Get away from me, you selfish pig!

(*Back to normal.*)

MOLLY. Fred!
FRED. Molly!
JIM. Arlene!
ARLENE. Fred!
FRED. Molly!
JIM. Fred!
ARLENE. Jim!
MOLLY. Arlene!

(*LIGHTS GO TO BLACK amidst the raging argument.*)

END OF PLAY

EAST
MONROE

East Monroe was presented in a revue titled "Multiple Fractures" which opened at the Déjà Vu Coffeehouse in Hollywood, California on May 26, 1978, directed by John Forman, performed by Ned Van Zandt.

<u>CHARACTERS</u>

A MAN

EAST MONROE

By Ross MacLean

(*It is an apartment. It looks nice. In center of the living room is a mannequin arm on a stand. This is the way it looks for some time. Then a MAN walks in.*)

A MAN. Ah ha! So there you are. If you keep this up you're going to find yourself without a home.

You sniveling idiot. How dare you treat me like that!

All right. Now. Tell me. Which one did it?

(*He holds the arm by the shoulder, walking in front of the sofa, pointing it at imaginary people.*)

A MAN. Is this the one? This one? Yes, you do look guilty enough. No? Oh.

(*He looks at him suspiciously and moves on to the next one.*)

A MAN. This the one then. No? Then who? Tell me then, who???

All right. Stop this, please stop this. You've no right to torment me this way. I'll throw you out. I will. I can't take this anymore.

(*The arm hits him in the face and the man throws it across the room.*)

A MAN. Oh, so that's the way it's going to be. You coward, I see you hiding. Come out here. I see you now. You can't hide. Jellyfish— you inconsistent rubbish— I'll show you who's in charge.

(*Now he begins to wrestle with the arm. The arm knocks him down, they tumble. The arm hits him in the back of the head, but the man reaches quickly behind him and pulls it around,*) *strangling it by the wrist. It drops. The man sits a second, exhausted. Then the arm sneaks up and hits him on the leg. The man is very scared. The arm moves up and hits him on the chest. The man is terrified.*)

A MAN. No! NO!

(*He kicks the arm across the room. He looks at it, fearful and sympathetic.*)

A MAN. I'm sorry. Oh please, I'm sorry.

(*He retrieves the arm.*)

A MAN. I really didn't mean—

(*He tries to cradle the arm, but it hits him in the face.*)

A MAN. NO! NO!

(*A third and fourth time he is hit.*)

A MAN. I'm sorry. I'm sorry I said what I did. I didn't mean it. You know that.

(*The arm has stopped beating him. It begins to gently stroke his face.*)

A MAN. Oh thank you. That feels so much better. It hurts so.

How could I talk to you that way? How could you believe me? But it's all over for now. You know I'll never leave you. Now or ever.

END OF PLAY

FOOD

Kip Savage, Steven Nelson and Jean West in *Food* produced by the Fourth E Company at the New York Theater Ensemble, NYC. Photo credit – John R. Hill.

Food was first performed at the Deja Vu Coffeehouse in Hollywood, CA on September 14, 1978. The production was directed by Ellen Nickles. The cast was as follows:

Mack....	James Purcell
Bonnie...	Concetta Tomei
Carol....	Alyce Heath
Joe.......	Dy Lowell

Food was subsequently produced in New York by the Fourth E Company at the New York Theater Ensemble, directed by Bonnie Young. The cast was as follows:

Mack.....	Steve Nelson
Bonnie...	Sharon Ferry
Carol......	Jean West
Joe.........	Kip Savage

SYNOPSIS

Financial pressures strain family relations at the dinner table: how much support can they be expected to give?

CHARACTERS

MACK (m)   Blue Collar Worker

JOE (m)   Admin type, will speak up but is quick to appease. Married to Carol.

CAROL (f)   Old-world values housewife, expects to be supported.

BONNIE (f)   Mack's wife. Friendly, resigned quality.

SETTING

A dinner table and four chairs. Surroundings are optional.

FOOD

By Ross MacLean

(*MACK, JOE and CAROL are seated at the dinner table. JOE and CAROL eat vigorously. MACK has no plate. He is annoyed by that.*)

JOE. Mmm! Mmm! What fine spaghetti. It's quite... tender. Yum, tender. Just... delicious, to tell the truth.

MACK. (*Yells to the kitchen.*) Where's my dinner?

CAROL. Maybe she's busy with something else, Mack. Here, have some of mine.

MACK. Bonnie!

CAROL. I wouldn't say this is actually delicious. But it is healthy. That's what matter most.

MACK. What matters most is that I have mine.

JOE. You'll get it. Or take hers.

CAROL. Why mine?

JOE. You offered. Not mine.

MACK. Not yours? Whose is it now anyway? Didn't I pay for it, while you were on your ass in the unemployment line? You'll take someone else's, and you'll give away someone else's...

JOE. (*Insincere.*) Do you want this?

MACK. No, I don't—

JOE. He's right, Carol. Give him some of yours.

MACK. I don't want what I gave you. I want mine.

(*BONNIE enters.*)

BONNIE. Here you go Mack, I'm sorry you had to wait. I made it the way you like it.

MACK. Ah, Bonnie, thanks. It took long enough.

BONNIE. You don't mind that I serve our guests first.

MACK. Why should I?

BONNIE. I'll sit down in a minute, don't wait on me. The rest will be done pretty soon.

(*She exits. MACK pokes about his plate.*)

MACK. I hate spaghetti.

CAROL. Then why do you have Bonnie make it?

MACK. I didn't ask her to. She does the shopping.

CAROL. Is this the best she could do?

MACK. Yesterday it was macaroni.

CAROL. The cheese made it OK.

MACK. Day before, beans.

CAROL. It takes a chef's talent to make a meal of beans... work.

JOE. It was good here three weeks ago. That meatloaf.

MACK. We all ate the meatloaf. This is spaghetti.

JOE. I think it's good. If you need your plate cleaned, put it in front of me.

MACK. You would, wouldn't you.

CAROL. Confidentially, don't let Bonnie know I suggested this. You should speak with her about more careful meal planning. Too many starches are not good. A proper diet should draw from each of the basic food groups every day. It takes a balanced diet to maintain strong mind, body, and spirit.

JOE. What's spirit? Time to work and sleep's all you need. And food to keep the engine going.

MACK. I notice your engine doesn't do a heap more than shovel your mouth full.

JOE. (*Simultaneous protest.*) You asked us over!

CAROL. (*Simultaneous protest.*) He's unemployed! Your temperament wouldn't be unbalanced if your meals were.

MACK. Maybe I should speak with Bonnie, see what's the problem.

JOE. Uh huh, do that. I see it's a problem, but I've got to say that what you've given me, or us, that's here on this plate, I appreciate.

CAROL. Yes, me too. Thanks so much, Mack.

MACK. Could I turn away my own sister?

JOE. I should also point up, Carol, how good he's been to you by making sure that you're fed well. Like... should I bring it up? The meal three weeks ago?

CAROL. Oh, that meatloaf! Wasn't it the best!

MACK. Yeah...

CAROL. The crispy slices of bacon on the top— brown, crusty outside...

MACK. But, uh... it wasn't specially for you, exactly.

CAROL. Tender on the inside, pink, juicy, with the onions and the peppers—

MACK. She made that for me!

JOE. And the asparagus!

CAROL. Fresh, not canned.

JOE. But the corn— and the homemade bread. There is nothing in the world like the smell of homemade bread. Carol, I wish you could make that.

CAROL. I could never top Bonnie's.

JOE. Cut in half, with a big pat of butter melting through the loaf...

MACK. (*Remembering ecstasy.*) Oh Lord...

JOE. Yes, it was.

MACK. This spaghetti...

CAROL. Not like three weeks ago.

MACK. No, it's so dry, or sticky, or... bland. That's it: bland.

JOE. Maybe Bonnie's making some bread. That would make up for it.

CAROL. No, we could smell it.

(*BONNIE enters.*)

BONNIE. Here you go folks. Eat well.

(*She sets down a basket.*)

MACK. (*Dismayed.*) Crackers!

BONNIE. (*Obviously.*) Yes.

JOE. Mmmm!

BONNIE. We're out of bread. I hadn't noticed before now. I thought these would be... acceptable.

JOE. Thanks a lot Bonnie. Is there oleo?

(*He is passed some, and sets to business.*)

CAROL. I have always, *always* loved saltines. Good choice, Bonnie.

BONNIE. Carol, relax. You don't need to go on like that. I'll sit down for a minute while the—

MACK. You mean you're finished? There isn't more?

BONNIE. Yes there's more. I just wanted a bite before it gets too cold. Nothing will burn.

MACK. Excuse me.

CAROL. Wonderful meal Bonnie. We were all discussing it.

JOE. Yes, wonderful. Especially the one a few weeks ago: meatloaf.

BONNIE. Oh that...

CAROL. Just delightful spaghetti. It's the sauce that puts it over, that's what I always say. What would have made it just complete is some of that fresh-baked bread. We were kind of wondering about that.

BONNIE. There wasn't time to make it today. Don't worry, the dinner doesn't stop here. I've got a dish coming that's quite special.

MACK. Is it better than the spaghetti?

BONNIE. Much better.

MACK. It better be.

BONNIE. Eat, don't complain.

JOE. Spaghetti has never been one of my favorite dishes either. Until tonight. All the same, some meatloaf would have been nice.

MACK. Bonnie, what's with it? How come this stuff? How come the macaroni? Or those beans?

BONNIE. (*Embarrassed, doesn't want to answer.*) Well, Mack, you know the budget is tight and the markets are high...

MACK. Where does it all go? And not that I want to make you feel bad, but your meal planning is making me sick. I got to keep healthy don't I?

BONNIE. This is quite healthy.

MACK. There's no vitamins in this dough. It's all paste.

CAROL. It's not that bad.

MACK. So how come Bonnie'? Isn't it your responsibility to take care of me? And this— crackers!

BONNIE. It's just a substitute—

MACK. Substitute hell.

BONNIE. We... We can't afford meat.

(*Silence.*)

MACK. (*Simultaneous.*) What do you mean we can't afford meat,
I gave you—
JOE. (*Simultaneous.*) We don't mind Mack, it's OK—
BONNIE. We just don't have the money. I did the planning, and
we've had all the best meals earlier this month. With your
paydays being so far apart, if we don't plan carefully... the
supply dwindles.
MACK. But I gave you—
BONNIE. We don't have it.

(*Embarrassed silence, as MACK looks at JOE and CAROL.*)

MACK. (*To BONNIE.*) You used up all the—
BONNIE. All.

(*Pause. Everyone continues eating, except BONNIE, who
continues looking at MACK. When MACK resumes his eating at a
regular pace, then BONNIE takes a bite.*)

BONNIE. I understand, and I apologize.
JOE. (*Simultaneous.*) It's all right.
CAROL. (*Simultaneous.*) It's good, really!
MACK. (*Simultaneous.*) Mmmphrf...
BONNIE. It's only the first course. There is more to come, and it's
worth the wait.
JOE. Don't be embarrassed, Bonnie. We know what you're capable
of. We were all caught up thinking about the meal three weeks
ago.
BONNIE. The meatloaf.
MACK. You know, the night he was... uh... discharged.
JOE. Yes.
BONNIE. This is a humble effort, in comparison.
JOE. But no less kind.
BONNIE. I only have so much. If I don't keep buying food, I'm
sure to run out. You understand, don't you?
MACK. But there is an endless supply of food.
JOE. (*While chewing.*) It will always be available, you don't need
to be afraid of that.

CAROL. (*Her mouth also stuffed.*) Don't talk with your mouth full, Joe. (*She swallows, and continues.*) Like you say Bonnie, when it goes, it's gone. You can't beat that. Joe, why he worked at that print shop a year and a half, and when they let him go, that was it! Of course, there is unemployment, but after that's gone, then what?

JOE. I'll be working by then.

CAROL. But in the meantime? I know we have income, but it's a flat ninety-five a week. He can't put in overtime. That's the limit.

JOE. There's a light side though, which I'd like to point out, and that's that I've seen nothing but the better side of people. People have been very good to me, ever since I've been on the skids.

BONNIE. You can count on us, till you get back on your feet.

CAROL. Thank you.

JOE. And then what?

MACK. And then you take care of yourself, I suppose.

JOE. I suppose after I return to the working world, it'll be the last I see of good people.

MACK. The last you'll see of charity, anyway.

BONNIE. No, there needn't ever be an end to that.

JOE. There is a limit to everything, I'm sure of that. And when it's gone— "Cest la vie!"

MACK. (*Irked.*) "C'est la vie." Bonnie, I've had enough—

BONNIE. There's more coming when it's ready, not till then.

CAROL. Won't you tell us what it is?

BONNIE. It's my all-out favorite.

JOE. Strawberry shortcake?

MACK. Or chocolate pudding, a whopping bowl covered with whipped cream.

CAROL. No— a chocolate cake, with cherries and walnuts and a big scoop of peppermint ice cream on top.

BONNIE. No, you're way off track.

MACK. What I wish it could be is a two-inch slice of prime rib, with gravy— and lobster, and a big cup of melted butter.

JOE. No— asparagus and cheese sauce, with fried chicken, with the skin all crunchy and battered—

BONNIE. I don't think anyone heard what I said.

MACK. My best meal ever was the time I ate in the classiest restaurant in all of Santa Monica. That was for a bowling awards ceremony in 91. And we had porterhouse! Mashed potatoes! Drowning in butter, fresh beans. All the wine I wanted. God, I ate like a pig that night. That's the night I got my trophy. Best player, fourth division.

JOE. People eat best when they're celebrated.

CAROL. Every meal is a glorification to the body.

MACK. Isn't it Bonnie?

BONNIE. Usually.

MACK. So what have you got for us? Go get it, is it ready?

BONNIE. I'll see.

(She wipes her mouth, then exits.)

CAROL. Mmmm… This food tastes better and better as it goes.

MACK. Why?

CAROL. All the talk of fancy dinners got me excited.

MACK. It only reminds me of the crap I'm being forced to consume.

CAROL. Oh no. With a bit of imagination, the spaghetti becomes... oh, I don't know... Heaven!

MACK. Uh huh...

CAROL. And the saltines: Bread!

MACK. Yeah, with a bit of imagination, these crackers taste like food from a foreign land. Like the Sahara Desert.

JOE. It's all OK, we shouldn't complain. There are others with less.

MACK. And there are others with nothing, who still have as much anyway, aren't there Joe?

JOE. Yes, that's true.

CAROL. He's said thank you over and over. Do you have to humiliate us both for it?

MACK. Is that what I'm doing?

JOE. Now Carol, he's not bothering me, really.

MACK. I'm doing my best, why not?

JOE. You're just short tempered tonight.

CAROL. Joe, how can you just sit there and take that abuse?

JOE. I understand, Carol, it's OK.

MACK. Sure he understands, it's simple. Eating trash is better than not eating at all.

CAROL. It's not trash. Bonnie's a good cook.

MACK. All you got to do is swallow your pride and you're fed. I'd never stoop to pity, that'd put a hole in my stomach right there.

CAROL. Is that pity, that you'd be good enough to help us out?

MACK. No, it's pitiful the way he'll take it. Hear him grub and whimper how "tasty" all this shit is. I haven't had such a lousy menu in a hospital.

JOE. You don't know. I know how fortunate it is for a person to sit at a table and have something to eat. I've seen people fight over the trash bins downtown. I've seen old men at market checkstands, with just a few cans of pet food.

MACK. Aw, make me weep. My heart can't stop to bleed. Tasty is it? Bland garbage.

CAROL. You have no appreciation of what the good Lord put before you.

MACK. *Bonnie* dished up this crap.

CAROL. It's not crap!

MACK. I worked for this meal and I deserve better.

JOE. But Mack, it really is very good.

CAROL. Why are you so mean? We were *invited*.

(*MACK pushes himself from the table.*)

MACK. You guys make me want to barf.

(*He exits. CAROL leans across the table and speaks urgently to JOE.*)

CAROL. Eat faster! (*She takes a bite herself.*) Then we won't seem like such pigs in front of him. I swear I don't ever want to take another bite in this house again. Get out there tomorrow and go to the unemployment office. Check that job board, go to the agency, hit the streets, all the department stores you can find. Try the souvenir shops even, just don't let me suffer another week of this humiliation.

JOE. I've been all over town, I've said I'll do anything.

CAROL. Everyone can't reject you. The papers are crammed with want ads, you can't give up. So what if a thousand places tell you no? All you need is the thousand and first to tell you yes.

JOE. It's degrading. I can't it depresses me. It doesn't do any good.

CAROL. Oh! You are a disgrace. We're lucky my brother has a weakness for incompetents.

JOE. Well your brother has a lot more than—

CAROL. Stuff your mouth so I don't have to listen to your stupid words.

(*He does. MACK re-enters.*)

MACK. Ah. Stricken I see. Burning with guilt. Frozen with shame. In deep consideration of your state of distress.

(*This is sarcasm: JOE and CAROL have never stopped eating.*)

CAROL. Is your stomach any better?

MACK. Nothing wrong with me.

(*He seats himself and resumes eating.*)

JOE. I'm sorry if we—

MACK. I don't want you to be sorry.

CAROL. He appreciates how you—

MACK. I don't want gratitude.

JOE. (*Making no move to leave, but angry.*) Maybe if we left—

MACK. You got to stay and finish your meal.

CAROL. Well thank god for that.

JOE. You see Mack, I'm flat broke, with not enough for the laundry, let alone—

MACK. I don't care, I don't want to know, I don't want to hear about it. You were invited to dinner, by all means, have it. I told Bonnie we'd help you folks out till you get back on the breadline. We're not going to take that away, so relax. But it's been three weeks, man! How long's it going to take?

CAROL. Three weeks isn't—

JOE. (*Tries to interject but his mouth is full.*)

MACK. I never, in the five years I lived in this house, been served such tripe as I have in the last couple days. And tonight— this is my limit you understand, my limit! Don't misunderstand. I like eating crap as much as the next guy. And I'll always call it crap, cuz I know it when I see it. But you know, I think you folks actually like this garbage.

CAROL. (*Simultaneous.*) No, it's not that—
JOE. (*Simultaneous.*) Don't call it garbage.
MACK. Sit here and see you two pump that rot down your gullets like it was candy, when you know sure as hell we had *banquets* only a few weeks ago.
JOE. Quality cheapens day by day, there's no denying that.
MACK. Maybe that's what you've been accustomed to, but it's not that way with me. I've been working for years to get to a certain plateau, and now that I got here I want to sit on it, but what happens? Stuff is disappearing! For some reason, I decide to help out a family member, and what happens but I find he's pulling me into his boat!
CAROL. He is not!
JOE. It's kind of you to help us, but—
MACK. No it wasn't kind of me! Stop saying that, you make me feel like a blinking asshole.
CAROL. Maybe you aren't as stable as you'd imagined, did you think of that? Maybe there's something wrong with you.
MACK. You bet there's something wrong with me. That I'd stop to help you guys out, that's what's wrong with me. That I assumed you folks would take care of yourself.
CAROL. Oh, now aren't we hearing it! Poor hard working Mack, the saint and martyr, being dragged into the ditch with his good intentions— and with his relatives! You are invaluable aid to us Mack, but you are by no means supporting us. Sure we'll take your help if you offer. And we'll stop any time you say. Just say so, Mack. Say when. Three weeks is not a whole lot.
MACK. Enough to run me broke.
CAROL. It's not my fault you don't make enough money. Ask for a raise. Get another job or something.
MACK. (*To JOE.*) Did you hear that? Was she talking to me or you?

(*JOE can't reply, his mouth is full. He nods in an acquiescent fashion: "Well yes but...")*

CAROL. And you leave my Joe alone.
MACK. Do you really want me to Carol? Do you think I should?
JOE. I'll pay it all back as soon as I can. Write it down somewhere. What do you want?

MACK. Food!

CAROL. Right in front of you.

MACK. Pfa! I don't know what Bonnie's up to in the kitchen, but if it's no better than this I think I'll kill her.

JOE. Isn't that a little extreme?

MACK. Ha ha. No, it's not.

JOE. Oh...

MACK. All right. I see I'm just making you uncomfortable, which is not what I want to do. I'm trying to move you to action, so you'll get back on track. And I can't imagine how you'd want to advance yourself when you're so ready to accept this crap.

JOE. But I wasn't lying, I really do—

MACK. No, no, don't start in on that. This is garbage Joe. It's unhealthy stuff, do you understand? No good. If you admit to what you really, honestly think of this meal, and this goes for you too, Carol, we'll all be in much better shape. What do you say?

JOE. Um. The spaghetti itself is excellent. Well cooked, but not mushy.

MACK. (*Groans.*)

JOE. But the butter *is* a little...

MACK. Rancid?

JOE. Yes. And the sauce, well... Carol's done better.

MACK. And the milk, how about the milk?

JOE. It's starting... to... go sour.

MACK. Atta boy (*Gives him a hearty slap on the back.*) Let's dig in!

CAROL. Thank god you're such a bastard, Mack. Now we can finally face some facts.

MACK. I'll say. Gimme some crackers.

JOE. Oh, I can breathe easier, now that I don't have to pretend this is anything more elaborate than tripe.

MACK. Tripe! You said it! God, it feels good to be honest, don't it?

JOE. I'll be honest, but I won't say it feels good. I mean, look what you've made me eat.

MACK. You don't like it, get your own, pal.

CAROL. What the hell's he supposed to do, huh?

MACK. Get off his duff, for starters.

CAROL. You pig, next time you want to play Mr. Charity, make sure you have something to offer.

MACK. I *did*, when I started.

JOE. So what if this stuff is lousy. It's still perfectly good food.

MACK. You think so?

JOE. Better than nothing.

CAROL. And that's all it's better than. Look Joe, be logical. You work, you eat. You better have some luck this week, because I don't want to have another meal in here, can you do that for me?

MACK. I second that.

JOE. Well, uh, are you sure now, because, I don't mind eating here, all things considered.

CAROL / MACK. Yes!

JOE. Can't we wait and see what Bonnie has up her sleeve?

MACK. Cripes… Bonnie!

BONNIE. (*Off.*) Coming Mack!

MACK. Where's my dinner? What have you been working at for us all, huh sweetie pie? (*To JOE and CAROL.*) Going to make us sick with more of your awful rot?

(*All snigger, though JOE remains hopeful.*)

MACK. More creations from your hot little stove?

BONNIE. It's just about ready—

MACK. I hope it's something terrific.

CAROL. And remember Joe, be honest. If she brings out anything that's going to make us sick, then we'll— then we'll—

MACK. You'll what?

CAROL. I'm ready for a good dessert.

(*BONNIE enters, with tureen.*)

BONNIE. It's ready, at last. I've been simmering this for seven hours. It's all home made, from scratch. It took me an hour just to prepare the vegetables. The rest of the time it takes to cook the beans.

(*She sets the bowls before them.*)

BONNIE. This is an old family recipe, and I like to make it whenever things get difficult. Years it's been in the family. My mother taught it to me, and my grandmother taught it to her.

MACK. Not the soup.

BONNIE. Yes.

MACK. Soup?

BONNIE. Why? What's wrong?

MACK. You never think, you never remember. Don't I tell you every blue moon you make that that I hate it?

BONNIE. Taste it.

MACK. Don't remind me! Aw.... Where's the substance? Where's the solidity?

BONNIE. I thought you liked it.

MACK. That concoction's a crime to Mulligan.

JOE. I'm sure it's very tasty and filled with lots of good—

CAROL. Will you shut up!

MACK. Bonnie, what's going on here? Are we that poverty stricken?

BONNIE. Try some. Please. There's onion in it. I know you like onion.

MACK. (*Near whining.*) Aw sheesh...

CAROL. Why this looks... quite interesting Bonnie.

BONNIE. You'll love it. I hope so. You still have room, don't you?

JOE. Oh yeah. No problem there.

MACK. Yeah, that's our Joe.

CAROL. What is this Bonnie? Are you and Mack getting into health food now?

BONNIE. No, just healthy food.

JOE. No what she meant was how come there's no meat in any of this?

BONNIE. I thought we discussed that earlier.

JOE. You mean you really are broke?

MACK. What do you think I've been talking about, huh?

JOE. I thought maybe you didn't want to serve good meals any more while we're still here.

BONNIE. Don't you like soup?

JOE. Oh yeah, I love soup— (*MACK glares at him.*) Sometimes.

BONNIE. I'm sure this will be one of them.

MACK. If it is, you can have mine.

BONNIE. (*After hesitation.*) I'm doing my best with what I have to work with.

MACK. You're doing a poor job in spite of it.

CAROL. (*Remarking.*) My, this is soup, isn't it

BONNIE. Yes. It's never made with any meat stock.

CAROL. I don't suppose you have any broth in there do you? This is a little thick.

BONNIE. It's supposed to be that way.

JOE. I guess I'll taste some. Mmm. This looks— (*MACK glares at him.*) hot. It's good this way. Sticks to your ribs.

MACK. Or your throat.

BONNIE. (*Embarrassed.*) Mack—

MACK. Can't you use a little flair, or some inventiveness?

BONNIE. It's a family recipe, I can't change it— it's been in the family for generations!

CAROL. It's not that bad, once you get started.

BONNIE. What do you expect me to do?

MACK. Don't give me any, for openers.

BONNIE. But it's all I have.

MACK. Then get something better.

BONNIE. With what?

CAROL. (*Simultaneous.*) She can't do anything, don't yell at her Mack. This is Joe's fault entirely. If he hadn't been laid off, we wouldn't be in this mess.

MACK. (*Simultaneous.*) You see what she brought, don't you Joe? You ready to decide what you want to do now?

JOE. The soup is not all that bad!

BONNIE. Can't we forget about it and count our blessings?

MACK. OK! (*Points to himself.*) One! *Now* what?

CAROL. Dammit Joe, how can you eat with all this trouble you've caused?

JOE. Bonnie's right. We should count our blessings.

MACK. I counted and came up short.

CAROL. Where's my purse? I'll straighten this out. You pigs sit right here. I'm going to the corner, and when I get back I better see three hungry faces.

(*She exits in a huff. A brief pause. MACK needles JOE.*)

MACK. What now Joey? She was embarrassed enough to split. What are you going to do, sit there?

BONNIE. Let him be. He is a *guest* in this house.

MACK. Yeah, I'll let him be. Let him sit there another three weeks and see if we still got a table to eat off of.

BONNIE. But he can't take care of himself or your sister, so what are we supposed to do? I don't mind having a little less if we can help them out.

MACK. Sure Bonnie, let's hand out a little bit of everything we got. There's hungry people everywhere. I'm one. You're one. Don't we count?

BONNIE. No. There is enough here for everyone— and there is nothing wrong with what is on your plate. Nothing.

MACK. Don't you remember what you were cooking only a very few weeks ago? Isn't there a definite drop in quality, wouldn't you say?

BONNIE. That's not important. We still have what we do have. Make use of it.

MACK. We'd still have what we *used* to have if it weren't for—

BONNIE. It was your invitation, so don't blame them, and don't blame me. It was a loving gesture, at the time.

MACK. I've changed my mind! Look, he's still at it. Doesn't even stop if we talk right in front of him.

BONNIE. Why should he stop? You don't want it. It's not good enough for you.

MACK. I deserve better.

BONNIE. You *want* better.

MACK. Same thing.

BONNIE. If Carol and Joe will eat what I give them, they're welcome to it. I made this soup— cut it and cooked it with my own two hands.

MACK. Is it that important to you?

BONNIE. I made it myself.

(*MACK looks at her and weakens. Almost sympathetic, almost understanding. CAROL bursts into the room, returned from a bloody conquest. She holds up a paper bucket and announces:*)

CAROL. Take-out chicken!

MACK. All *right!*

JOE. Where did you get the money?

CAROL. I had it. Unemployment comes Wednesday?

JOE. Yeah.

CAROL. We got two dollars and eighty cents to last us two days.

JOE. –I better get a job this week.

MACK. Well, did you hear that? All hell's breaking loose. Let's get this table cleared.

(*He starts dumping food off the plates.*)

BONNIE. (*Stunned.*) Mack!

MACK. Come on, Bonnie—

(*He confiscates her food, dumps it out.*)

BONNIE. My soup—

MACK. Forget about that, honey. Have some of this.

CAROL. It was real good soup Bonnie, but I'm not in the mood for it tonight. You'll have to give me the recipe some time.

BONNIE. It's a family recipe.

(*CAROL is passing out paper plates and napkins.*)

JOE. Gimme one too.

CAROL. Here you are, sit still.

MACK. Hey Carol, this is terrific. God I really appreciate this.

BONNIE. That food shouldn't have been wasted.

MACK. Come on Bonnie, forget about it, OK?

BONNIE. But I made that for all of you.

CAROL. You can make it again some time. But now have some of this.

JOE. Yes, it's important you put good things in your body. Keeps you alive.

MACK. –and kicking!

CAROL. Eat up Bonnie. They make it best on the evening shift.

JOE. How can they make it so good all the time?

MACK. Cripes, they only make a couple thousand pieces a day.

JOE. Well, I'm gonna start. Don't hold me back!

MACK. You got a plate, and there should be eighteen pieces of bird in there. Dig in.

CAROL. I'm serious about that soup now.

BONNIE. It's a family secret. I don't give it out.

CAROL. Let's all forget about everything, and just concentrate on one important occasion:

MACK / JOE / CAROL. Dinner!

(*All begin stuffing themselves, except BONNIE, who pokes at her plate rather dejectedly.*)

MACK. I could eat this stuff till the break of day!

JOE. I could eat it the rest of my life.

BONNIE. You can eat it until the bucket's empty. (*She takes a bite.*)

CAROL. I really did enjoy that soup Bonnie. The dinner was tremendous.

JOE. It was very good.

MACK. Just have that chicken, honey. Everything's all right now. Yep, everything is just fine.

(*They continue eating, LIGHTS FADE.*)

END OF PLAY

DELUSIONS
REVEALED

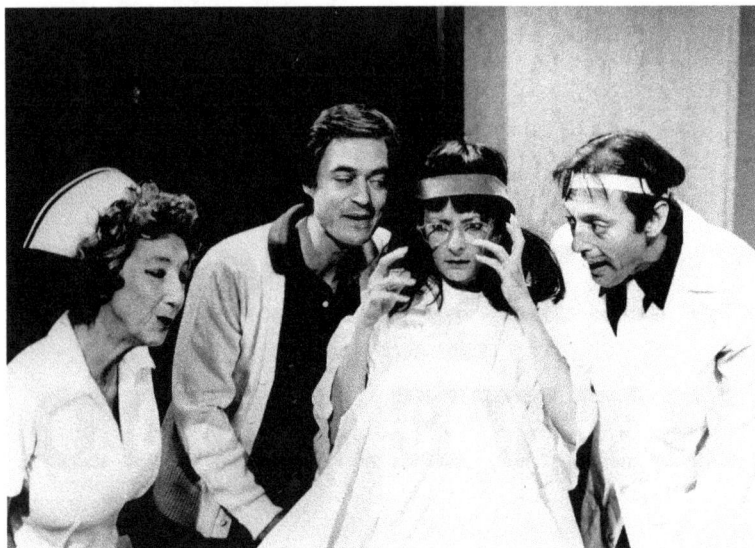

Francis Bey, James Dybas, Susan Barnes and Robert Glaudini in *Delusions Revealed*, Oddysey Theater, Los Angeles. (1980)

Delusions Revealed was presented in a revue titled "Multiple Fractures" which opened at the Déjà Vu Coffeehouse in Hollywood, CA on May 26, 1978, directed by John Forman. The cast was as follows:

Jenny.......	Anya Cronin
Donald......	Karl Honaker
Doctor......	Michael Bossier
Nurse.......	Kristina Callahan

It was next produced as part of "The Great American Playwright's Show" at the Oddysey Theater, Los Angeles, opening on November 1, 1980, directed by Victoria Hochberg, with the following cast:

Jenny.......	Susan Barnes
Donald......	James Dybas
Doctor......	Robert Glaudini
Nurse.......	Francis Bey

SYNOPSIS

Former hippies meet the consequences of their past: Were they really building a better future generation?

CHARACTERS

JENNY (f)

DONALD (m)

DOCTOR (m)

NURSE (f)

SETTING

Jenny's bed in a hospital room.

DELUSIONS REVEALED

By Ross MacLean

Scene: A hospital room.

NURSE. Good morning Miss Conlin. I heard it was quite a delivery last night.

JENNY. Yes, the doctor said that births like mine always amaze him.

NURSE. As it was told in the doctor's lounge, he described you as being tighter than a Scottish Jew. We all had quite a laugh.

JENNY. I was not nervous. I want my child to know from the start the he will be subject to strict discipline.

NURSE. I see. You know, your child probably will have a harder life than others. I really shouldn't say, but it won't be entirely due to your protective instincts.

JENNY. What do you mean, Nurse?

NURSE. Well, I probably shouldn't say...

JENNY. That's stopped you from nothing before.

NURSE. Yes, but this is a surprise I think Doctor should handle.

JENNY. Nurse! There's something you're not telling me— is something wrong with my baby?

NURSE. (*Starts giggling.*) Oh, I really can't say. You'll have to wait for Doctor! (*Exits giggling.*)

JENNY. I bet something terrible has happened. I haven't even seen the tyke yet. They're just playing tricks on me. That's all it is. Just a cruel, sick joke.

NURSE. Miss Conlin, the father is here to see you.

JENNY. Let him in then. I'm afraid to look.

DONALD. Hello Jenny.

JENNY. Hello Donald.

DONALD. Well. It's happened.

JENNY. Have you seen it?

DONALD. No, they said I should wait.

JENNY. Do you think it is beautiful?

DONALD. I'm sure it is Jenny. In its own way...

JENNY. What do you mean? Why do you talk in that tone? Do you know something I don't?

DONALD. No Jenny, it's just that I was thinking...

JENNY. Yes?

DONALD. Well Jenny... Do you remember those years ago when I first met you?

JENNY. Yes, at the peace rally in 1970.

DONALD. Those were carefree days, weren't they Jenny?

JENNY. We demonstrated in faith!

DONALD. We enjoyed ourselves– in excess.

JENNY. It worked– the war ended, they came home and we're still together!

DONALD. But... Our actions have turned on us.

JENNY. What is it Donald? Is it that you— no longer love me?

DONALD. No Jenny, it's not that— Frankly Jenny... it's the drugs.

(*SOUND EFFECT: EEEEEEEEEEEEEEEEEEEEEEEE!*

The NURSE appears.)

NURSE. Good afternoon Miss Conlin, the Doctor is here to see you now.

JENNY. Afternoon– afternoon? It's been a day and a half and I haven't seen my baby yet? Something is wrong. Something is terribly, terribly wrong.

DONALD. Calm yourself Jenny. You know it's only been a few hours. The doctor is here to straighten you out.

NURSE. Probably I shouldn't say, but I'd say he's too late.

JENNY. Show him in, Nurse. And get out of my sight, please.

DONALD. I want you to know Jenny, that whatever happens, I'll be at your side.

JENNY. No, no, it's not supposed to be this way. It should be joyful, it should be a blessing. It shouldn't be frightening to have a child. Not for a few years at least. Could I have made my mistake too soon?

DONALD. It happened years ago Jenny. We read the reports, but how could we have believed them?

JENNY. Where is the Doctor? Is he waiting for me to go into full frenzy before he brings me some drugs?

DONALD. Drugs! Drugs! Don't say that word in front of me! If you only knew...

JENNY. What is it Donald? Do you know something I don't?

DONALD. Well Jenny– I haven't seen the baby, but I heard what caused the– what caused the – the–

JENNY. Oh Donald!

DOCTOR. Good morning Miss Conlin.

JENNY. Morning? Morning? Am I waking from a nightmare or into one? Tell me I'm real Doctor, someone has to.

DOCTOR. It's all right Miss Conlin, calm down. How are you feeling?

JENNY. Doctor, I'm worried. Everyone has been acting so strangely, I'm afraid something terrible has happened. I haven't seen my baby yet. Where are you keeping him?

DOCTOR. Don't worry Miss Conlin, we have it in special care, and it is doing fine.

JENNY. It? It? Why this It? What is "It?"

DOCTOR. We haven't determined its sex yet Miss Conlin, but I can assure you that is only a minor concern at this point.

JENNY. At this point? At this point??? What is going on! Help me, tell me what is going on. I want to see my baby.

DOCTOR. Now Miss Conlin, you know by now that your baby is somewhat unique, and you know I can't let you see it until you are in a fitting mood.

DONALD. But Doctor, what is a fitting mood? She's hysterical now.

DOCTOR. That's close. The less in control of her senses, the easier she'll be able to believe the horrible tragedy which she has created.

JENNY. No! No! Don't talk that way. It's my baby, it's beautiful. It's beautiful because it's mine!

NURSE. You may talk that way now, but your snobbery will not hold in the neighborhood.

JENNY. Oh!

DOCTOR. Quiet Nurse. Miss Conlin, I'm afraid your baby is not regular at all.

DONALD. Is it that bad?

DOCTOR. In fact, it is worse.

NURSE. Don't panic Miss Conlin, you'll get a kick out of it once you get used to it.

DOCTOR. Nurse!

JENNY. It's OK Doctor. I can be a strong woman when I need to be; I can take it.

DOCTOR. Well Miss, you've–
JENNY. Yes?
DOCTOR. You and this man here, you've–
DONALD. What?
DOCTOR. What I mean to say is... um..
JENNY. Come on Doctor, be strong. We are.
DOCTOR. Your baby, Miss Conlin, is...
NURSE. Hurry up and get to the good part!
DONALD. Quiet you!
DOCTOR. Miss Conlin, I'm afraid, due to your past experiences, that your baby is... your baby is...
ALL. YES???
DOCTOR. Excuse me, I need some water! (*He exits.*)
JENNY. Oh, wouldn't you know! What is going on here? Is it true that this could be the ugliest day of my life? When will it ever end?
DONALD. I'll bear it through with you Jenny, trust me. It's just like we're waiting for them to call our number at a raffle. We know we'll hear our number.
NURSE. What a number!
DOCTOR. I'm back. Forgive me, I've never had to do this before. Miss Conlin, you've just given birth to a seven-pound eye.

(*Silence.*)

NURSE. What do you think of that, sweetie!
JENNY. No! No! What did I ever do to deserve this?
DOCTOR. You took acid Miss Conlin. L.S.D. Remember?
JENNY. No, no no no no...
JENNY'S VOICE ON RECORDING. (*While flashback characters materialize.*) Yes, yes, I do remember. I see it all now, I remember. That day before the rally... I never would have known. I never gave it a thought. I see it all as it happened...
FLASHBACK DONALD. Hey Man, what ya smokin?
FLASHBACK JENNY. Bananas man... cool hi hi hiiiiiii....

(*He hands her a large sugar cube.*)

FLASHBACK DONALD. Here babe, try some of this. It will TURN * YOU * ON *

FLASHBACK JENNY. Oh wow, oh wow– It's beautiful man. Love! Love!

(*Flashback dissolves.*)

DOCTOR. Was it really beautiful Jenny? Think about it. Vital chromosome damage. Was it all that beautiful?

DONALD. I'm sorry Jenny.

JENNY. Goodness, the guilt, the pain I feel I feel nothing but the guilt and the pain. What will I do with all those booties I knitted? I don't know anyone who plays golf.

DONALD. Don't worry about a thing Jenny. We'll see it through.

JENNY. Oh Donald, my dear Donald, how sweet. We'll see it through together. We were busy living, we couldn't know what we were creating for the world. Some of it was good! –and some of it.... we did it, and we must love it all the same. You will stay with me?

DONALD. Of course I will.

NURSE. What a couple of flakes!

JENNY. Oh shut up Nurse, and bring me my baby.

DOCTOR. You actually wish to see it?

JENNY. Of course. I don't care what it may be. I will love my baby.

(*The NURSE brings it in, wrapped in blanket.*)

JENNY. My god, my god... I've give birth to a flashback.

DONALD. I suppose, Jenny, this cancels our hopes for a concert pianist. Oh, why were we so careless? Why didn't we think?

JENNY. How will I care for it? What should I feed it?

DOCTOR. Murine?

DONALD. We will make a good home for our little Iris!

NURSE. There is a bright side to all this. There is something for you both to be quite grateful for.

JENNY. And what is that?

NURSE. It was not born blind!

(*BLACKOUT.*)

END OF PLAY

HYAENA

Curt Pesicka and Tony Catanese in *Hyaena*, The Changing Scene, Denver, CO. (1991)

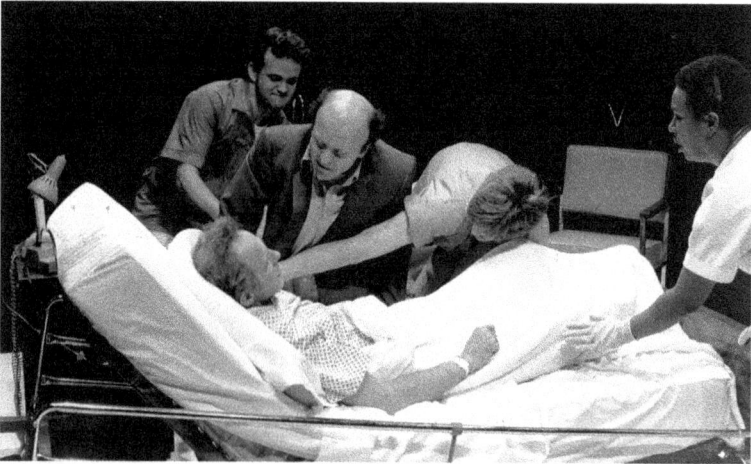

William McNulty, Michael Hartman, Christopher Franciosa, S. Scott Shina and Daryl Swanson in *Hyaena* at the Humana Festival, Actors Theater of Louisville. (1992)

Hyaena was first produced on January 10, 1991 by The Changing Scene, Denver, CO. Directed by Tricia Stevens, the cast was as follows:

Hyaena............	Curt Pesicka
Patient.............	Tony Catanese
Wife...............	Toni Brady
Friend..............	Andrew Pollet
Nurse...............	Kendra White

Hyaena was subsequently produced at the Humana Festival, Actors Theater of Louisville, on February 18, 1992. Directed by Mladen Kiselov; set design by Paul Owen; lighting design by Mary Louise Geiger; and costume design by Laura A. Patterson. Dramaturg, Michael Bigelow Dixon. The cast was as follows:

Hyaena........	William McNulty
Patient........	Michael Hartman
Wife...........	Kathryn Layng
Friend.........	Mark Shannon
Nurse.........	Sandra Sydney
Aides.........	Christopher Franciosa,
	S. Scott Shina,
	Daryl Swanson

What the critics said:

THE 1992 HUMANA FESTIVAL, Actors Theatre Of Louisville

"A strongly gripping evocation of a world of twisted values that successfully forces viewers to re-evaluate their own. Under Mladen Kisselov's tight direction, William McNulty gave a harrowing performance as the Hyaena."

London Financial Times

"The lead character in Ross MacLean's HYAENA is a lurking hospital visitor who feeds on the death experiences of patients, an unusual and unsettling premise worthy of further development."

Variety

"HYAENA emerged as the festival's most quietly disturbing play ... one that hints at the possible consequences of living in a society that clinically detaches itself from emotional realities."

American Theatre

"Disturbing. It makes the audience think, which renders HYAENA highly successful."

The Louisville Cardinal

"One couldn't walk away from Ross MacLean's HYAENA without letting the thoughts and images conveyed toss and turn about in one's head... HYAENA ranks merit."

Backstage

"Mr. MacLean has created an extraordinary character in this metaphorically carnivorous stranger."

The Washington Times

"Chilling, thought provoking... It is a fascinating portrait drawn by MacLean's play. HYAENA will fuel a lot of discussion and some thoughtful insight."

The New Albany Tribune

"Remarkably unsentimental… This tough-minded writer deserves respect."

Theatre Week

SYNOPSIS

In the closing weeks of a terminally ill patient, a most peculiar visitor hopes to accompany him through his final passing.

CHARACTERS

HYAENA (m)

PATIENT (m)

WIFE (f)

FRIEND (m)

NURSE (f)

AIDE (m)

SETTING

The main playing area is a hospital room, with hospital bed center, and a tray table and night stand on either side. There is also a small functional sink. If possible, a window upstage, showing only sky and indicating time of day by varying shades of light or dark. Downstage left is a small area with a couple chairs, indicating a waiting room. Downstage right is a small counter and stools, indicating the hospital's coffee shop.

HYAENA

By Ross MacLean

ACT ONE

Scene One

(*A hospital room. Pleasant. Single bed. Window. Nightstand, tray table, closet. IV pole stand by the bed, with tubes attached to PATIENT. A trash can near the bed.*

The PATIENT, a man in his late 40's or older, lies in bed, talking in his sleep. The HYAENA stands nearby, a care-worn man in an ill-fitting jacket, observing the PATIENT and the activity of the NURSE, who is throwing medicine bags and other paraphernalia into the trash.

The hospital P.A. system announces the end of visiting hours.)

PATIENT. Yes... yes... No...

HYAENA. Talking in his sleep. That's new, I think. Always seems to be answering questions. Does it mean anything?

NURSE. Does he get restless? Shakes?

HYAENA. Not that I've seen. (*He nudges the PATIENT.*)

NURSE. Let him be. He's had some excitement today.

PATIENT. Was I...? hmmm...

HYAENA. I woke him once. He couldn't remember anything.

(*The AIDE comes in to take the dinner tray away.*)

HYAENA. (*To the AIDE.*) No, leave that please. (*To the NURSE.*) Around the comer, the door was closed. How is the woman in the other room?

NURSE. She's not here any longer.

HYAENA. Did she go home?

NURSE. No.

HYAENA. I see. When did this happen?

NURSE. Earlier this afternoon. I'm sorry.

HYAENA. (*Discretely makes a note in a little book.*) Did you notice the hour?

NURSE. After two sometime.

PATIENT. Yes... yes... No... No...

HYAENA. Too bad. Did you see anything.

NURSE. She was alone so I imagine it was peaceful.

HYAENA. Yes. So you've no idea of the exact time? (*She disregards the question.*) She was doing so well...

NURSE. Sometimes patients go through a recovery stage where their functions return to normal for a period.

HYAENA. There was a very nice photograph of one of her birthdays. She offered it to me once, but I didn't know if she was serious or not... She had no family. Who would I ask about that?

NURSE. You could speak with the desk downstairs. Usually it gets thrown out.

HYAENA. I see. Thank you.

PATIENT. Over this way... oh, that's so nice... this way.

(*The HYAENA looks through the papers on the PATIENT's tray table. Cards and unopened mail. One he opens and reads.*)

PATIENT. No. Different lines. That way, different lines. Ahh... ahh...

(*The NURSE goes. The PATIENT starts looking around. Until he gets revved up, it is hard to tell the difference between sleep and waking in this person.*)

HYAENA. Are you awake? Are you with us?

PATIENT. Oh it's you. What are you doing here?

HYAENA. Reading your mail. This one has a little bear on it, in a washtub, can you see? (*Reads.*) "I hope that you will get well soon / You know I really care it / Will be such fun when this is done—" (*Opens the card.*) "You shouldn't have to bear it."... and there's a drawing of the bear hopping up, showing his little backside. From— (*The PATIENT takes the card from him.*) Oh, your hands are free! They were under the blankets, did they change the IVs after I left last night?

PATIENT. No, they took off the boards and put in longer tubes. This morning at quarter to five, at their convenience. Is everyone gone?

HYAENA. No one's here. I would never have opened this if I'd known you could do it yourself.

PATIENT. How long have you been here?

HYAENA. I've been here about twenty minutes.

PATIENT. Why didn't you wake me?

HYAENA. I like watching you sleep.

PATIENT.... I don't know why. What time is it?

HYAENA. It's after seven.

PATIENT. Morning or evening?

HYAENA. Evening.

PATIENT. You're late.

HYAENA. I hear you had some activity today.

PATIENT. I got out of bed today, the first time in weeks. I got my exercise. Once around the ward.

HYAENA. So you're getting better!

PATIENT. It's amazing how weak you become. Got to start getting better, it's now or never. Only made it part way, then I had to come back and fall asleep. That was around... when? And didn't wake up until you got here.

HYAENA. Part way around and part back, that counts as once around the floor.

PATIENT. What's that?

HYAENA. Your dinner.

PATIENT. Bring it to me!

HYAENA. I wasn't sure if you'd be ready for it or not.

PATIENT. What kind of shit did they bring me this time? (*Whines.*) Oooh, and it's cold!

HYAENA. I could bring you something from outside if you like.

PATIENT. No. So it's cold. Good. That'll be just fine, that's just as well. Nothing wrong with that. (*Looks over tray. Change in mood again.*) Why do they do this! Will you look at that, why do they even bother.

HYAENA. It has been here a while.

PATIENT. (*Change in mood again. He sorts out what he will or won't have, throwing most things into the trash.*) These are good. This can go. This can go... This can go out. What's this...? (*Takes the lid off a paper cup.*) I can have this soup.

HYAENA. Is that all you're going to have?

PATIENT. Do you want it? Aaaaugh...! (*He throws the spoon down.*)

HYAENA. That's not enough.

PATIENT. It's enough all right. But what's it for? You idiot—!

HYAENA. Easy now, easy... Try something, at least. Drink this.

PATIENT. You.

HYAENA. (*Takes a salad.*) I'll take this if you take that. (*The PATIENT accepts it.*) I hate to see natural food go to waste. (*Eats a shred at a time, with his fingers.*) They say there is no food value in this, but if it comes from the ground, I think there must be something worthwhile to it. Don't you?

PATIENT. No.

HYAENA. You missed a beautiful day out today.

PATIENT. (*Flat.*) Did I.

(*PATIENT turns on the television, and lays down to sleep again.*)

HYAENA. So many people out, walking here and there, finally out of their heavy coats, trying to go without their light sweaters... which they have to keep putting back on— Enjoying the day. Running here and there...

PATIENT. (*Flat.*) Sounds delightful.

HYAENA. Does it upset you? To hear about life outside?

PATIENT. I don't get any visitors anymore. Only you.

HYAENA. Doesn't your family look after you?

(*PATIENT looks at the ceiling with impatience.*)

HYAENA. I do my best. (*PATIENT isn't responding to his food.*) Your soup.

PATIENT. What do I need food for? Once around the floor and sleep.

HYAENA. If that's the best you can do. I passed another patient while I was leaving yesterday. Very young. She was surrounded by flowers. Orange and yellow tulips, violets, pink roses and blue daisies.

PATIENT. Oh? What's her name?

HYAENA. She had someone with her, so I couldn't find out. My age. A parent, maybe, a relative of some type. It's hard for me, when they're looked after. But then, she's new.

PATIENT. What happened to that other friend of yours? The one that was in the other bed?

HYAENA. Before you were put in this private room?

PATIENT. (*Protesting that he was isolated. Though he was.*) I asked for this room. Yes.

HYAENA. (*Disinterested.*) He's fine now, I imagine...

PATIENT. Do you still see him?

HYAENA. He's better now, so I don't see him so much.

PATIENT. Seemed like a nice guy. (*Turns off the television.*) I get tired of the television. Usually I only sleep. What was his name?

HYAENA. What difference does it make? He wasn't a close friend of mine, you're not going to see him again. And like I told you, he's fine now.

PATIENT. Sorry. OK. I just sometimes... miss the company.

HYAENA. I'm sure. You haven't noticed my new jacket.

PATIENT. It doesn't look new.

HYAENA. A gift, from a friend.

PATIENT. Oh.

HYAENA. It was left in the ward closet, family forgot about it, apparently. I know he would have wanted me to have it.

PATIENT. Fits funny.

HYAENA. I could have it altered, but it wouldn't be the same.

PATIENT. (*Looks at his ring.*) My friend gave me this. Years ago.

HYAENA. I've noticed it. It's very nice. Why don't you wear a wedding band?

PATIENT. I gave it to my wife, thought it would be safer, you know, around here; but I still got— (*Starts throwing food away again.*) I can't take this. Here, you have it.

HYAENA. Oh no, I couldn't thank you.

PATIENT. Did I just ask you that?

HYAENA. No.

PATIENT. Then to the garbage, where it came from. (*Coughs a bit.*)

HYAENA. You want some water?

PATIENT. (*Reaches for water himself.*) Did I ask for water? What do you think I am, helpless? Let a man do for himself, for chrissakes.

HYAENA. Of course.

PATIENT. Uh. I didn't ask for water, did I?

HYAENA. No. Just wanting to be helpful.

PATIENT. Yeah. You never met any of my family, or friends, have you.

HYAENA. I'm shy about that, usually. I feel more comfortable when I have you to myself.

PATIENT. You should meet my wife.

HYAENA. No one has ever wanted me to meet anyone they actually know. Is there a special reason?

PATIENT. My mind's going. The doctor was in to see me, I was answering a question, and— I knew what I meant to say, but what came out was... just bizarre.

HYAENA. Could that be from the medicine?

PATIENT. I don't know.

HYAENA. What did the doctor say?

PATIENT. I clammed up. Didn't want him to think something else was going. I'm not ready to believe it myself.

HYAENA. I see.

PATIENT. So, maybe if you were here, to... fill in the gaps. Maybe she won't notice if I...

HYAENA. Fail?

PATIENT. I'm getting better. One step forward, two steps back.

HYAENA. I'll be right here with you.

PATIENT. My other friend, Jerry. Haven't seen him in weeks. And he stayed by me with this whole thing. When it was new.

HYAENA. People drift off, like you say.

PATIENT. We grew up together. Went to the same schools. I have to talk to him.

HYAENA. What about?

PATIENT. Oh some personal things. Just want to talk out... some private stuff.

HYAENA. It's OK if you don't want to tell me.

PATIENT. He'll be back. In bad times, people pull together. (*Coughs a bit.*) Seems to.
HYAENA. There was a man here earlier.
PATIENT. A visitor?
HYAENA. You were sleeping.
PATIENT. (*Starts to get excited, angry, almost panics.*) What did he look like?
HYAENA.... I don't know.
PATIENT. It was a man?
HYAENA. About your age. A little dumpy. Light hair, thinning, I think...
PATIENT. – That was Jerry !
HYAENA. He didn't leave a name. I just said that you needed your rest and I— I sent him away.
PATIENT. But you stayed here yourself
HYAENA. They might have taken your dinner if I hadn't.
PATIENT. I haven't seen him in— Oh, I wish you would have told me... We've been friends all my life.
HYAENA. Call him.
PATIENT. I can't do that. I used to, all the time. If he wanted to see me he would have— Oh forget it. (*He's close to tears.*) Shit. Darn. Oh, and this awful dinner, and it's cold besides.
HYAENA. Did I do something wrong?
PATIENT. Forget it. Just forget it.

(*He's showing tears now. The HYAENA becomes cheerfully helpful.*)

HYAENA. Don't make yourself so upset. He'll be back.

(*He fluffs the PATIENT's pillows, though the PATIENT is uncooperative.*)

PATIENT. Will you just leave me alone, please.
HYAENA. –I can't do anything right! (*He makes as if to leave, then turns back.*) How was I to know he wasn't someone from your family or something. I was only thinking of you.
PATIENT. Well, you screwed up.
HYAENA. I won't let it happen again.

PATIENT. Please, if anyone, ever, comes in to see me, I want to see them!

HYAENA. Understood. Got it. Never again.

PATIENT. Thanks.

HYAENA. (*Tries to make a joke.*) It might have been someone from the income tax.

PATIENT. It doesn't matter. Nothing matters.

HYAENA. (*Picks a book off the PATIENT's table.*) What's this?

PATIENT. Another lady on the floor gave it to me. Weeks ago. How to heal yourself with nothing but thought. If you read it, it all makes perfect sense. She was just down at the corner, I think, haven't seen her in a while either.

HYAENA. Do you know how it worked out for her?

PATIENT. (*Shakes his head.*) I was going to start today, but I fell asleep. Well, once around the floor, that's pretty good in my condition.

HYAENA. It's nice when a special person gives you something.

PATIENT. And you can learn more about, you know, death, without having to actually experience it or anything.

HYAENA. You're going to avoid that?

PATIENT. You're like all those other living people, you don't understand what it means to—

HYAENA. Please, please don't— I do understand, believe me I do.

PATIENT. It might not seem like much to you, but it's progress. I was even thinking, when I get out of here, I'm thinking about joining a health club. Take some classes. Isn't that a good idea?

HYAENA. Oh, it's noisy in those places. All the people leaping around, it drives me nuts. I'd rather... (*PATIENT silences him with a cold look, then continues.*) If you think it's possible.

PATIENT. Of course it's possible. Why, when I think of all the things I've wanted to do... It's funny, I have seen so many movies, you know, where they tell you over and over again how simple life is, and how we should do what we want. And I never got it. Now, I got it. I know why people don't want to be around me, I'm not any fun. But it's my fault, I can change that.

HYAENA. Now you shouldn't think that way. You've always held an interest for me.

PATIENT. A change is coming. I can feel the difference.

HYAENA. Good. Would you like to take a walk?

PATIENT. What for?

HYAENA. You said you're feeling stronger. Why waste it?

PATIENT. But I haven't really started the book yet... And I tried already today...

HYAENA. Without me.

PATIENT. (*Frightened.*) Well. Maybe.

HYAENA. Maybe just as far as the corner. See what you missed.

PATIENT. Right. OK. Sure.

HYAENA. Good.

PATIENT. Get my robe then. Are you sure it's all right?

HYAENA. I think, as long as you have me with you. (*Taking hold of the IV pole stand.*) Here, should I hold this? So you don't get the tubes tangled up?

(*The PATIENT fumbles in trying to get up, places his hand in the dinner tray. The HYAENA will get a sponge or wet paper towel and wipe him down.*)

PATIENT. You know, maybe this isn't such a good idea.

HYAENA. I can do it for you.

PATIENT. I better not. I want to rest first, read the book later, after breakfast.

HYAENA. You're sure you need me here then.

PATIENT. It's morning isn't it?

HYAENA. Evening. Seven thirty.

PATIENT. At night?

HYAENA. Yes.

PATIENT. I was dreaming when I woke up, about riding a bicycle.

HYAENA. Oh?

PATIENT. It felt so real, so I know it's possible. I think that's why I was dreaming it.

HYAENA. Possibly. Where were you riding?

PATIENT. Nowhere. By myself.

HYAENA. Not through a park? Down a country road?

PATIENT. No. Just through space I guess. Blank. Free. Quiet.

HYAENA. Outer space?

PATIENT. (*Throws soup cup into the trash.*) I said no, how many times do you want me to repeat it. Take this stuff away. Everywhere you suggest is a no, and there's a long list of 'em. Understand? It was a dream anyway, why bother?

HYAENA. Maybe we could find the meaning.

PATIENT. –Of something that never happened. Idiotic pastime. What time is it?

HYAENA. I just told you. (*As he sponges the PATIENT's hand.*) That's such a nice ring, you really shouldn't wear it here.

PATIENT. Stop, I can take care of myself.

HYAENA. I've upset you enough. It's time to go.

PATIENT. Leave me alone from now on. I don't want to see you here again, OK?

HYAENA. I can come earlier tomorrow.

PATIENT. Good-bye!

HYAENA. Oh, I almost forgot— your, uh— friend...? Mitchell?

PATIENT. Jerry. Yeah yeah. What about him?

HYAENA. He left you this note.

PATIENT. Now you tell me! Now you remember!

HYAENA. It's been a nice visit.

PATIENT. Call him for me— call him, I can't—

HYAENA. Good-bye.

(*The HYAENA leaves. The PATIENT, agitated, probably knocks the phone off the table trying to reach for it. He falls back in the bed.*)

END OF SCENE ONE

SCENE TWO

(*Hovering high above the PATIENT's bed are shiny mylar balloons with yellow "happy faces" on them, or "Get Well Soon!" in bright cheerful letters, tied to the bed with gay ribbons and bows. The tray table is cluttered with festive foil boxes, Chinese ring puzzles, a Rubiks cube; general items of mental torture. The television is on [screen facing away from the audience, no sound]. Noise from the hospital is quite apparent; Footsteps, bells, phones ringing, carts wheeling, and constant uneasy murmur of conversation. The PATIENT lies in bed. Room is ill-lit, and the curtains are closed.*

The HYAENA appears at the doorway, tentatively holding a bouquet of flowers.)

HYAENA. Oh, you're up. I was just going to look in and go on.
PATIENT. No, come in. Come in.
HYAENA. So. Your family's been to visit.
PATIENT. They're awful. Just awful. Was I asleep?
HYAENA. Yes.
PATIENT. How long?
HYAENA. Did you have your dinner yet?
PATIENT. It's morning isn't it?
HYAENA. Evening. Six forty-four.
PATIENT. At night?
HYAENA. Your family loves you a lot, I can tell.
PATIENT. Stupid, stupid people. They don't know.
HYAENA. Don't know what?
PATIENT. Those are nice. Are they for me?
HYAENA. No, actually. They're for the other patient, the girl. With the flowers?
PATIENT. Oh.
HYAENA. She doesn't have as many, they've faded. I thought she'd appreciate a few. How are you feeling?
PATIENT. I may be going home soon.
HYAENA. Oh...?
PATIENT. The doctor said I was showing signs of progression—
HYAENA. Of recovery or illness?

PATIENT. (*Balks, insists.*) Why would he say that?

HYAENA. Of course. Go on.

PATIENT. Said there was nothing more they can do for me here, that I'd be just as well to let it run its course at home.

HYAENA. (*Distressed.*) Oh. Oh, This should be good news. You uh... weren't having any of the other problems? Your thinking?

PATIENT. Not that I know of. I'm glad you showed up. I did want to see you before I go home.

HYAENA. You'll be missed here. Nurses, doctors, I mean. Mostly.

PATIENT. The bed won't stay empty.

HYAENA. If you want, I'd still be happy to take care of you. As long as you're ill.

PATIENT. Why would they do that? Why would they send me home if I wasn't well? I'll have my family to look after me.

HYAENA. Yes, that's what they're so good at, aren't they.

PATIENT. Home... And my own clean bed.

HYAENA. Since you don't need me, I'll be moving along then.

PATIENT.... So soon?

HYAENA. I want to get these to the new girl. She's not well.

PATIENT. Take me. I can be an example. Is she on this floor?

HYAENA. She still had people with her— I did go there first, but it sounded like they might leave soon.

PATIENT. When I was new I always had flowers. Sit down a minute. If you want, you could put those in some water, there's a vase.

HYAENA. To what do we owe your freedom? Have you been reading your healing book?

PATIENT. Some of it's really interesting. It says colors can attract certain things. (*He starts flipping through the book.*) There's a part—

HYAENA. What are you looking for?

PATIENT. Wait, wait— oooh— Woo! This makes me dizzy. (*Takes in the balloons and the puzzles. Nudges one of them towards the HYAENA.*) Ever work one of these? (*Despair.*) This is no world of mine, I'm getting out of here. (*He opens book again.*) They have a grave sight for me on a hillside. There is a shipyard nearby.

HYAENA. Did you like boats?

PATIENT. Do I like boats. Do you mean "Do I like boats"? I'm right here.

HYAENA. Sorry. Do you like boats?

PATIENT. I used to. I need to see Jerry. What if he comes and I'm not here.

HYAENA. Wouldn't he find you at home?

PATIENT. He shouldn't wait so long. We've got something to discuss.

HYAENA. Tell me.

PATIENT. Well, we go way back you know.

HYAENA. Uh huh. What. Tell me.

PATIENT. It's because of him that we met.

HYAENA. Who.

PATIENT. (*Laughs it away, mild.*) Don't bother, you wouldn't understand.

HYAENA. I don't need to.

PATIENT. In the book it says... I don't know why I get so scared all the time— Here. (*Hands book to HYAENA.*) It talks about how people can do miracles. This story here— about a man who pulled his wife out from under an automobile? Lifted it up by himself to save her? And I think this book was printed in '63, cars were a lot heavier then. Proves how much power there is in us all. We just have to learn to use it.

HYAENA. And I suppose it offers instruction on where this power lies.

PATIENT. When we're challenged, we have it. In adversity, we release this— strength.

HYAENA. Well then, why don't we get you out of this bed, and we can go upstairs to see that new patient. Would you like to?

PATIENT. I might.

HYAENA. Then let's get you moving.

PATIENT. Good! Right! (*Sits up, places legs over the side of the bed, pauses.*)

HYAENA. Need help?

PATIENT. No, I just thought. She might not want company.

HYAENA. Here then— just come this far. This will be for you.

(*He pulls a flower from the bunch and lays it on the windowsill.*)

HYAENA. Come over and put it in the vase.
PATIENT. Sure. (*But he doesn't move.*)
HYAENA. What is it?
PATIENT. (*Seems immensely happy and content with the world.*) You know, sometimes I want to get up and go walking around. And sometimes I just don't.
HYAENA. Maybe we should rest.

(*The HYAENA lays the PATIENT down.*)

PATIENT. That might be nice. It's not time. It's coming though. When the time comes, I'm really going to surprise you. Adversity isn't strong enough yet.
HYAENA. Would you like to go back to sleep?
PATIENT. Watch. When it gets really bad... You'll see. (*Pause.*) Sometimes I wonder if I'm having a dream, and I slip away, how will I know the difference?
HYAENA. If I was with you, I could let you know. Some die alone, because living people are afraid to be around them; they think the dying person tries to take a part of them when they go. That possibility doesn't frighten me.
PATIENT. Where's my— I want to call the nurse—
HYAENA. What do you need that I can't give you?

(*The HYAENA comes to the bedside.*)

PATIENT. I am going to live!
HYAENA. There is that possibility, but being realistic—
PATIENT. Get out, get away from me!
HYAENA. Some say in dying, we become closer to God.
PATIENT. The further I get from God, the better!
HYAENA. (*Easing the PATIENT back down.*) Relax. You said you were going back to sleep,

(*The HYAENA places a hand over the PATIENT's chest, the PATIENT has a coughing spasm.*)

HYAENA. Stay calm, stay calm. I'm not frightened, why should you be?

(*With great care, the HYAENA lays the PATIENT down, makes the bed around him, maybe wipes his face with a cloth*)

HYAENA. Think of it: No one should have to suffer like you. In the next world, you'll see how life is meant to work, you will have the answers. You could... be a means to heal people. You could come back to me.

PATIENT. (*He's too weak for volume, but he speaks with intensity.*) Do you think that I might be the first person to die? Do you think no one else would have thought of that first? Who do you think you are, you're no friend of mine, who do you think you are?

HYAENA. I'll go. I'm going.

PATIENT. You're no one, you're some jackal, some hyaena, you're some stranger who used to visit someone else in a room I'm not in anymore! Get out! Get out!

HYAENA. Forgive me. Please forgive me, I never want to give you anything but comfort. It's all I know how to do.

PATIENT. Get out! Get out!

HYAENA. (*As he gathers his things.*) I'm sorry. I'm going. Lay down, rest. Please if you have any last thought in your life, please: forgive me. I won't come anymore. Thank you.

(*The NURSE appears in the doorway. He takes a last look at the PATIENT, then bolts quickly past the NURSE, who goes to the PATIENT's bedside. The curtain is pulled across, concealing the PATIENT from view.*)

END SCENE TWO

SCENE THREE

(The HYAENA is now seated at a table in a Greek coffee shop. Extending his fingers into a small coin purse, he counts his money. He talks to himself and an unseen waitress.)

HYAENA. No, I don't think I'll have lunch today. I have a friend in the hospital. The coffee will have to be enough. Uh, Miss— *(The waitress has walked away. Sharply.)* Miss! I'd still like some more. *(With irritation.)* Isn't Sandy working today? Oh, she did? I'm sorry... I didn't know. When did she...? Oh, that's a shame. She was always real. *(The waitress has left.)*... to me.

(He pokes about the table, spills coffee, tears a bit of his napkin to dab it up with. Lonely business.)

HYAENA. No one keeps these jobs very long. It's so hard to develop any... acquaintances. It's not like when I was— No, I never was, was I? But my parents— Ah, now they used to talk about what a neighborhood was like! Used to know everyone, and everyone's business. Sounded wonderful.

(The waitress has returned)

HYAENA. Oh, I was saying how my parents told me about this neighborhood from years ago.

(Waitress: "Where are they now?")

HYAENA. My parents? Dead. It used to sound like it used to be wonderful. And now Sandy's gone. She was here a long time. Almost three months. Her mother died you know.

(Waitress: "Recently?")

HYAENA. No, just after she started. Beautiful funeral.

(Waitress: "Oh, are you a friend of the family?")

HYAENA. Me? No. I just like to give comfort where I can. And her father was in the hospital. Very unfriendly man. Sandy really— surprised me. Said I had no business going... [to visit her father...]

(*The waitress has gone off again. He carefully collects crumbs from a muffin, and presses them back in. Examines the check. The waitress returns.*)

HYAENA. Of course dear, I know you're busy. What is your name? Kathleen. Oh, how nice. Now I can't leave you a big tip today— "Kathleen". I have a friend in the hospital, he's very sick. Oh, I can't say what with. That's a very personal question. But I'll make it up to you. You look fairly young. How is your family, dear? Are they all living? Don't let me bother you, you'll get used to me. My name? You really want to know? Aren't you sweet. It doesn't matter. You'll get used to me, and you won't even notice I was here.

(*The waitress has gone. The HYAENA picks up the check and exits.*)

END SCENE THREE

SCENE FOUR

(*Outside the door to the PATIENT's room, the WIFE. stands with the FRIEND.*)

WIFE. Wait for me.

(*The FRIEND leaves. The WIFE takes her place at the bedside.*

At this point, all the PATIENT's inflections have a trace of question in them: his "Come in, come in" sounds like a person calling into an empty house, to see if anyone is still living there.)

PATIENT. Come in! Come in! We're all waiting to see you.
WIFE. (*Hesitantly.*) It's me?
PATIENT. Oh, it is you. I thought it was... Hi. Sit down. Close to me. I was afraid it was that— I thought you were that man.
WIFE. What man?
PATIENT. That man that comes around. You've seen him before. He's here all the time. Hangs over me in the bed. I've even seen him in here at night sometimes. Tries to take me places. Horrible man. You know who he is.
WIFE. I'm sure. Is he... here now?
PATIENT. Well look around, you tell me. Do you see him?

(*WIFE cautiously shakes her head.*)

PATIENT. Good.
WIFE. How are you feeling?
PATIENT. Oh, I don't know.
WIFE. You look well.

(*PATIENT gives her a look that says she's full of shit. WIFE begins to remove a large envelope from her bag, but reconsiders, giving him something else instead.*)

WIFE. I have... Well— Here, I brought you this. (*She hands him a little snow globe.*)
PATIENT. What is it?

WIFE. It's a souvenir of Atlantic City.
PATIENT. Something about that place sounds familiar... I don't know why... Did we ever go there?
WIFE. Don't you remember?
PATIENT. No.
WIFE. Oh...
PATIENT. What do I do with it.
WIFE. It's a snowstorm, dear. You—

(*The PATIENT has no idea what the object is or is for. The WIFE takes the PATIENT's hand, and turns the globe over. The PATIENT gives a weak cry of delight.*)

PATIENT. Oooooh...!
WIFE. I hoped you'd like it. I was thinking of you. I really was.
PATIENT. I haven't heard from Jerry. No more. Do you ever see him?
WIFE. Why do you ask?
PATIENT. I called his office. They said he went away for the day.
WIFE. I thought you couldn't use the phone.
PATIENT. The nurse, she dialed me. For me.
WIFE. Did they say where he went?
PATIENT. Yes, to— now why can't I remember it, I— Did you see anyone in the hall? A man?
WIFE. No.
PATIENT. What was I just trying to remember— Snow? You know: You just said it... I'm sorry, I— can't say what I think— always. It's a struggle.
WIFE. I'm glad everyone got a chance to see you the other day. I know it was hard on you, but they all really enjoyed themselves.
PATIENT. Yes, well...
WIFE. I love you.
PATIENT. Be close to me.

(*She gets nearer, but is edgy about touching him. She fumbles to get some papers out of her purse.*)

PATIENT. I wish I had you to hold while we sleep. I need you.
WIFE. Something else I brought.

PATIENT. Did you see Jerry there?
WIFE. Well— No. Why would I? I didn't really go there.
PATIENT. Then where did you get this?
WIFE. Jerry gave it to me. To give to you.
PATIENT. How is he?
WIFE. Who?
PATIENT. Jerry! He went to Atlantic City! You saw him, he gave me this.
WIFE. He only went for the day.
PATIENT. Why hasn't he come by? We have some very important things to talk about.
WIFE. So do we.
PATIENT. Something's wrong here... Are you cold?
WIFE. Are you?
PATIENT. There was a sudden chill in the room, don't you feel it? I wonder if... What's behind that door?
WIFE. Nothing. That's just the closet.
PATIENT. There's something in there... For me...

(*The WIFE cautiously goes to check.*)

WIFE. There's... nothing. Your robe.
PATIENT. Bring it to me, will you. I'm cold.

(*She does this, and sits him up and helps him into it.*)

PATIENT. No one takes care of me anymore. I called him and they said he wasn't in, so I thought he was coming here. He said he would come back, I don't know why he's avoiding me. I haven't seen him for seven months.
WIFE. You've only been in the hospital five, dear. Off and on.
PATIENT. And you haven't been here. At all.
WIFE. I just felt like getting away, thought that a little escape would be... good for me, you know... I've been getting so... depressed.
PATIENT. So go to Atlantic City.
WIFE. No! What makes you say that— I couldn't do that... with you here...
PATIENT. Could have gone with Jerry. He went.

WIFE. That would hardly be appropriate. Have you seen anyone else?

PATIENT. Just that— that hyaena. That blood-sucker. You know who he is, you just don't remember. Would you look under the bed?

WIFE. What for?

PATIENT. See what's under there. The uh— the uh— Takes me, to walk. You know. Freedom peddles.

WIFE. Your slippers.

PATIENT. Put them on, will you? Oh, that's nice. That's nice... You're so good to me. Not like—

WIFE. I don't want to talk about it.

PATIENT. We don't have to talk. You don't know how it feels to have you here. I love you. Hold me.

(*The WIFE obliges.*)

PATIENT. Don't let go of me. Never let me go. (*When he finally lets her go.*) I get so much strength from you.

WIFE. We haven't got much time. I was talking to the doctors. They said—

PATIENT. Oh! Are you taking me home?

WIFE. (*Freezes up.*) What.

PATIENT. Isn't that what you came for?

WIFE. You're not well enough.

PATIENT. I won't be any trouble.

WIFE. Later maybe. Next week.

PATIENT. A week?! No, now, I want to go now.

WIFE. You're making me feel bad. Don't. (*Discreetly wipes her eye.*) I know I haven't been here, but it's not because I've forgotten about you. It's just that—- I have the house to take care of, and no one to help— There is no reason, is there?

PATIENT. Let's not fight now. There isn't time.

WIFE. I'm not fighting. I've been in touch with the doctors over the phone, so I... I know what's happening. They said you were sleeping almost all the time, so I haven't— I thought I should let you rest. (*PATIENT seems to be drifting off to sleep.*) Are you all right?

PATIENT. Yes... Fine... You want to lay down with me?

WIFE. I don't think I could. We'd better do this now; these are the papers from the bank. Your signatures were a little messy on the last ones, so they asked if you would do it over.

PATIENT. What for? Why?

WIFE. They couldn't read it.

PATIENT. What do I do with this?

WIFE. Sign it.

PATIENT. My name you mean?

WIFE. You always make this so difficult, I can't keep coming back and back for this same thing— Don't do this to me! All the—

PATIENT. Wait till I'm home. One week.

WIFE. Now. Practice once, I'll help you.

(*He has little motor control; his hand goes any direction.*)

PATIENT. Oh, look at what's happening, come on you! I can't even— My own—

WIFE. (*Gently helps him.*) Let me hold you.

PATIENT. (*As he signs one paper, then another, through the whole stack.*) Is this what you want. This is all you came for.

WIFE. (*Strong and patiently, throughout.*) Easy now. Steady.

PATIENT. Take it all— off! You can't take my— paper, my money, my spoon, it's all yours anyway. Call the— teacher.

WIFE. There is no teacher.

PATIENT. Teacher says write everything down, a hundred times till tomorrow.

WIFE. That's right. Everything's going to be OK. It's just one less thing to take care of. One less thing... (*She sorts through the signed papers.*) That's the end of it.

PATIENT. You're not going to come see me anymore, are you.

WIFE. You make it so difficult! How much do you expect me to put up with! It's hard on me too, can't you see that?

PATIENT. You don't think of anyone but yourself.

WIFE. You're all I think of, or can think of, you're like nothing but one helpless—! Oh God, I love you. You must know that.

PATIENT. (*Dies a little.*) Take your pa— (*Says with great difficulty.*) pppages. Papers! I've signed them. Get!

WIFE. This isn't a good day. I'm sorry to have put you through all this. But it will all be over and we can start again tomorrow, all right?

(*PATIENT withholds response.*)

WIFE. I'll come back every day from now on. Every day.

PATIENT. He's waiting. He'll be here any time.

WIFE. Who's waiting?

PATIENT. You know.

WIFE. I'm not letting you threaten me. I'll come back.

PATIENT. When?!

WIFE. You're going to have days ahead. Beautiful days. And I will be here, with you. I will. OK?

PATIENT. (*Private. Alone.*) Thank you.

(*There is no embrace of any kind. She leaves. She joins the FRIEND at the side of the stage; they go off.*)

END SCENE FOUR

SCENE FIVE

(*The PATIENT is now hooked up to many tubes, IVs and medicine bags, catheters, oxygen hoses. He sits up, confused in the tangle. The HYAENA stands in the doorway.*)

HYAENA. Hello? Hello? (*PATIENT moans in restless sleep.*) Do you need help? I've come for you.
PATIENT. Wha—? Huh?
HYAENA. Did I wake you?
PATIENT. It's you. Oh— Good. Get my bags.
HYAENA. Where.
PATIENT. In the closet. Do you have any money?
HYAENA. Yes. What happened?
PATIENT. Call a cab. I'm going home.
HYAENA. Did the doctor say it's OK?
PATIENT. Yes, I've got to get home, I want to get home—-

(*He struggles to get out of bed. He manages to pull himself to a standing position.*)

HYAENA. Wait now, wait...
PATIENT. My bag should be all packed. (*Looks over the HYAENA's shoulder.*) Who's that?
HYAENA. Who?
PATIENT. Don't answer him. My family is going to meet us at the —intersection, and we'll all— we're all going to —swimming. Let's go, it's time to go.

(*The PATIENT begins carefully walking away— but at any turn or step, he remains lost.*)

HYAENA. I don't think that's a good idea. We should ask the nurse. Here, sit down. You'll hurt yourself... The tubes... Be careful...
PATIENT. Let go! We've got to go! Let go—!

(*He tries to push and fight, but the HYAENA gently, gently, guides the PATIENT towards the bed.*)

HYAENA. We will. Come this way, sit and rest. Don't get excited...

PATIENT. Don't make me lay down too!

HYAENA. I won't.

PATIENT. Home. I want to be home. Tell them to go away.

HYAENA. Who?

PATIENT. Can't stay. Don't make me stay.

HYAENA. I understand perfectly. You should just stay until... (*Notices the IV.*) just until you finish your medicine. Then I'll look for a cab.

PATIENT. Should we? Oh. All right. The medicine. Yes.

HYAENA. Were you dreaming? Just now? When I came in?

PATIENT. Have to get home. Something isn't right. Must see what it is... went wrong. Can you stay?

HYAENA. Thank you. How do you feel?

PATIENT. Sick.

HYAENA. Uh huh... Uh huh.

(*The HYAENA waits for a further response. There is none. He tries to lay the PATIENT back down in bed.*)

PATIENT. No, No, don't make me. I don't want to go, I—

HYAENA. Do you want to sit up?

PATIENT. Chair. Let me into the— I want—

(*The HYAENA lifts the PATIENT from the bed, and sets him in a chair.*)

HYAENA. Is that better?

PATIENT. Oooh, I'm sick...

HYAENA. What's it like? (*Pause.*) What is it like?

PATIENT. I don't know.

HYAENA. I wasn't really sure if you'd want me here or not. When I was here last— what happened?

PATIENT. I don't know.

HYAENA. You don't remember?

PATIENT. No.

HYAENA. Were you in another—

PATIENT. Why do you bother me with questions!

HYAENA. They told me nothing. Ignored me. Made it seem like I was no one.

PATIENT. Give me something to drink.

(*The HYAENA does this.*)

HYAENA. I just tried to see a very dear person who's been suffering for some time now, two floors below. First the door was closed, but then a nurse came out and then four people went streaming into the room, candy boxes, magazines, balloons, I looked in at some new person sitting there, dazed as I was. I went to the nurse's station to ask, but I saw the cardboard box, they were sealing it with masking tape— and I felt desperate to get up here to you. These things can happen so fast, we never know at what exact moment. No one understands like I do how fragile life is, and how precious friendships are.

PATIENT. Let go of my hand. What are you talking about. Fix my pillow.

HYAENA. I know you said your friend gave you that ring. Have you made a will yet?

PATIENT. (*Looking just behind the HYAENA's shoulder.*) Don't come now, I'm not tired.

HYAENA. Are you talking to me?

PATIENT. They are sending me for cleaning.

HYAENA. Who?

PATIENT. I'm going to have my organs cleaned, I'm not going to have any dirt in my body at all.

HYAENA. Have you—

PATIENT. (*The PATIENT is in delirium. He seems to be answering questions.*) No.

HYAENA. (*Does not catch on to what's happening at first.*) Would you like some more water?

PATIENT. No.

HYAENA. (*He realizes what is happening to the PATIENT, but goes on anyway.*) What I wanted to ask is, have you made out a will?

PATIENT. No.

HYAENA. I think it's time you did. (*Eyeing the ring.*) You have a lot of very nice things, I'm sure.

PATIENT. No.

HYAENA. That ring is just beautiful. I hope you don't think I'm too... brash or something, but we are, after all, pretty close now. Since all my visits...

PATIENT. Yes.

HYAENA. So, let me ask you something very delicate about that ring. It isn't much. Can I ask?

PATIENT. Yes.

HYAENA. I want it.

PATIENT. Yes.

HYAENA. Can I really?

PATIENT. Yes...

HYAENA. Are you sure?

PATIENT. No... Yes... No...

HYAENA. Oh, thank you, you don't know what this means to me. I have many friends, you know. Oh, I couldn't count them.

PATIENT. Yes...

HYAENA. I always try to count them. None of them have ever given me anything. Not like this. You don't know what this means to me.

PATIENT. Yes.

HYAENA. Maybe I should keep it for you. Hospital staffs have been known to...

PATIENT. Yes.

HYAENA. No, I'll wait. But the will— You did make one.

PATIENT. No.

HYAENA. You didn't?

PATIENT. Yesterday, I thought.

HYAENA. This is important to me!

PATIENT. Let's go over the head for nothing. Over the head for nothing.

HYAENA. (*Trying to understand.*) Over the head for nothing. Over the head for nothing...

(*The NURSE enters, quite routinely, and begins to take his pulse.*)

HYAENA. (*To NURSE.*) We're good friends. I have many friends.

(*The NURSE, after taking pulse, quickly checks other vital signs, then urgently leaves the room. The HYAENA carefully lays the PATIENT back, pulls the sheet up, then the blanket. Then he sits aside the PATIENT and talks to him.*)

HYAENA. I believe you can understand what I'm saying. Can you answer me?

(*The PATIENT is silent.*)

HYAENA. You're dying. Do you know that? I know I can talk to you honestly. If you are dying, I am going to let you. It's OK. The world will go on without you. I am not going to call the nurse. Let go, and join what is probably a supreme being, I guess, one greatness, or something or another. Something like that. Uh... die. Let go now, while I'm here. It's OK. I am right here...

(*The PATIENT closes his eyes, and sinks into rest.*)

HYAENA. He's doing it! He's doing it! It's really happening! I'm right here, I'm right here!

(*He places a hand on the PATIENT's chest.*)

HYAENA. Our father, who art— no— Yea though I— I mean, The Lord is my shepherd, I— I'm really here! For the first time, I'm really actually, I get to be—

(*The NURSE returns, with a DOCTOR and an AIDE. They surround the PATIENT.*)

AIDE. I'm sorry, you'll have to go now—
HYAENA. I'm supposed to be here. I've been here every day, but I've never seen you before.
AIDE. You have to go now!
HYAENA. Don't make me go, we're good friends. I'm supposed to be here...

(A curtain is drawn, separating him from the PATIENT. Dismayed at being torn from this experience, he cries out.)

END OF SCENE FIVE

SCENE SIX

(*CONTINUOUS. The HYAENA is back at the coffee shop, giddy, disturbed, aflame with his favorite form of anxiety.*)

HYAENA. I'm here, have you forgotten me already? Would you rather I didn't sit in your section, I won't be here long. I just came from the hospital, no menu please. Visiting hours are over, but I'll try again later. I'm starving, but I can't afford— well, I have some time, timing is very important, and I need my strength. Like all living things— Ha! (*He observes a nearby customer.*) You know what? I want what that man is having. Yes, that's what I'll have. Bring me that. (*He laughs nervously.*)

(*BLACKOUT.*)

END ACT ONE

ACT TWO

SCENE SEVEN

(The FRIEND and the WIFE are seated in the room. The NURSE and the AIDE are changing the bed, an involved procedure of covering the bed with several layers of plastic, absorbent pads and sheets, as well as sheets and pads for diapering the PATIENT.

The PATIENT is propped in a chair, covered with a sheet, useless.

When the bed is ready for his return, the WIFE makes no move towards her husband. The FRIEND begins to lift the PATIENT, but backs away. The AIDE comes forward, and he straps the PATIENT into bed.

This activity is carried out during the following dialogue.)

WIFE. It's been two weeks. He's finally come out of it today.
FRIEND. What time?
WIFE. What time, nurse?
NURSE. Around five this morning.

(The NURSE begins disconnecting the PATIENT's tubes.)

WIFE. Thank you. (*To FRIEND.*) Around five this morning. Why do you ask?
FRIEND. I don't know. I just want to know.
WIFE. So now you know.
FRIEND. You've made a difficult decision.
WIFE. I've always said I'd want the same for myself. It's strange, isn't it. Look. Nothing in there. An object.
FRIEND. Maybe we seem the same to him.
WIFE. We shouldn't talk. He could be listening.
FRIEND. Is he able to talk?
WIFE. I don't know. (*To NURSE.*) Is he able to talk?
NURSE. He said a few words this morning.
WIFE. (*To FRIEND.*) He said a few words this morning.
FRIEND. There were some things I wanted to say.

WIFE. I'll leave you alone with him.

FRIEND. You don't want to stay?

WIFE. Nurse, I thought he was being taken off everything.

NURSE. There's nothing in this one. It's just a solution to keep the vein open if we need it.

(*NURSE will exit whenever she is finished, the FRIEND and WIFE pay no more attention to her duties. The AIDE will get the PATIENT into bed alone.*)

WIFE. OK. Thank you. (*To FRIEND.*) Doesn't the smell in here bother you?

FRIEND. Piney. Like chlorophyll or something.

WIFE. It smells like death.

FRIEND. I don't think of those things. It's hard to understand, isn't it?

WIFE. I have no intention of understanding it, it's none of my business. That's for doctors. People like us should stand clear. It's all his now. Look at him.

FRIEND. Difficult.

WIFE. If I could believe it was really him I'd probably be more upset. But I can't. It's not. It doesn't look like anyone I ever knew.

FRIEND. I'm surprised you'd think that.

WIFE. No you're not. You're surprised I'd say so out loud. What amazes me is he seems completely unable to die. That's what I would do. If I found myself in that condition, what other choice would there be? I would say to myself, well, we've reached the end of it, and now it's time to die. And I would. Polite and simple. If it were me, I would want it over.

FRIEND. Will you stay a minute?

WIFE. No.

FRIEND. I thought you'd want to speak to him.

WIFE. It's all been said.

FRIEND. Nothing you want to say?

WIFE. I want to go. We should leave here—

FRIEND. I know it's hard to face situations.

WIFE. (*Angry, turns on him.*) I have been here constantly, day after week after month! Where have you been? Who's afraid to face situations? —I can't stand the smell. I'm going.

FRIEND. You'll need the keys. (*WIFE balks.*) We took my car.

WIFE. Right.

(*She gets the keys from him, and exits. The FRIEND stands there a minute. Takes in the room. Slowly draws the visitor's chair up to the bed, and sits, leaning over the rail to look at the PATIENT. Breathing is labored and noisy. The HYAENA appears at the door.*)

HYAENA. (*Almost sharply.*) Will you be long?

FRIEND. (*Startled.*) I don't know. I guess.

HYAENA. (*Enters brusquely.*) They told me at the desk the coma lifted.

(*The FRIEND stands. The HYAENA regards him with a cold shoulder.*)

HYAENA. I suppose you want to be alone with him.

FRIEND. If it's all right.

HYAENA. I'll wait.

(*The HYAENA goes. The FRIEND checks his appearance in the mirror. Then looks back at the PATIENT in the bed, through the mirror. Going to the PATIENT, he takes a photo from his wallet, and compares the two images, then and now. He sits at the bedside, and folds his hands for prayer. The HYAENA has appeared in the doorway, observing silently. The FRIEND draws a breath and is about to speak—*)

HYAENA. (*Gently.*) It's OK to talk.

(*The FRIEND turns around.*)

HYAENA. You don't have to wait for him to come to. He can hear you. I'll leave you alone.

(*The FRIEND returns to his position. Takes an honest look at the PATIENT, and his heart begins to break.*)

FRIEND. God, dear God... Can you hear me? I'm sorry. I'm sorry this is happening to you, and I...

(*The HYAENA discreetly appears at the doorway. Acts as if he's waiting to come in, but is eavesdropping and spying on this man's awkward efforts.*)

FRIEND. Everything's taken care of. I'm looking after your wife. When guys ask about you, I've been telling them... (*He looks over his shoulder, the HYAENA steps away. He continues.*) I don't know what to say. (*Sits for a moment.*)

HYAENA. (*From the doorway.*) Excuse me. Are you his brother?

FRIEND. We're not related.

HYAENA. Do you want more time? Go on then. I understand. It's better to express yourself now. It makes grieving easier when it's over.

FRIEND. Are you with the hospital?

HYAENA. No, I'm just a friend, like you. Go on. (*He steps away.*)

FRIEND. Are you awake? How are you, fella? (*There is no response.*) Can you hear me? Hey. Hey. You there? —Ooooh, this is a crime. It's not right. Close your eyes then, if you—

HYAENA. (*Invasive. Annoyed.*) I'm going to come in, if it's all right with you.

FRIEND. He's not responding.

HYAENA. He's asleep.

FRIEND. His eyes are open.

HYAENA. It's the medication.

FRIEND. Oooh. Strange. He— He's... sick.

HYAENA. Everyone here is.

FRIEND. I remember you from a few weeks ago.

HYAENA. I don't know from where. I've never seen you.

FRIEND. I was here. I left a note.

HYAENA. Maybe. I have a lot of patient-friends here, I don't try to remember the living.

(*The PATIENT is beginning to revive.*)

PATIENT. (*Struggles to articulate.*) Wha... wha... (*General moaning. Doesn't need to be too loud.*)
FRIEND. —Is he all right?
HYAENA. I think he senses that I've come to see him. —Oh, maybe he did describe you to me. His life-long friend, or something. From childhood? (*The FRIEND smiles.*) You're very awkward. It's hard on everyone. You might feel guilty letting go of a friend, but they need you to do it. Friends... are a person's last connection to the life they have known. In these final days, he might find it less painful to be around a strange person.

(*He pours a cup of water and brings it to the PATIENT's lips.*)

PATIENT. (*Barely articulate.*) Who's here?
FRIEND. He said "Who are you."
HYAENA. My name's not important. Your friend is here.
PATIENT. (*Identifies the FRIEND. Does not want to see him.*) Go away.
FRIEND. What did he say?
PATIENT. No. Over.
FRIEND. I think he wants to spend time with me.
HYAENA. You never know what a sick person thinks...
FRIEND. He doesn't sound too good. —If you don't mind...
HYAENA. Maybe I'll leave him to you for a while. I have another friend on the next floor who isn't doing so well. Of course, I'd only heard that he'd come out of the coma a few minutes ago. I shouldn't appear too eager.
FRIEND. Who should I say was by?
HYAENA. He knows I won't leave him alone.

(*He exits.*)

FRIEND. It's OK. He's gone. I'm here now.
PATIENT. (*Distressed that the HYAENA has left.*) Oooh...
FRIEND. (*Approaches the bed cautiously.*) Are you all right? (*PATIENT turns his head.*) Hi.
PATIENT. Where have you been?
FRIEND. How are you doing?
PATIENT. Sick. I'm very... sick.

FRIEND. (*Awkward.*) I'm glad to see you.

PATIENT. You were supposed to be here... You said you would come right back. Where are we? I mean, when is it?

FRIEND. (*Not sure he understands.*) You mean now? It's Thursday. Late.

PATIENT. God I'm sick. When's the last time you were here? You promised me, and then—

FRIEND. I didn't realize what condition... Next time, I'll know better.

PATIENT.... Next time.

FRIEND. Well, in the future. (*The PATIENT is gesturing towards him.*) What do you want?

PATIENT. Have to tell you. Have to talk to you.

FRIEND. What about?

PATIENT. (*He doesn't know. Can only repeat.*) Have to tell you. Have to talk to you.

FRIEND. Yeah... ?

PATIENT. The other— where did he go? Is he coming back?

FRIEND. I think so.

PATIENT. Good. What's happening? I— I don't know what's happening.

FRIEND. You were unconscious. For a couple weeks.

PATIENT. Was I? I don't believe it, it's like nothing happened. I don't know what's going on...

FRIEND. I'm sorry, can you speak up?

PATIENT. What—?

FRIEND. What did you say?

PATIENT. I don't know...

FRIEND. I've been thinking about you.

PATIENT. Where's— My wife hasn't been here. She's stopped coming. No one can stand to be around me. Have you seen her?

FRIEND. Did you have something to say to her?

PATIENT. No. She doesn't care any more. No.

FRIEND. Why do you say that?

PATIENT. I just know. Have to let it all go.

(*PATIENT struggles to sit up. The FRIEND helps him. He might be careful to place his hands in folds of blankets or sheets when handling the PATIENT.*)

PATIENT. Oh, thank you, that's much better... When I get out of here, it's all going to be so much different...

FRIEND. Are you getting out? I mean— did the doctors— ?

PATIENT. Oh, it's going to be so nice, and clean, and wonderful, you know. Just like it was at Sonoma. Is there any more coffee?

FRIEND. I— I'm sorry, I can't understand you.

PATIENT. Then-just-speak-up! That's all you have to do. OK?

FRIEND. OK.

PATIENT. There. Then it's no problem. What I wanted to tell you— maybe you know this— it's hard for me to talk— I'm so weak, and I... well, you know. Don't [*make me*] explain. OK?

FRIEND. Yes?

PATIENT. I've written her out of my will.

FRIEND. When?

PATIENT. Yesterday.

FRIEND. Why?

PATIENT. She was in here, she came in here and she stole everything from the dresser. That one right over there. So I couldn't go home. She wants me here. So I'm done with her.

FRIEND. That's ridiculous. She loves you more than—

PATIENT. Oh, what do you know, you're just like she is.

FRIEND. You don't know what you're saying; she couldn't have been here yesterday, she was with me.

PATIENT. Why?

FRIEND. She just was.

PATIENT. Then the day before, I get mixed up—

FRIEND. About two and a half or three weeks ago she was here, with statements from the bank. Before that she was here almost every day, now I see what she was talking about. I don't think you understand what a strain she's been living with!

PATIENT. Strain. Get out.

FRIEND. No.

PATIENT. You're done. You forgot, she forgot—

FRIEND. I came by once, the people here said there was no use in hanging around. I stood by you for a few minutes. It didn't seem to make any difference, so I left.

PATIENT. No, no she was right there, I remember seeing her, standing right there— !

FRIEND. She couldn't have been.

PATIENT. She did, she had a row of cones, all around the bed, and she wouldn't let me step on them, the— about this high, and when they turned— when they turned off—

FRIEND. Listen to me, you're talking nonsense.

PATIENT. I am too, why can't you understand me? You're trying to get away, aren't you.

FRIEND. No— Let me get someone, I don't know what's happening—

PATIENT. Don't leave me!

(*The HYAENA appears at the doorway.*)

HYAENA. Are you ready to see me?

FRIEND. Something's wrong with him—

(*The PATIENT breaks into a horrible coughing spasm. The FRIEND doesn't know what to do.*)

HYAENA. (*Comes in.*) Maybe I should—

FRIEND. I'll take care of him.

(*The HYAENA glides into the room, standing near the head of the bed. He moves little, says nothing, sees all.*)

FRIEND. Should I get you some water?

(*The FRIEND finds the emergency cord and pushes it, then starts to pour a cup of water, but stops and looks out into the hallway.*)

FRIEND. Nurse?

(*He disappears. The PATIENT doesn't know what is going on. He reaches for the water but spills it and it drips all over himself. The FRIEND returns.*)

FRIEND. The nurse will be right here. (*Re-pours another cup of water and holds it out to him, over the bedrail.*) Do you want a drink of water? Huh?

PATIENT. (*Tries to cry out, but hasn't the breath—*)

FRIEND. Hey, relax! Settle down, you're making it worse— Calm down, buddy— stay calm till help comes—

(*He tries to put a hand on the PATIENT's chest, but the PATIENT pushes him away. The FRIEND is repelled, he hangs near the door, looking for the NURSE to come.*)

FRIEND. Aw cripes, what am I supposed to do? (*To the PATIENT.*) Hey, don't panic, you're only making it worse!

(*As he watches out the hallway, the spasm resides, finally, and the PATIENT will breathe heavily, but normally. The NURSE arrives.*)

NURSE. How is the patient?
FRIEND. Coughing spell— it was horrible!

(*The NURSE moves past him, and checks the PATIENT; turns off the emergency light.*)

FRIEND. I was — he really scared me, I thought he was going to— I thought I was going to faint!
NURSE. Fever is starting. Breathing isn't very good. I'll call the doctor, maybe I can bring him an injection.
FRIEND. Thanks nurse.

(*She exits.*)

PATIENT. Oooh.
FRIEND. You OK now?
PATIENT. Oooh, my head...
FRIEND. Gee. It's all over now. It'll get better. The worst is behind you, OK?
PATIENT. This is it. This is the end of it.
FRIEND. Don't talk that way. There's always hope.
PATIENT. It's all done with. All done. All done.

(*He repeats this phrase, continually, until he falls into rest. The FRIEND sits silently, not knowing what to make of it. He knows it's over, and he would like to leave. The NURSE returns, with syringe.*)

FRIEND. Do you know how much longer he has?

(*The PATIENT hears this question, does not respond verbally.*)

NURSE. No.
FRIEND. (*To NURSE.*) What's in that?
NURSE. Something for the fever. It will help him rest.
FRIEND. I'd like to talk to him more though. Don't you have anything that will make him more... you know, better?

(*She doesn't hear the FRIEND's question to answer it; just gives him the shot. The P.A. System announces the end of visiting hours.*)

NURSE. It's OK, just a shot to help you sleep. It doesn't hurt at all... (*To FRIEND.*) He's got to be kept quiet.
FRIEND. Thank you nurse.

(*The NURSE leaves the room once she is finished. The FRIEND doesn't know what to do. He creeps around, puts on his jacket, gathers any magazines or bags he may have carried in with him. It is important that he has physical possessions to hold on to, to affirm that he is a member of the living world.*)

FRIEND. I'm going to leave you now... (*There is no response.*) It's time for me to go.

(*He starts to leave, then realizes he may never see the PATIENT ever again. He says a quick, silent prayer, then goes out the door. The HYAENA is standing outside the door, he watches the FRIEND pass. Then the HYAENA enters. Outside, the FRIEND pauses, looks back. The HYAENA stands in the doorway, to prevent him from coming back in.*)

HYAENA. So you've said your goodbyes?

FRIEND. For today, yes.

HYAENA. When do you plan to see him again, then? I'm sure he's going to want to know.

FRIEND. Uh... Soon. I have someone waiting for me—

HYAENA. I'm sure I understand. Good-bye.

FRIEND. If he wakes up, tell him—

HYAENA. What.

FRIEND. (*Approaches the HYAENA.*)... I shouldn't be shouting down the hall, the place is loaded with sick people... Listen, if he wakes up, tell him I love him. No, just, tell him I... I left.

(*He exits quickly, awkward and in a hurry. The WIFE meets him in the hallway outside the room.*

The HYAENA sits alongside the PATIENT, and strokes his head.)

WIFE. What's the matter?

FRIEND. He's in bad shape— bad shape.

WIFE. I know.

FRIEND. I wasn't expecting anything like this. Why didn't you tell me?

WIFE. I thought you understood.

(*She goes into the hospital room. The HYAENA is close to bedside, soothing the PATIENT.*)

WIFE. Oh! Excuse me—

HYAENA. It's all right. Come in. Come in. Are you his wife?

WIFE. Yes. You must be with the hospital?

HYAENA. Unofficially.

WIFE. What do you mean "Unofficially"? Are you supposed to be here?

HYAENA. I care for the dying. I have many friends here.

WIFE. You must be very kind.

HYAENA. I've been seeing him for weeks. Your husband is a very special one at the moment.

WIFE. Is he all right?

HYAENA. He's better now. Yes. Had a little spell. Fortunately I was here. The nurse gave him a shot.

(*The PATIENT stirs. He's doped, and out of it. Not much life left in him. He raises his head.*)

PATIENT..... Barbara?
WIFE. (*To herself, with a sigh of anger, or tension, or sadness.*)... God.
HYAENA. Go ahead, speak. He's talking to you.
WIFE. (*She makes no move to him.*) What is it dear?
PATIENT. (*Can't speak. Does anyway. All that comes out is:*) Aaah. Wuaa. Uuoaah. (*He flips his hand about helplessly, then lays his head back down.*)
WIFE. Don't talk. I'm not really here. (*To HYAENA.*) I've got to go.
HYAENA. Of course. Uh— You are his wife, aren't you? (*She nods.*) Of course you are, you just said so. Uh— There is something I wanted to discuss with you, if I ever got to meet you. And by now, obviously, I have. I would like to be included in the funeral, if you have no objections.
WIFE. I— haven't made— or thought about— yet— the—
HYAENA. There will be one, won't there?
WIFE. What?
HYAENA. A funeral.
WIFE. Oh, I'm sure there will, eventually. Be. One. I really have got to go— (*She goes to the sink, quickly rinses her hands.*)
HYAENA. Most people are afraid of death. I see it all the time. People need love when they're sick. People need a lot of love. That's a property I've found that I happen to have a lot of. A lot I can give away. When I leave your husband, I visit other patients on other floors.
WIFE. I think you'd find other things to do with your time.
HYAENA. I do. That's why I go to the other floors. Sometimes it seems they're even worse off, but they're all really the same.
WIFE. In what way?
HYAENA. Left alone.
WIFE. People have lives to lead. It's not simple, I have so much—

HYAENA. I know. It's very painful; believe me, I know. So please, don't worry. I'll be here.

(*The PATIENT again tries to speak, while the HYAENA strokes his hand.*)

PATIENT. Whuaao... aaoweh.

HYAENA. (*Gently, with love.*) Be still now. (*Back to WIFE, secretly begs.*) So, in your plans, over the next few weeks, if you would, maybe, just, try to... remember me...?

WIFE. (*Misunderstands, and nods in agreement. Then:*) I don't suppose I'll see you again.

HYAENA. I'll be with him at least as long as he's here. He is dying, you know. But, since you aren't going to be here, I have a card—

FRIEND. (*Calls from the door.*) I'm waiting.

WIFE. (*Tactlessly avoiding taking it.*) He'll last a while longer.

(*She steps near the bed to look, but not too close, in case the PATIENT should look back.*)

WIFE. Oh God...

HYAENA. (*Steps between the PATIENT and the WIFE, begins tucking the PATIENT in, raising sheets unreasonably high to interfere with her view.*) Comfort is what they need about now. That's really all we can do, he probably doesn't know who you are anymore. Or me either. But of course, I'm used to it...

WIFE. I'm going.

(*She almost rushes from the room. The FRIEND is there to catch her, they embrace.*)

FRIEND. It's awful, isn't it?

WIFE. It's not awful, I am awful—

FRIEND. Now now now... (*He tries to embrace her, she pushes him back.*)

WIFE. No!

HYAENA. (*To PATIENT, with gentle, delicious urgency.*) They're gone now, you don't have to worry about seeing any of them again.

PATIENT. (*Weary. Resigned. Dead.*) Let's be finished. Let's be finished. Let's be done. Let's be done. (*He may repeat this, feebly.*)

HYAENA. Look at me. Can you understand what I'm saying? Is time getting close? (*He lifts the PATIENT, making him upright and comfortable.*) I'll be right here. Right here. Right here...

(*Lights dim on the hospital room. The WIFE and the FRIEND meet outside, and walk to the waiting room.*)

FRIEND. This illness is terrible, I didn't realize what a toll it's taken on you—

WIFE. I'm fine, it's him it's ruined!

FRIEND. That— That person in there is no one we ever knew. It used to be, but—

WIFE. How can you be so stupid!

FRIEND. I'm not, I was being— I meant to—

WIFE. Shut up, you don't know what you're talking about, you don't know anything.

FRIEND. Don't yell at me, it's not my fault. I shouldn't have come here, I don't know what I was expecting. I wanted to remember him like he used to be, when he was—

WIFE. What do you mean, "Used to be"?!

FRIEND. A few weeks ago.

WIFE. He's not de— he's still here, there's always a chance he'll come through, we can't forget that!

FRIEND. Darling. There's not.

(*Silence for a beat. The WIFE almost breaks down, but she is still more angry than grief-stricken. All actors: Avoid tears in any of this.*)

WIFE. I can't do it. I've had enough. There's nothing more to do about it. I thought I could see him through to the end, but—

FRIEND. That's not necessary.

WIFE. He just keeps hanging on, and on! It makes it seem like—
as long as I keep showing up, he still has something to— I
mean— Just now, he even sat up and started to try and talk
again... I just don't want to hear it anymore.

*(The AIDE enters the hospital room, replaces ice water, removes
dinner tray, if there is one, while the HYAENA looks on.)*

FRIEND. I wish I hadn't seen him like this. But I tell you what I'm
going to do: I'm going to pretend this didn't happen, it's not right
to remember him as anything but what he used to be. That's the
right thing to do. Remember him only as being alive, and
strong. And healthy. And then: we can forget about this.

WIFE. I don't care anymore. I just don't. I wish I did, but at this
point I can't see his death as being anything more than a
convenience.

FRIEND. *(He takes her in his arms.)* You are bad. *(He kisses her.)*

WIFE. Don't say that. Am I?

FRIEND. You are the most evil *(He kisses her tenderly.)* selfish,
(And again.) wicked, *(And again.)* callous, *(And again.)* black-
hearted, *(And again.)* sensitive... *(And again.)* Don't worry. I'll
never leave you.

*(Wrapped safely in his arms, he leads her off. Lights up again on
the PATIENT and HYAENA. A shadow crosses the window, and a
wind softly blows the curtains. The AIDE leaves the room, if he is
still in there.)*

HYAENA. *(Looks up.)*... Are you still here? Are you with us?

NURSE. *(Enters.)* Visiting hours are over, you should be getting
on.

HYAENA. Oh, no. I never leave my patient-friends. I have to be
here to keep watch.

NURSE. Rules. Please cooperate.

HYAENA. Of course.

(He remains. The NURSE leaves.)

HYAENA. Are you hearing any music? Can you hear me? Talk to me. Please? Can you open your eyes? Make a sound then. Come on, make a sound.

(*He shakes the PATIENT. No response. He shakes him again, until he cries out.*)

HYAENA. Like that. Good. Talk to me.

(*The PATIENT moans.*)

HYAENA. Good.

(*He feels the PATIENT's pulse, he puts his hand on the PATIENT's chest. Places his ear on the PATIENT's chest, then moves up. He leans closely over the PATIENT, placing his hand over his mouth to feel for breath; he gets up and fetches the room odorizer. Places it at bedside. Closes door. Places chair against door, then removes it. Closes window curtains. Turns down lights, sits near bed. Gets up. Turns all lights on.*)

HYAENA. Does that hurt your eyes? (*He holds the PATIENT by both hands.*) The reports are always different, and it's never happened to me, so I don't know. But do you hear music? There's supposed to be a long dark tunnel and some light, a really bright light.

(*The PATIENT opens his eyes, and slowly sits up.*)

HYAENA. Look right into my eyes. This is where you can come back to when you leave. Into my eyes. Right to me. I'll always be here. Take a part of me, so you can always find your way back, so I can always go beyond with you. So you won't be lost, ever. So I will never be alone. You can come back. You will always be able to come back.
PATIENT. (*Looks around, weakly.*) No. No. No.
HYAENA. The world will always be here. And with me, you can still have part of it.
PATIENT. Don't want. Don't want. No. Finish.

HYAENA. Live in me. Live in me.
PATIENT. Turn. The propellers. Backwards. Turn all. The propellers. Backwards.

(*The NURSE enters.*)

NURSE. It's time. You have to go.
HYAENA. No! Don't make me now!
NURSE. Is he all right?
HYAENA. Of course he is, you said so yourself, leave me alone, I always stay as long as I want.
NURSE. This is a hospital and the patient needs privacy.

(*The HYAENA grabs the PATIENT's hand, wants the ring. Knows he can't take it while the NURSE is there.*)

HYAENA. But I have more... things to do.
NURSE. Hospital rules. You can't stay here. It's time to go.
HYAENA. I can't go yet. Five more minutes.

(*The NURSE leaves.*)

HYAENA. If you're here tomorrow, I'll be too. Don't leave without me, please don't leave without me. Don't forget about me—

(*The NURSE returns with the AIDE, who confronts the HYAENA, bodily ejecting him.*)

NURSE. Come now. It's time.
HYAENA. No, please don't make me...
NURSE. Come away.
HYAENA. I still— have—
NURSE. Let go! Come away now!
HYAENA. (*Urgently to the PATIENT.*) Remember me— Remember me—
NURSE. It's time.
HYAENA. Don't push, I'm going— Don't make me—
NURSE. Come now. Come along … !

HYAENA. I'm supposed to be here! Don't forget me. I'm supposed to be here! (*To the PATIENT, desperately.*) Remember me! Remember me!

(*The AIDES step in, and the HYAENA is rudely and roughly escorted out. The NURSE waits impatiently at the door, and pulls the drape on the PATIENT.*

LIGHTS OUT, and we hear the magnified sounds of the hospital. Sounds become very loud, then soften, and become the sound of birds and morning traffic. Lights come up on the HYAENA, extremely fatigued, sitting at the table at the coffee shop.)

END SCENE SEVEN

SCENE EIGHT

(*HYAENA is agitated, giddy, and maniacally writing notes to himself, gulping coffee.*)

HYAENA. No more coffee, what time is it? The hospital opens in, it's still another twenty minutes. They wouldn't let me in. They don't know who I am. I am very important there, I have... Notes. (*Returns to his scribbling.*) God I'm afraid I've missed it—

(*The unseen waitress appears. He jumps, knocking over a glass of water.*)

HYAENA. Oh! You startled me, yes, I better have more thank you. My friend. In the hospital. He's dying. No, not yet. I waited all night. I'm afraid I may have missed it. Or him, I should say. Yes, they do call the family. But I'm not. No one calls me, they don't even know who I am. Thank you. I'm touched. I appreciate that. Leave me alone please, I'm busy. I'm excited. I'm upset.

(*The waitress leaves, he writes excitedly, keeping reigns on his giddiness.*)

HYAENA. "Return to hospital. Sit in chair. Keep close look at his eyes... —What do I do if he's still unconscious? I've got to be able to see into his eyes. (*Writes more.*) "Look at eyes. Figure out how when I'm there. Synchronize breath. Be prepared to hold it." (*Looks at watch.*) Time now is eight-forty-eight. (*Writes more.*) "Keep mind totally clear at The Moment, note every observation. Hold patient by both hands. Spirit exits through head. Keep palms open and inhale to make connection... "

(*LIGHTS COME UP on the hospital room area. The WIFE and the FRIEND are there, the bed is empty. There is a great sense of relief about them. They listlessly clean out drawers of the nightstand, and remove the few articles of clothing.*)

WIFE. When they called this morning, I knew what it was, even before the phone rang. Funny. Just minutes before, I could actually hear him talking to me.

FRIEND. It's been an ordeal. But it's over.

WIFE. I got hold of Janie.

FRIEND. Oh?

WIFE. She said Brian hurt himself chasing a beachball.

FRIEND. Are she and Bill coming out?

WIFE. Ken's going to pick them up at the airport Sunday. I asked them to leave the kids home; there's not much for them to do at a funeral.

(*The HYAENA appears at the doorway. He halts when he sees what has happened.*)

HYAENA. Oh my god. Oh my lord...

(*They halt briefly. The HYAENA says a quick, silent prayer, and then the FRIEND and WIFE privately go about their business. The HYAENA goes wearily to his visitor's chair.*)

HYAENA. Were you with him?

(*They freeze up, they don't want to talk to him. The WIFE looks over shoulder and shakes her head.*)

HYAENA. Was anyone? (*He is ignored.*) Oh no. I was just around the corner, they wouldn't let me in any earlier. I wanted to stay the night. You remember me, don't you?

(*He goes to the bedside, and runs his hand over the sheets, feeling.*)

HYAENA. Aaaah. He's gone. Nothing left. No. Nothing left. Is there. —Do you have— he wanted me to have—

FRIEND. What?

HYAENA. Nothing.

(He continues fingering the sheets, seems to be searching through them to find the ring. The FRIEND and the WIFE leave. The HYAENA closes the door once they are gone.)

HYAENA. Are you in here? I feel something, give me a sign, some indication. Life is all around me, I can feel it— just let me try and concentrate and find which part of it was yours—

(The NURSE enters. She opens the curtains and sunlight floods the room. She begins to strip the bed.)

HYAENA. I — I hear he was alone.
NURSE. I found him myself.
HYAENA. What time? Nurse, what time?
NURSE. Just before eight o'clock, I guess.
HYAENA. The exact time. I must have the exact time.
NURSE. Time on the certificate is seven thirty-eight.
HYAENA. You just said you—
NURSE. Found him. He expired some minutes earlier.
HYAENA. Seven thirty-eight, what was I doing. I'd been— fighting with the guard, seven thirty-eight, then I went to the coffee shop, *(Flips through book for notes.)* seven three eight, seven three eight three— *(Finds note.)* eight forty eight, eight four eight, eight three seven— probably at the moment— *(He seems to strike his own alarm. Fires out a laugh of amazement.)* Ha! At the— At the moment I was— that was just before I spilled the water! I HA! I felt something, tug at my elbow, a jolt, hahaha, the water just: Spilled!
NURSE. We have another patient coming in soon.
HYAENA. Certainly nurse, I understand.

(The NURSE leaves.)

HYAENA. I've done it. At last. I think. Yes: At 8:37, the water spilled!

END OF SCENE EIGHT

SCENE NINE

(*Continuous. HYAENA is back at the coffee shop, happy, agitated, almost at peace with himself.*)

HYAENA. My friend? In the hospital? Yeees, that one. He died. Thank you, you're very kind to say so. We had become very close, and you know, I think we still are. Maybe people don't really leave— well— I won't say any more. Yes. Oh, I can't rest, I have another friend, a girl, I should bring her flowers this afternoon. Bring me some hot water, with nothing in it. Charge me for a tea, I don't mind. Yes, life does go on. Perfectly hateful, isn't it? So many people, and all of them, so much in need... —I will look at the menu, do you mind? Suddenly I am so hungry!

(*Freeze, and a quick BLACKOUT.*)

END OF PLAY

THE
COCK
MACHINE

TOP: Johnny Blaize Leavitt, Tisza Cher-Rie Evans, Stacey Turner. BOTTOM: William Modean and Rodney Ladino in *The Cock Machine*, Theater for the New City, New York. (2002)

The Cock Machine was first performed at Theater for the New City, New York on January 31, 2002. Directed by the author, the cast was as follows:

The Professor....................	William Modean
Moe................................	Jack Fitz
Mr. Climsby............................	Johnny Blaize Leavitt
Mrs. Climsby...........................	Tisza Cher-Rie Evans
The Woman Who Wants A Happy Life....	Johanna Buccola
Jacqueline..............................	Allison Tilson
Joe Hercules............................	Kila Packett
Minister Barley.........................	Edward Harding
Delilah Barley	Bobbi Owens
Barney Terwhilligher	Paul Weissman
The Baby Seal..........................	Danielle Montezinos
Bertha..................................	Carrie Thomas
Sonia...................................	Stacey Turner
Mayor Lucky/Bag Man/Judge..........	Rodney Ladino
Man in Hospital/Coroner..............	Andrew Cohen

SYNOPSIS

In attempt to win back a lost love, a man invents a self-improvement device which wreaks havoc on the moral lives of the town.

CHARACTERS

THE PROFESSOR (m)	A Humble Inventor.
MOE (m)	His Assistant.
MR. CLIMSBY (m)	Head of the Patent Office.
MRS. CLIMSBY (f)	His Wife.
THE WOMAN WHO WANTS A HAPPY LIFE (f)	
JACQUELINE (f)	A Wonderful Lady.
JOE HERCULES (m)	A Fitness Expert.
MINISTER BARLEY (m)	A Good Man.
DELILAH BARLEY (f)	His Daughter.
BARNEY TERWHILLIGHER (m)	Her Suitor.
THE BABY SEAL (m)	
BERTHA (f)	Head of "Women Against Fur".
SONIA (f)	Animal Rights Advocate.
MAYOR LUCKY (m)	
BAG MAN (m)	
JUDGE (m)	
MAN IN HOSPITAL (m)	
CORONER (m)	

SETTING

There are multiple places and locations in this comedy, don't try and build a fixed set. Most settings and set pieces should be light-weight cardboard or plywood cut-outs, colorfully painted, that can be quickly and effortlessly taken on or off by the performers themselves. In style, refer to old burlesque sketches from the 30s or 40s.

COCK MACHINE

Rude Comedy by Ross MacLean

ACT ONE

Scene 1 – At the Patent Office

(*MOE and THE PROFESSOR are speaking to CLIMSBY, the Chief Patent Officer, an efficient man at a desk.*)

CLIMSBY. Gentlemen. (*The intercom buzzes.*) I'm in a meeting Grindel, hold my calls. Gentlemen. (*He coldly examines a folder and pauses before addressing THE PROFESSOR and MOE.*) I hope you will notice, I want you to appreciate the fact that I use the term "Gentlemen" with you; I do so to maintain the dignity of the patent office.

MOE. Much obliged, pal. We got—

CLIMSBY. Climsby to you, sir.

THE PROFESSOR. You give out the patents, right?

CLIMSBY. For all original inventions. Over the course of my career, I've seen every conceivable creation and all their improvements. Do you remember the pop–top can? I approved that.

MOE. I thought there was always pop–top cans.

CLIMSBY. No. We had to use can openers.

MOE. Life's been better since then.

CLIMSBY. Do you remember Ginsu knives? I approved that.

MOE. Pretty sharp.

CLIMSBY. Do you remember glow–in–the–dark disco apparel?

MOE. Very bright.

THE PROFESSOR. You approved that, I suppose.

CLIMSBY. I did. Silicone breast implants?

MOE. I approved that!

THE PROFESSOR. Now Climsby, unless you are telling me you were the inventor behind these creations, I see no reason to puff yourself over these approvals!

CLIMSBY. Let me explain Mr. uh—

MOE. Hiram. He's the Professor.

CLIMSBY. I'm sure. People can build and dream to their heart's content. But unless someone approves of their creation, someone like, oh, let's say ME... Unless there is approval, then people's dreams can and will rot in darkness. I am the force to reckon with here.

THE PROFESSOR. Climsby what we have here will be a revolution to mankind, a means of "dignity," as you said, for the world population.

CLIMSBY. No one in history has had the bald immorality to bring what you have wrought.

MOE. A cock machine!

(*CLIMSBY's intercom buzzes.*)

CLIMSBY. Is that what you call it?
MOE. Yeah, a cock machine!

(*CLIMSBY's intercom buzzes.*)

CLIMSBY. Hold my calls!!
THE PROFESSOR. I wouldn't describe it to the public in those terms, Mr. Climsby, uh, sir. The SX–70 is an exercise device, suitable for the health club or the home. It's singular function is to... enlarge the male organ.

CLIMSBY. Permanently?
THE PROFESSOR. Oh, yes sir. What use would it be otherwise?
MOE. And it works like a charm, Climsby, a balls–out charm.

CLIMSBY. I don't want to know about this indecency. I don't know where you people get the time to think up these inventions, it's a lapse in your fear of god, or maybe you just have too much money. Take your penis enlarger out of my office.

THE PROFESSOR. Respect! Respect, Climsby, you paper–pushing pip squeak! I'll not stand here and have you insult science!

CLIMSBY. You call it science. I call it pornography!
MOE. Pornography??? It's your own body.

CLIMSBY. My private body, which no one knows about— almost, usually. God gave me this body—

THE PROFESSOR. —And I can add to it!

MOE. It's like that old saying: Build a bigger mousetrap, you'll catch a bigger mouse. Get a bigger weenie, you'll catch... a bigger mouse.

CLIMSBY. (*Spluttering.*) If god had wanted me to have a — !!! Big—??! Fat——??! —If god wanted me to have one of those, he would have given me—

THE PROFESSOR. — an SX–70!

MOE. Look at these results. Before…

(*MOE passes him a folder, which he takes two photos from. One measures 3x3.*)

MOE. After.

(*The second photo measures 6x9.*)

CLIMSBY. Leave my office. I am done with you for the day!

THE PROFESSOR / MOE. What?!

CLIMSBY. I have no need of your device, I am a married man.

(*CLIMSBY's buzzer rings.*)

CLIMSBY. I'll be just a moment, hold my calls.

THE PROFESSOR. I don't think you realize the importance of my invention!

CLIMSBY. Importance? Don't make me laugh! I am important.

MOE. Yeah, you might be. But how big is your dick?

(*CLIMSBY's intercom buzzes.*)

CLIMSBY. Grindel! I told you— Mrs. Climsby! (*To MOE and PROFESSOR, panicked.*) My wife! (*On intercom.*) Send her away! Get her out, I'm in a very important meeting! I don't want to see that—

(*MRS. CLIMSBY enters.*)

CLIMSBY. Grindel? Hold my balls. (*To MRS. CLIMSBY.*) Hello dear.

MRS. CLIMSBY. Don't give me that! I waited a full hour!

CLIMSBY. Lunch!

MRS. CLIMSBY. There I am, sitting alone at the Mean Cabaret!

CLIMSBY. I'm sorry Darling, I forgot. As you can see, I'm in a meeting right now. These gentlemen—

MOE. You did ask us to leave, maybe this isn't the best time—

CLIMSBY. Don't Move!

MRS. CLIMSBY. Good afternoon gentlemen, I'm Mrs. Climsby... (*They exchange introductions.*) Please excuse me for the interruption, but I just need a few minutes to talk to this (*Turns back to CLIMSBY.*) Cheese–brain! —Two more geniuses at your mercy, likely holding something to improve life as we know it but Ha! Good luck if they do, with a clerk like you guarding the gate.

CLIMSBY. I am not a clerk.

MRS. CLIMSBY. A man of with no accomplishments of his own, imagining he's as important as the gizmos he greenlights. Did he tell you about the diet mineral water? The karaoke machine for the deaf? The pet rock? What have they been taking up your time with that's so fascinating you could forget about me?

MOE. A cock machine. Expands the male... you know.

MRS. CLIMSBY. Does it work?

(*PROFESSOR nonchalantly lets his coat fall open.*)

MOE. Not an implant!

THE PROFESSOR. All natural!

MRS. CLIMSBY. (*Sparkles. Politely.*) Charming. (*Then wheels on CLIMSBY, sharp.*) Of course YOU have no need for anything that could do that!

CLIMSBY. I was made in God's image!

MRS. CLIMSBY. Of course you were. (*Briefly, to MOE and PROFESSOR.*) I love him all the same. (*Back to CLIMSBY, mean, Kramden wind–up.*) He thinks he's important to commerce, he thinks he's important to industry, he imagines he has some value in the stream of creation and then he leaves me alone in the finest place in town. (*She bats him with her purse.*) Do you know who saw me there? Wanda McGillicutty, and you know what a mouth she has.

CLIMSBY. (*Cold.*) Besides your complaint, do you have anything to offer?

(*She pulls a foil swan from her bag, and slams it on his desk.*)

MRS. CLIMSBY. Roast Beef! I know: you'll be working late. I'll see you at home.

(*She strides out, angry and hurt. CLIMSBY fuddles, but maintains his demeanor.*)

CLIMSBY. Show yourselves out. I want my sandwich.
THE PROFESSOR. Now Climsby. Sit down here with me, and we'll talk. Man to man. Moe, will you excuse us?

(*MOE stands downstage, pretends not to listen.*)

THE PROFESSOR. I see the difficulties you face. You have worked very hard. You have achieved and acquired many things. But are you happy with what you've got? You probably turn down the lights before undressing, don't you.
CLIMSBY. (*His voice shuddering.*) I— I have to wear pajamas.
THE PROFESSOR. My wife left me on our wedding night!
CLIMSBY. No!
THE PROFESSOR. Yes!
MOE. Uh–oh: here we go…
THE PROFESSOR. There was, in the early summer only a few short years ago, a delicate, mature woman, with flowers in her hair. I worked for a medical appliance maker at the time. She dispensed the paychecks. And her name... was "Penny".
CLIMSBY. Penny?
MOE. Yeah, I worked there too. Go ahead boss, tell him all about... Penny.
THE PROFESSOR. We fell in love. Became engaged. Happiness was mine— until the night of our Honeymoon!
CLIMSBY. And where was that?
MOE. You don't need to know, it was in a motel anyway, wasn't it professor, the Silver Moon or something…
CLIMSBY. It would be some coincidence if it was, that's where I went on my honeymoon. The Silver Moon in Niagara Falls.
THE PROFESSOR. (*Ready to explode.*) Niagara Falls!

MOE. Oh, not again: this is such an old bit with him— (*MOE restrains him.*) Forget the night, if you have to talk, tell him about the day, the hillside, the chapel...

THE PROFESSOR. It was a simple ceremony. The "I do's", the rings... and our little honeymoon suite. A beautiful night together, and out the window we could see the moon spilling over the water. (*He gasps a bit before he can carry on.*) In the motel I stood proud before my newfound bride, and yet— words fail me Climsby—

CLIMSBY. Oh yes. There is nothing so beautiful, as the moon over Niagara Falls

THE PROFESSOR. Niagara Falls!!!! Slowly, I turned down the sheets... But quick-as-a bunny she high-tailed it to the parking lot, and was never seen again! "Penny, what's wrong?" I called as she fled— AS IF I DIDN'T KNOW!!! I tell you Climsby, I got SO mad, I just wanted to— to grab someone! (*He grabs CLIMSBY.*)

MOE. (*To CLIMSBY, he steps back.*) You're on your own now!

THE PROFESSOR. And shaked him up! Smack him inna noggin! Threw him to the ground, and kicked his brains from here to Sunday!!! (*CLIMSBY has been severely beaten. PROFESSOR becomes calm again.*) But I didn't.

CLIMSBY. No?

THE PROFESSOR. (*Calm again.*) Instead, I dedicated my life to developing this, the machine which can give comfort to every man, woman and child over the age of twenty-one. Today, I have confidence. I have self-respect. I have large sexual organs.

CLIMSBY. Get out of my office. Get out before I throw you out!

THE PROFESSOR. Why? What did I do?

MOE. The honeymoon incident, boss.

THE PROFESSOR. Oh no...

CLIMSBY. Your interview is done!

MOE. What about our patent?

CLIMSBY. You don't get one, not from me.

MOE. But my future—!

THE PROFESSOR. My wife—!

CLIMSBY. (*Dismisses them.*) My ass.

MOE. (*Hands him a card.*) Our card—

CLIMSBY. (*Takes it.*) Good–bye!

THE PROFESSOR. Aw, petunias! (*They exit.*)

Scene 2 - On The Streets Of The Town

(*MOE and THE PROFESSOR walk to the lab, they pass the general public on Main Street.*)

MOE. You gotta learn to control that temper, boss…

THE PROFESSOR. Bite my temper! I think the world will be better off if they accept what I have to offer!

THE WOMAN WHO WANTS A HAPPY LIFE. Who could ever cure the ills of this society? All I ever wanted was a happy life, but look at the people on this city street: Tension and misery, everywhere you see. Waah! Waah!

BAG MAN. (*Wagging a piece of fuzzy material.*) Windows cleaned! Spare change? Cigarette?

THE WOMAN WHO WANTS… He has no money! And what about these young lovers? Can they find happiness in a world so tormented? Can they really?

BARNEY. Do you have to go to choir practice, Delilah?

DELILAH. It's not that I want to. But you know how daddy feels about it.

THE WOMAN WHO WANTS… I hope they find love and happiness. Lord knows, I never have.

BARNEY. I have something very important to ask you.

DELILAH. Can't talk now, gotta run. I'll meet you in the park at four! (*Gives him a wholesome peck on the cheek, and runs off.*)

THE WOMAN WHO WANTS… Now he's all alone. Just like me. Here's Lady Jacqueline. All the time the Professor was locked away working, she sat across the street looking out her window with a wistful sigh…

BAG MAN. Spare change? Want to buy this fluffy cloth?

GIRL A. Hrumph! It's artificial! I only prefer reality, like the spring freshness of my bottled Evian water.

BAG MAN. Up your ass! Help me! Fluffy cloth for sale! Fluffy scrap o'cloth!

LADY JACQUELINE. Professor? Moe?

THE PROFESSOR. Who's that?

MOE. Wake up boss, that's Lady Jacqueline, lives across the street. He's been working hard.

LADY JACQUELINE. It's nice to see you out again. I haven't seen you since you left on your honeymoon. How's your wife?

THE PROFESSOR. (*Pulls himself up straight with indignance. JACQUELINE notices bulge in his trousers.*) She left me!

LADY JACQUELINE. I'm so sorry. I can't guess why.

MOE. Painful story. Don't ask about it now.

LADY JACQUELINE. Then may I invite you to my home for a private dinner. I've always admired you, there never seemed an appropriate time.

THE PROFESSOR. (*Brusque.*) I'll let you know.

BERTHA. Good sir, I believing in helping out the homeless: Let me buy that fabric.

BAG MAN. Fifty cents. It's fake.

BERTHA. Thank goodness. We both support wildlife.

BAG MAN. I don't give a shit. Got a cigarette?

BERTHA. If you're going to use this money for cigarettes, I won't buy! (*Out front:*) Tobacco is not healthy for children and other living things.

BAG MAN. Gimme the four bits and get out.

BERTHA. Here's two dollars. Buy yourself a warm meal. This will make a nice cover for my bicycle seat.

BAG MAN. Wanna come to my hotel?

BERTHA. Typical man! (*As she runs away.*) And I thought he would be grateful!

THE WOMAN WHO WANTS... (*To THE PROFESSOR.*) Do you really think you can change the world? Do you really?

MOE. Take a walk, sister.

THE PROFESSOR. Lock the door, Moe. I've had all I can take of the world for this day.

(*They retreat into the lab. Street scene clears.*)

Scene 3 - At the Professor's Laboratory

THE PROFESSOR. Home. Alone. A failure. What's the use...?

MOE. I know how you feel boss. Lemme check the mail: Gas bill. Electric bill. Phone bill. Rent bill. Insurance bill.

THE PROFESSOR. We're broke!

MOE. We need money! No response to the ads? Aw, balls!

THE PROFESSOR. What ads?

MOE. Get your head out of your butt! I placed ads for the Cock Machine in a few national magazines with reply cards, remember? It seemed like a safe way to sell until we got the patent and could set ourselves up legit.

THE PROFESSOR. (*Referring to a magazine.*) No response to my personal ad?

MOE. (*Flips towards back of magazine and reads.*) "Sparky, intelligent, well–hung inventor seeks the beautiful but small–minded cunt who dumped me?" Nah.

(*There's a knock at the door, THE PROFESSOR answers.*)

THE PROFESSOR. What?

RADIO MAN. I'm from Radio Station KOOK! I have brought you a check for Fifty Thousand—

THE PROFESSOR. (*Shoves him away, engrossed in his personals ad.*) Get out. (*Goes to the SX–70.*) My wonderful machine. My SX–70. All that time, gone to waste.

MOE. What waste? Machine gives you a big dick: you got a big dick. What do you want?

THE PROFESSOR. It was supposed to bring her back.

MOE. You don't have to put all your eggs in one basket, Prof. You got other inventions, just as good.

THE PROFESSOR. Like what?

MOE. The automatic shoes. (*THE PROFESSOR gives a look.*) They'd work if you put a little more time into them.

THE PROFESSOR. (*As he puts them on.*) Maybe I've given too much for this one dream. A dream too grand for the unwashed masses.

MOE. Cut your beef. Just put them on low speed, and try to keep your balance.

THE PROFESSOR. Automatic shoes to take you wherever you want to go: they do all the walking: all a person has to do is keep standing…

MOE. Give it a shot.

THE PROFESSOR. Here goes nothing… (*He switches them on, walks around for a few steps before running into a wall and falling down.*) Aw, petunias!

(*There is a pounding at the door. MOE goes to answer.*)

MOE. Yes?

CLIMSBY. OK wiseguys, remember me? I want to try that cock machine!

MOE. It's Climsby.

THE PROFESSOR. Salvation!

MOE. Just a minute there, Climsby. Why the change of heart?

CLIMSBY. Well, you have to realize that a man of my position has to keep up a certain a level of authority...

MOE. To mask the simple nature he really possesses, of course.

CLIMSBY. Whatever. And that for me to approve the machine might imply to my superiors that I would actually need such a device...

MOE. Which no one really needs—

THE PROFESSOR. But everyone wants!

CLIMSBY. Perhaps. And if my superiors ever felt I was somehow... unworthy, well, I could lose my job. I was looking over my bruises suffered during your... graceless attack, and I said, my body will look fine once they clear up. Then I looked a little more closely, and decided, perhaps there might be some further improvement that could be made on my physical self.

THE PROFESSOR. Absolutely!

CLIMSBY. So I thought I would drop by and offer to test the efficacy of the SX–70 in order to make a full evaluation before I— Oh hell with it, just let me on the machine!

MOE. Nah, we need to take a minute to discuss the details.

CLIMSBY. I can't wait. My wife's birthday is next week, and I want to surprise her. Is this the machine? (*As he mounts it.*) It seems my feet should go here, and... Well look! This instruction panel is finely illustrated, with a backlit quartz digital display. Even a child could learn to use this.

MOE. Don't rush things, Climsby. You should always consult your physician before starting an exercise program.

CLIMSBY. Is there anything else I need to know?

THE PROFESSOR. (*Checks CLIMSBY.*) You've got your penis in backwards.

CLIMSBY. Ah! Thank you. That's much better... (*He begins exercising enthusiastically.*) How long does it take before I start seeing results? (*He looks down, excited.*) —Never mind!

MOE. Before you get too carried away, chum, what about our patent?

CLIMSBY. In my back pocket.
MOE. (*Retrieves it.*) Professor, we are in business.

(*There is a knock at the door.*)

THE PROFESSOR. Yes?
POSTMAN. Mail delivery!
THE PROFESSOR. Who would be sending mail at this time of day?

(*He opens the door, and is weighted down with a huge sack of multi-colored envelopes.*)

THE PROFESSOR. What is all this?
MOE. Mail orders, Professor. Look at the responses: (*He pulls out different colors of cards.*) Sports magazines. Poetry journals. Women's reading, and Men's companions.
THE PROFESSOR. My dream, my gift to the world... and people want it. I'm so full, my heart— my heart is about to burst.
CLIMSBY. (*On cell phone.*) Grindel? Cancel my appointments. I won't be back in today.
THE PROFESSOR. Moe, can you imagine how it will be to see smiles on the face of everyone in town? All men will have pride in themselves, and in their children. And in their children's children... Men will wave to each other on the street.
CLIMSBY. It really works! Yippeeeeee!
THE PROFESSOR. Our time has come! To work!

(*BLACKOUT!*)

Scene 4: In the City Park

THE WOMAN WHO WANTS... Well, they might think they've found the key to happiness, but watch how it only causes more hurt feelings than there already are in the world: Here we are in the city's prettiest park. At this time of year, it's so touching to see a boy and a girl so much in love. But I know it's going to fail: Take care, young lovers— Wah!

DELILAH. Barney.

BARNEY. Delilah!

DELILAH. I'm so glad to see you, I could hardly wait for choir practice to end! I've written you this poem:

BARNEY. "Roses are Red, Violets are Blue, The lord in his heaven, the fish in the zoo—

DELILAH. (*Finishes for him:*) They all dream what I dream: You, you, you!"

THE WOMAN WHO WANTS... *The magnificence*!

(*She clutches her breast and leaves, greatly moved.*)

BARNEY. That was nice, Delilah. And I have something for you.

DELILAH. A ring! Barney, does this mean what I think? Is this for me?

BARNEY. Yes it is, Delilah. If you will be my bride.

DELILAH. Can I believe it? "On Sunday, the twenty-fourth of June, Miss Delilah Barley will become:

BARNEY. "Mrs. Barney Terwhilleger!" What do you say?

DELILAH. Barney Barney, I am so excited! And I have something for you too! It was going to be for your birthday, but now it will be: for Our Wedding Night. (*She hands him a colored envelope.*)

BARNEY. (*Reads:*) "Men— Increase the size of your penis"— What does this mean?

DELILAH. It's the new SX-70 expansion system, I read about in my diet and health magazine. It says here about—

BARNEY. I thought you liked me.

DELILAH. I do! But it says here you can double your cock size in just ten days, and I just thought that you— any man—

BARNEY. You surprise me, Delilah. Frankly, I expected better from a minister's daughter.

DELILAH. Here comes Joe Hercules.

(*Enter JOE HERCULES.*)

JOE HERCULES. Hey there Barney. Hi Delilah. I haven't seen you at the club for a while. And I'm teaching a low-impact abdominals session in just a few minutes.

BARNEY. I thought Yablonski had that class.

JOE HERCULES. Dale moved away to the next town. I teach the abdominals now. Hey, I see you ordered one of those new cock machines.

DELILAH. The SX-70.

JOE HERCULES. I ordered one for myself. I'm trying to get an exclusive license for the club.

DELILAH. Does it really work, Mr. Hercules?

JOE HERCULES. That's not a very nice question for a girl to ask— That'll have to be private information between us guys, eh Barn?

BARNEY. I'm not so sure, Mr. Hercules.

JOE HERCULES. How would you two like to come by for a free workout? As my guest.

DELILAH. I would love to— I haven't exercised in some time, and I'm getting flabby. Barney—?

BARNEY. I don't think I better. I'm a little tired now and—

DELILAH. Not even if you come with me?

JOE HERCULES. Starting an aerobic fitness plan could increase your pep and vim. That's why I teach the class.

(*DELILAH decides to try and make BARNEY jealous. She presents herself to the gym instructor.*)

DELILAH. What about my breasts? I'm not wearing a bra, and I'm worried that too much jumping could harm their shape.

JOE HERCULES. For an older woman, that might be something to look out for, (*He cups her breasts and squeezes them deliciously.*) but yours appear to be... quite firm. (*He sees Barney looking hurt.*) Oh! Hey Barney, excuse me. I don't want it to look like I'm making moves on your girl.

BARNEY. Don't worry about it Joe. It's not as if we were— engaged.

JOE HERCULES. All right then. The class starts at four, and then I need to stop by City Hall to see about acquiring a few Cock Machines for the club— I've really got to move out.

DELILAH. I only need a minute. (*Goes to Barney.*) I'm going to the low-impact abdominals. I wish you'd come along.

BARNEY. Why bother. I can see what's important to you.

DELILAH. I was only trying to make you jealous. I... I guess I tried too hard.

BARNEY. Don't try and explain.

DELILAH. If that's the way you feel. I'm sorry Barney. I guess you'll be wanting this back. (*She returns the ring.*)

BARNEY. So! So you really don't care!

DELILAH. What about my needs?

BARNEY. I'm not man enough for you.

DELILAH. You've always been man enough for me, Barney. It's just that— I've given you everything I could. I only thought that, with the SX-70, I could give you something you've never had.

JOE HERCULES. Ready Delilah?

DELILAH. (*Painful parting.*) Good-bye!

(*JOE HERCULES slings DELILAH over his shoulder, and as he trots off with her, she waves goodbye to BARNEY.*)

THE WOMAN WHO WANTS... Didn't I tell you it would fail? Oh, if only I was wrong for once, then I would be so happy. But of course, that will never happen.

(*END OF SCENE.*)

Scene 5: On the City Streets, but in a Bad Part of Town

(*The muck and mire of the bigger world swells up again: People rush about the stage, cursing and running into each other. When that clears away, we are in the slums. The BABY SEAL enters. He is wearing a hunter's cap.*)

BABY SEAL. (*Sings.*)
I'M A LONELY BABY SEAL IN A GREAT BIG WORLD
PITY ME,
PITY ME,
PITY ME!
WHEN THE HUNTERS KILLED MY VILLAGE ON THAT
SNOWY DAY,
I HID BENEATH AN ICEBERG AND IT SAILED AWAY
NOW I WANDER ALL ALONE IN THIS COLD, STRANGE
PLACE:

PITY ME,
PITY ME,
PITY ME!

(*A BAG MAN wakes from the garbage.*)

BAG MAN. Hey— got a dollar?
BABY SEAL. A dollar? Are you crazy?
BAG MAN. Hey buddy, help me out. Come on.
BABY SEAL. I'm sorry. I don't have any spare change. Can you tell me—

(*Two BUSINESSMEN enter, in suits with brief cases.*)

BUSINESSMAN #1. It's a really big deal. We've made a conversion offer of seven point nine basis points against the value of the shares.
BUSINESSMAN #2. Pretty risky in today's market. —What have you heard of this new outfit, the Supercock Manufacturing Company? Supposed to grow a bigger—uh—uh—

BUSINESSMAN #1. Wouldn't touch it, wouldn't touch it. God knows I don't need any help there, heh heh—!

BUSINESSMAN #2. Not saying that I do, not saying that I do, heh heh!

BUSINESSMAN #1. Does it work? Not that I'd try it...

BUSINESSMAN #2. Haven't seen. Not that I'd look!

BUSINESSMAN #1. Say, you get a look at Linda, new chick works with convertible debentures? Quite a rack!

BUSINESSMAN #2. Hey. I would sure love to convert her debentures!

BUSINESSMAN # 1. Haw haw haw.

BUSINESSMAN # 2. Haw haw haw.

BABY SEAL. Can you tell me where I am?

BAG MAN. Where you from.

BABY SEAL. Antarctica.

BAG MAN. Got a cigarette?

BABY SEAL. What's a cigarette?

BAG MAN. You mean to tell me they don't have cigarettes in Antarctica? Shit, you ain't lived. Here. (*He gives the BABY SEAL a cigarette.*)

BABY SEAL. Thanks. Got a light? (*He gets it.*) Hey, this is nice. Can I have another one for later?

BAG MAN. Fifty cents. Smokes 're only free the first time.

BABY SEAL. I'll go without. I've never been a moocher, and I'm not gonna start now. But I sure am hungry...

BAG MAN. What do you eat?

BABY SEAL. Fish, mostly. Have any?

BAG MAN. I might. Got any money?

BABY SEAL. Yes! But, I have to save it... For a very special reason.

BAG MAN. (*He starts searching his coat pocket.*) Ya know. You're not like the average guy I meet.

BABY SEAL. (*Edgy.*) I'm not?

BAG MAN. When I look at you, I get a warm feeling all over. I start thinking of things...

BABY SEAL. (*Frightened, backing away.*) Yeah?

BAG MAN. Yeah: (*Plucks off the BABY SEAL's cap.*) —things like fur coats!

(*He pulls out a bludgeon and the BABY SEAL runs off in terror.*)

BAG MAN. I almost had him. Now I'll freeze tonight. What a terrible life, what a terrible world. If only the members of the government looked out for the cares of all men!

(*He exits, much aggrieved.*)

Scene 6: At the City Bureau of Business Permits

(*SONIA stands at a desk in the Civic Licensing Bureau. MOE and HIRAM stand before her.*)

SONIA. Here's your permit, Ms. Hildebrande. Your Organic Granola Salon will be quite an asset to the mall, good luck with it.

MOE. Is this where we apply for a business permit?

SONIA. Yes it is. Have you filled out the appropriate paperwork?

MOE. Right here. (*He hands her a long form, and she browses it.*)

SONIA. A cock machine? Now see here sir, I am a staunch defender of our animal citizens as well as the human ones. All species deserve equal employment, and I'm not willing to see my barnyard friends replaced by mechanical chickens.

THE PROFESSOR. It's not about chicken.

MOE. It's about salami!

SONIA. Denied.

MOE. It's not a farm project. We want to open something more like a— gymnasium—

THE PROFESSOR. Or a clinic—

MOE. A facility where men can come to — expand their physical capabilities...

SONIA. Not interested. It is my job to protect the citizens from indecent businesses. Without my approval, you are S.O.L.

THE PROFESSOR. Shit–Out–of–Luck??? It's a cock machine! It's an amazing new device that can give men bigger penis size! (*SONIA is horrified.*) Longer! Thicker!

SONIA. Denied!!

MOE. Meatier!

SONIA. I'm vegetarian!

MOE. Ya got any men work this desk we could talk to?

(*BUSINESSMAN #1 enters.*)

BUSINESSMAN #1. What is all this noise about, Sonia?
SONIA. Nothing, sir. I'm trying to eject these two troublemakers.
MOE. We want to open a shop for our Cock Machine.
BUSINESSMAN #1. I've been hearing a lot about that. I won't go into details, but I can tell you, I've never been thrown out of bed! Haw haw haw.
BUSINESSMAN #2. Yeah, I'd hate to think what made you want to go and invent that, haw haw. —Does it work?
THE PROFESSOR. Of course it works, you imbecile. (*MOE calms him.*)

(*JOE HERCULES enters.*)

JOE HERCULES. What's going on out here? I've come to renew my permit.
SONIA. Certainly Mr. Hercules. As soon as I eject these troublemakers.
BUSINESSMAN #1. This is the man with the Cock Machine.
JOE HERCULES. The Cock Machine?
BUSINESSMAN #2. He invented it!
JOE HERCULES. I've been using it! Pleased to meet you! I'm Joe Hercules, owner of the town's largest fitness center. I was thinking of getting a few more for my club.
MOE. We're hoping to run our own operation.
SONIA. Denied!

(*The MAYOR enters, with POLICE CHIEF O'FLAHRETY.*)

SONIA. Here comes the Mayor! He knows all about decency, maybe HE can set you straight!
MAYOR. Good afternoon, gentlemen. What's all the ruckus?
SONIA. I've got it all under control, Mayor Lucky. I'm just trying to eject all of these horrible men. —If the kind Officer O'Flahrety could assist me?
O'FLAHRETY. What's the big problem here?
SONIA. These two gentlemen, the Professor and his assistant Moe, have invented a machine which they say enlarges the uh... "penis" of any gentleman.

O'FLAHRETY. Those things never work.

MAYOR. Oh really? Professor, Moe: Mayor Lucky. Pleased to meet you, I've heard something about your invention.

THE PROFESSOR. Have you now?

JOE HERCULES. Does it work?

THE PROFESSOR. Why do you think I'm here, of course it works.

SONIA. Officer O'Flahrety is right. Show them out please. I want to waste no more time over this tiny, little, insignificat—

THE PROFESSOR. That's my machine you're talking about! This has been my consuming passion for the past two years. And I promise, it can guarantee every man in this room increased penis size.

BUSINESSMAN #2. Haw haw haw. Do you expect me to buy that?

THE PROFESSOR. Yes. Next question.

SONIA. Denied!

SONIA. Has it been proven safe?

THE PROFESSOR. No ill effects have been seen.

MAYOR. How much increase can we expect to see?

THE PROFESSOR. As with any exercise device, the more you work, the more you can get. Of course, there are bound to be differences in one man and the next. But in its short time of study, a reasonable expectation shows to be an increase of approximately two pounds.

(*There is a great stir among the men.*)

SONIA. This is obscene! This is will corrupt our values and destroy the town! Mayor Lucky, do you really want to encourage such a business, after all you've done to clean up the city?

MAYOR. Would it be possible, Professor, to sample this invention?

MOE. Once we get our permit, sure!

JOE HERCULES. Sonia might have a point. My health club presently meets the fitness needs of the locals. And, who around here really needs a device that enlarges— well—

THE MEN. Not me, no way, uh–uh...

SONIA. What impact will this have on the environment?

THE PROFESSOR. None.

SONIA. What will it do for the workers in our community?

BUSINESSMAN #1. Dammit Sonia, don't start—

SONIA. Is this just another indulgence to the rich, white, male population? Or will it be available to all people, regardless of race or ability to pay?

THE PROFESSOR. It's intended mainly for use in our own facility, once we get the permit. Similar to a health club, I suppose, but with a more specific focus.

JOE HERCULES. Now wait a minute Professor. I already run the city's most profitable health club. As much as I support your product, I think my own club is quite enough for the citizens of this town.

THE PROFESSOR. Perhaps. But perhaps our operation will not conflict, but provide a space for a more exclusive clientele.

SONIA. As I suspected, Professor! When mere bread is out of the reach of the poor, owning a cock machine will be another taunt to their poverty, something ELSE they can never have, right up there with Christmas. If anyone gets to use your machine, then bigger dicks for all, I say! Bigger dicks for all!

THE PROFESSOR. What is she talking about?

SONIA. You bad, evil male! As if we women aren't victims enough, now you want to threaten us with further sexual horrors. And even that's not enough. I know what real hidden agenda you are promoting: The destruction of our wildlife.

THE PROFESSOR. What is she talking about?

SONIA. While homeless people sleep in our subways, and you don't care, men will be courting, maybe even marrying— womyn!

MOE. So what?

SONIA. Everyone knows that in their pathetic mating ritual, men seduce womyn with fur coats! I'm not blind, Professor! Your machine will escalate the murder of cute, helpless animals!

MOE. (*To THE PROFESSOR.*) Did I just miss something here?

SONIA. And did you think of those women Professor, draped in that —fur?

THE PROFESSOR. Absolutely. But without the fur—

SONIA. He wants us all naked! All the time! Your business permit is denied! Denied do you hear?

THE PROFESSOR. Think of the men in this community!

SONIA. Think of the women! How are my Sisters going to accommodate these monstrosities? Have you also built an invention to increase the female sexual organ to, say, five or six times its natural size???

(*All action halts momentarily; then every man present grabs SONIA and hurls her out the door.*)

MR. WISDOM. (*A solemn rebuke:*) Council, I draw the line here: Don't make fun of vaginas. My wife, god rest her soul, had one. You must never laugh at a thing like that.

O'FLAHRETY. Now good Mayor Lucky, the whole topic makes me jumpy. I'm not sure we need this thing within the boundaries of our fair city. After all, surely there can't be that much disparity among the male population.

BUSINESSMAN #1. What if there isn't? What if I just want more?

BUSINESSMAN #2. Oh, so you really need more, that's what you're really saying.

BUSINESSMAN #1. No, I didn't say that. I'm sure that I have quite enough to get by, thank you. I can say with confidence that I am comfortably "average" in that department.

MAYOR. Oh really? What is average?

BUSINESSMAN #1. Well... You must know.

MAYOR. Yeah, I think I do. Never mind.

O'FLAHRETY. Then how big is it, Mayor?

MAYOR. Don't bother me, O'Flahrety. At least as much as you. You know. Average. The better side of average. You know.

MOE. I don't think you do.

O'FLAHRETY. What's that you say?

MAYOR. Well Professor, you should have experience in this— How big is a man? On average?

THE PROFESSOR. (*Amazed.*) You don't know?

(*There is uncomfortable shifting in the room.*)

O'FLAHRETY. There's a fine Mayor for ye. Don't know what's in his own pants.

MAYOR. Most certainly I do O'Flahrety, but I don't know what's in yours. Go on then, YOU set the standard. (*Silence from O'FLAHRETY.*) Go on. You're the big bad police chief. Or are you afraid that you're less of a man than you should be? Out with it.

O'FLAHRETY. Four inches. (*Varied responses from around the room.*) That's right, and every one of 'em Irish. And what proud, fine Irish inches they are, I might add.

MAYOR. There we have it. Is there anyone who can differ with Officer O'Flahrety's statistics? (*No response. The MAYOR is smug.*) Then that must be the average size. (*Gloating.*) So I have nothing to be ashamed of.

THE PROFESSOR. Gentlemen, this is disgraceful. Listen to yourselves, desperately one-upping each other. And no one knows with what! It is a sorry fact, gentlemen, that after millions of years on this planet, no man in this room can even guess the average size of his own species!

A HUMBLE SOMEONE. Does it really work, Professor?

THE PROFESSOR. Demonstrate, Moe.

(*Utter silence as MOE approaches the downstage end of the meeting table. All are sharply attentive, and we hear nothing but the sound of MOE unzipping his pants. People fight to feign indifference, but can't. When he pulls himself out, a heavy thud sounds against the tabletop, and MOE stands on display. There is a storm of anxiety in the room: The men push themselves away from the table, some engage in impromptu "boxing", another does pushups. No one can harness their envy, and the torment persists until THE PROFESSOR approaches MOE from behind.*)

THE PROFESSOR. (*Softly.*) That's enough Moe. Put it away now. (*He takes a stance before them.*) Can you still laugh at the joint achievements of medicine and science? I want my business permit!

(*The men collapse pathetically, grabbing at THE PROFESSOR's cuffs, begging.*)

THE MEN. Gimme one! Gimme one! Gimme one!

THE PROFESSOR. (*Someone hands him the permit*—) Mine!!! (—*but THE MAYOR snatches it away.*)

MAYOR. No one gets this until I get it first. I should use it. Test it for safety.

MOE. Balls!

JOE HERCULES. I think the Mayor may have a point, gentlemen. I would suggest that, before you go off half–cocked, gently introduce the machine to the population in an established, controlled setting. Like my health club.

MOE. You're not riding on our backs!

THE PROFESSOR. Maybe just a temporary arrangement wouldn't be so bad.

MOE. Balls!

THE PROFESSOR. But the electricity bill? The insurance bill? The gas bill? The renewal for my personal ad?

BUSINESSMAN #1. See here, gentlemen! This invention can alleviate the suffering of hundreds, maybe thousands of men in this town. It's wrong to withhold a cure while you battle over money!

MAYOR. So Peebles: you admit to your inadequacy.

BUSINESSMAN #1. I'm fine enough, probably: but if I could do better, why shouldn't I? After all, my red sportscar is very expensive!

BUSINESSMAN #2. And I could have avoided getting the battleship tattoo on my back!

JOE HERCULES. And Mr. Mayor, you could stop smoking those expensive cigars!

MAYOR. Silence! Unless I get a private sampling of the machine, you will never open your Cockamamie Shop in this town.

MOE. Agreed!

THE PROFESSOR. But Moe—!

MAYOR. I forbid operation of your business based on moral grounds.

JOE HERCULES. You can still run it through my club.

MAYOR. I'll shut you down.

JOE HERCULES. If you interfere, I will inform the voters. You know half the town is a member of my health spa.

MAYOR. (*Considers...*) If you want to operate through Joe's gym, I can't stop you.

MOE. They got us over a table, Prof.

THE PROFESSOR. Fine, for now.

JOE HERCULES. Then the deal is settled. I'll give you space in my club, and pay you a percentage of the membership fees.

MAYOR. I expect a free membership.

JOE HERCULES. I'll give you a discount during off–hours, but that's my limit.

MAYOR. And before the city renews your permit, Hercules, there's a fee increase: a 75% surcharge is hereby applied by me! (*All are aghast.*) If you want to operate cock machines here, you'll have to reimburse the City.

MOE. What in hell for?

MAYOR. For using my citizens as research animals.

(*People begin to protest.*)

THE PROFESSOR. What a shame. I have an invention which can bring happiness to the world. And it is corrupted by greedy profiteers.

JOE HERCULES. Here's your money, Professor. Thank you, from the bottom of my heart. (*To the MAYOR.*) And here's your fucking seventy-five percent, you scumbag. Wait till you see who I vote for in the next election!

BUSINESSMAN #2. What about a membership, Joe?

JOE HERCULES. Membership rates have suddenly increased, 300%.

BUSINESSMAN #1. I don't care! I can sell my sports car!

BUSINESSMAN #2. I can remove my tattoo!

MOE. We can open shop!

THE PROFESSOR. I can find my Penny!

MAYOR. I can take that trip to Niagara Falls!

THE PROFESSOR. Niagara Falls! Slowly, I turned—

(*THE PROFESSOR begins to go into a fury, and chases them off the stage.*)

Scene 6A - Newsflash

NEWSBOY. Extra! Extra! Read all about it! Chief of Police Declares Four-Inch Mandate! Red tape delays release of SX-70, proven method of dramatically prolonging men's size! Special News Flash! Antonovichovich Furriers announce clearance sale to make way for new inventory! Prices slashed for Fabulous Bargains on fox, mink and chinchillas! Extra! Extra!

Scene 7 - Headquarters of the Women Against Fur

(BERTHA busies herself cutting and stretching her scrap of cloth to fit her bicycle seat.)

SONIA. It was terrible, Bertha! The men have this new weapon— They are all going to be hung like pythons.
BERTHA. Disgusting, I can't argue. But what do men's repulsive sexual organs have to do with the rights of animals? (*The phone rings.*) Women Against Fur.
MAN'S VOICE. Hey, yeah, I wanna complain— I ordered this pamphlet from ya, called "Women Against Fur"?
BERTHA. Yes?
MAN'S VOICE. Well there's no women in it at all, just pictures of deer hunts and seal hunts and stuff—

(BERTHA slams down the phone.)

SONIA. Men are men, and they must be stopped!
BERTHA. Take a look: here comes that Barley girl with the gym instructor.

(DELILAH and JOE HERCULES enter.)

DELILAH. Hi Ms. Bagley, Ms. Manniker. Daddy wanted me to return these pamphlets to you. He said regardless of what people do, the church should take a neutral stand on Animal Rights.
BERTHA. Typical male response.
DELILAH. I read the pamphlets though. I thought they were kinda neat. Except the pictures were gross.

BERTHA. —I haven't seen your boyfriend around lately. Are you available now?

DELILAH. No, Barney's just... doing other things. This is Joe Hercules, from the gym?

JOE HERCULES. Hello, ladies! (*BERTHA and SONIA give a frosty stare.*) I'll wait outside.

BERTHA. So you've taken up with someone else.

DELILAH. Ms. Bagley, Daddy doesn't like it when I talk about boys... Have you ever had to chose between someone you love, and someone who's built like a... farm animal?

BERTHA. Never!

SONIA. Are you wearing a belt, Delilah? A leather belt?

DELILAH. I guess I am.

SONIA. A cow died for that, Delilah. Do you know how that cow died?

DELILAH. Jolt of electricity through the head, according to your literature. Ick. Oh well, Daddy's waiting. Gotta run!

(*She exits*)

SONIA. There she goes, off with that gym instructor. He sided with the Cock Machine people. He's giving them shelter in his health club.

BERTHA. Sonia, I can't listen to you. We have our purpose, we cannot take dog legs, pardon the expression, into other areas of concern. There is nuclear war to worry about, there is the spread of disease. There is political torture. What is our contribution, Sonia, what is our cause?

SONIA. Fur?

BERTHA. Look at these photos— a bear trap, with one foot in it— a monkey, tied to restaurant table while the patrons eat his brain!

SONIA. Yeah but who did all this? The men, Bertha, the men!

BERTHA. I know Sonia, but I don't care! I know what men are like. Don't you think our own mission is important enough?

SONIA. We burglarized the furriers, and stole nearly their full inventory— We didn't sell the fur for profit, that's what a man would do.

BERTHA. And when we tossed those skins into the dumpster, Sonia, I was proud. Proud of the contribution. Sweet, baby animals are dying, Sonia. Not people: animals. We can't stop the fight now. (*The phone rings*:) Yes?

HEAVY BREATHING VOICE. What are your showtimes?

BERTHA. Showtimes? For what?

HEAVY BREATHING VOICE. For "Women Against Fur"—

BERTHA. We are NOT a movie!! (*Slams down the phone.*)

(*The BABY SEAL enters. He is wearing a pork-pie hat.*)

BERTHA. Hey! Hey you! No smoking in here. You're polluting my air!

BABY SEAL. Oh. Sorry.

BERTHA. What may I do for you?

BABY SEAL. I am looking for my mother. Can you help me?

BERTHA. What does she look like?

BABY SEAL. She was big and white and furry, with two big flippers and a nice soft tail.

BERTHA. Really?

SONIA. That doesn't sound like any woman I have ever seen. That sounds more like a great white seal, from the arctic region.

BABY SEAL. That's her! That's her! Where is she, I want to see her now!

BERTHA. Wait a minute. You are a baby seal, aren't you.

BABY SEAL. I— I might be. Would you hurt me if I was?

BERTHA. Heavens no! Why would I do a thing like that?

BABY SEAL. For my fur. The seal killers get $50 for one skin. (*Cautiously removes his cap as he speaks.*) The hunters got most of our village, but I escaped on an iceberg. I came to the city, because I have saved the $50 I need— well, forty-nine dollars and fifty cents actually, and I want to buy mama's fur back. Do you think— do you think I will find the right one?

BERTHA. I don't think so, my child.

BABY SEAL. Why not! I saved my money, I came all this way— (*Frightened, slaps his hat back on in defense.*) are you going to steal my fur too?

BERTHA. Oh my baby! God has led you to me. This is the world-wide headquarters of the Women Against Fur. You couldn't have chosen a safer place.

BABY SEAL. Really? Oh, boy!

BERTHA. Hey Sonia, look who we have with us tonight: A baby white seal!

SONIA. Aaaaaaawwwww!

BERTHA. Don't fear little seal. You are always safe here.

(*They hug the seal. End of scene.*)

Scene 8: At the Home of Minister Barley.

NEWSBOY. Extra! Extra! Read all about it! Controversial New Invention, SX-70 To Be Made Widely Available in Special Civic Ceremony! Chief O'Flahrety Condemns Enlarging Device! Read All About The Four-Inch Force That Backs Up City Hall!

MINISTER BARLEY. Over here, boy. I'll take one.

NEWSBOY. Thanks Minister Barley. You going to ask me in for ice cream?

MINISTER BARLEY. Not today Billy. I've given up smoking.

DELILAH. Thanks for walking me home, Joe. I really enjoyed the private session.

MINISTER BARLEY. Delilah!

DELILAH. Daddy!

MINISTER BARLEY. Kissing on the doorstep— What will people think! Come in this house, both of you.

DELILAH. Daddy, this is Joe Hercules.

MINISTER BARLEY. Where's your boyfriend?

DELILAH. I don't know if I'll be seeing much more of Barney, father.

MINISTER BARLEY. Oh? That's too bad. He seemed like a fine young man. Say, haven't I seen you in my church?

JOE HERCULES. Not for a while, Minister Barley. I run the fitness center.

MINISTER BARLEY. Yes, I thought so. Say, I read in the paper that your health club is the only one to have one of those new SX-70 units.

JOE HERCULES. I signed an exclusive contract. I'm having a membership special to keep up with my customer's demand.

MINISTER BARLEY. Shameful. Disgraceful. Does it work?

JOE HERCULES. I'd be happy to show you—
MINISTER BARLEY. Sinful. Sinful. Sinful.
DELILAH. Daddy, will you leave us alone?
MINISTER BARLEY. I'd like to speak to you privately, young man.
JOE HERCULES. Delilah, do you mind?

(*JOE HERCULES and MINISTER BARLEY go off. The doorbell rings. DELILAH answers.*)

BARNEY. Hello Delilah. Can I come in?
DELILAH. Barney! What are you doing here?
BARNEY. I just came... to talk. I've been thinking—
DELILAH. What is it, Barney?
BARNEY. Maybe I was wrong. Maybe my pride is too easily hurt. Maybe I should use the SX-70.
DELILAH. Maybe I was wrong too, Barney. Having sex with Joe Hercules was really terrific. But I love you. That's a big difference. And... if you really want the machine... then that difference doesn't have to stay so big.
BARNEY. You didn't cancel the order?

(*The POSTMAN enters, with a crate.*)

POSTMAN. Delivery here for Barney Terwhilliger, care of Delilah Barley! Sign here!
DELILAH. Just in time!
BARNEY. Thank you Delilah. I'm going to start using it right away!

(*The MINISTER and JOE HERCULES return.*)

MINISTER BARLEY. Good News Delilah: I've just enrolled in the health spa. Barney! I thought we would never see you again.
BARNEY. Not true, Minister Barley. In fact, I have come to ask for the hand of your daughter in marriage. That is: if she will have me.
MINISTER BARLEY. Wait— what's this big shipping crate?
JOE HERCULES. I recognize that— That's a cock machine.
DELILAH. It was just delivered.

JOE HERCULES. Say Minister Barley, I think that's terrific. Wait till the papers hear that even the town minister owns an SX-70. And here I thought you bought your membership from me just to try it out.

MINISTER BARLEY. Young man! You are gravely mistaken! Gravely! Who brought this box of hell into our home?

BARNEY. The Postman!

MINISTER BARLEY. (*Reads:*) Mr. Barney Terwhilliger! So! Sinful hedon! Hedon!

DELILAH. Daddy, what's wrong if he just wants—

MINISTER BARLEY. So the ignorance of sin has pervaded your sweet soul as well, has it? Foolish child.

DELILAH. Barney didn't buy it: I did, father. It was I.

MINISTER BARLEY. Is this true? Say it is true, and she is not a fitting wife. Say it is false, and you are not a fitting husband.

BARNEY. I paid for it, Minister Barley.

DELILAH. Barney, no—

MINISTER BARLEY. If he is only covering for you Delilah, you will be branded as the slut of this community. A disgrace to my preachings.

BARNEY. I paid for it, Minister Barley.

JOE HERCULES. Sir, I don't understand your indignance. After all, your inquiries about the gymnasium equipment were pretty specific.

DELILAH. I hate you! I hate you, you— hypocrite!

MINISTER BARLEY. See how you've broken this house with your lies? Someone may find out there is a cock machine under my roof. You can't marry my daughter Delilah. Get out of our home.

BARNEY. Minister Barley—

MINISTER BARLEY. (*To DELILAH.*) To your room.

DELILAH. (*Tears about to flow.*) ...Barney! (*She leaves.*)

BARNEY. At least— at least let me take this out of here. I hope I have room for it.

JOE HERCULES. You can store it at the club.

MINISTER BARLEY. You will leave that sinful apparatus here, young man.

JOE HERCULES. You shock me, Minister Barley. I can speak for the honor of both of these young people. And if you honestly believe in Truth, I could give the press some important details about your personal needs, and why you joined the health club.

MINISTER BARLEY. Do so and I will cancel my membership. I can always stop the check. You decide.

BARNEY. I'll tell everyone about you Minister Barley you villain— and I'll marry your daughter to boot!

MINISTER BARLEY. That's what you think! This whole cock-machine thing will be a dead issue, once I deliver my hell-fire and brimstone sermon! You will see what decent people think, you will see what decent people want; you will see what decent people will fight for!!!

Scene 9 - In the Church

(*The scene transforms to a Sunday Sermon, with MINISTER BARLEY addressing his congregation.*)

MINISTER BARLEY. People of the congregation, listen to me! Sin is among us, what are we to do? I had hoped to keep this from you, but the culprit forces me to expose him: I've just learned that Mr. Terwhilliger, the man courting my daughter! Has purchased a... an enlarging device, not for the church's organ, but for his own! Are we so ungrateful of God's gifts that we must distort ourselves? Is this not a gross perversion of nature?

MAN IN CROWD. The company's been sold out for weeks.

OTHER MAN. I'm on a waiting list.

MINISTER BARLEY. My message for today's sermon is *Shame!* We were made in God's image, that will have to be enough. If a man finds himself short of God's gifts, then that is your punishment. Learn to enjoy it. I want no one in my congregation indulging in this quest for penile enhancement.

MAN. What did you do with the machine? In case... Like... Maybe we should donate it to the poor.

MINISTER BARLEY. I will keep it safe in my home for several days, to inspect it for possible damage before returning it to the manufacturer for a full refund.

MAN. I'll give you a hundred dollars for it!

MINISTER BARLEY. (*Points finger in fury.*) Excommunicated! Out of my church! Good people, did you hear what this man had the nerve to offer me?

OTHER MAN. Two Hundred!

ANOTHER MAN. Two fifty!

MINISTER BARLEY. How did the devil get through these doors! Through your evil hearts, you swine! Repent! Repent!

YET ANOTHER MAN. Two sixty!

SOMEONE ELSE. Two eighty-five!

MINISTER BARLEY. What price my friends? What price can you put on shame? Guilt? Deformity? Death?

SOMEONE. Three Hundred!

ANOTHER BIDDER. Three seventy-five!

TROUBLE MAKER. Fuck the beggar, I'm stealing it for free!

MINISTER BARLEY. Keep your hands off my cock machine!

BARNEY. (*Leaps forward.*) Mine! I paid for it, mine!

MINISTER BARLEY. You've damaged the carton: Now I am forced to keep it.

BARNEY. Give it back thief! It belongs to me!

SOMEONE ELSE. Five hundred dollars!

(*A riot erupts. The pulpit disappears, and the scene transforms to the Grand Membership Drive at JOE HERCULES's Spa. While bright, joyous music plays, throngs rush to buy memberships. MOE and THE PROFESSOR oversee this event, happily observing the waves of cash.*)

Scene 10 - Outside the Jubilee Health Spa

CHORUS. (*Sings.*)
GIMME ONE!
GIMME ONE!
GIMME ONE!

REFORMED MAN. (*Sings.*)
I ADMIT I FELT SUPERIOR TO
SPANISH MEN AND BLACKS
BUT I'D ALWAYS SHRINK IN SHAME TO SEE
THE BULGE INSIDE THEIR SLACKS
I REPENT THE ERROR OF MY WAYS,
AND PREJUDICE MUST FALL:
A COCK MACHINE CAN REALLY MEAN
"EQUALITY FOR ALL!"

CHORUS. (*Sings.*)
GIVE US BIGGER DICKS FOR ALL,
WE ALL WANT BIGGER DICKS FOR ALL!
AND THAT'S WHAT PEOPLE WANT SO GIVE 'EM
BIGGER DICKS FOR ALL!
THE BIGGEST EARS IN HEAVEN HEAR
THE PLAINTIVE MALES CALL,
CRYING BIGGER DICKS! BIGGER DICKS!
BIGGER DICKS FOR ALL!
GIMME ONE!
GIMME ONE!
GIMME ONE!

WORRIED MOTHER. But the children, the children— What about the children?

(*A YOUNG BOY comes forward, backed by his PARENTS.*)

BOY. (*Sings.*)
MY MA WOULD ALWAYS NAG ME
TO BE MORE LIKE MY OLD MAN.
THE PROFESSOR MADE IT POSSIBLE
FOR ME TO SAY I CAN

I BROKE EVERY MAIDENHEAD IN SCHOOL,
THE GIRLS THINK I'M SWELL;
AND POP AND I ARE SO ALIKE
THAT MOM CAN HARDLY TELL.

CHORUS.	**CHORUS.**
GIMME ONE!	GIVE US BIGGER
	DICKS FOR ALL,
GIMME ONE!	WE ALL WANT BIGGER
	DICKS FOR ALL—
GIMME ONE!	

(*But the rompery grinds to a halt, interrupted by MINISTER BARLEY.*)

MINISTER BARLEY. This is sacrilege! Save us Lord, save us!
A JUBILANT. Nonsense, nonsense. (*Sings.*)
    IF THIS FABULOUS CONTRAPTION
    WAS MADE CENTURIES AGO
    IT WOULD REALLY LIVEN UP
    THE GREATEST STORY EVER TOLD:
    ADMIT IT, AIN'T IMMACULATE CONCEPTION
    PRETTY ODD?
    BUT WHAT IF JOSEPH WHIPPED IT OUT,
    AND MARY SCREAMED, "MY GOD!"

CHORUS. (*Sings.*)
    THEN WE'D HAVE BIGGER DICKS FOR ALL,
    WE'D ALL HAVE BIGGER DICKS FOR ALL!
    AND THAT'S WHAT PEOPLE WANT SO GIVE EM
    BIGGER DICKS FOR ALL!
    SWEET FATHER UP IN HEAVEN
    HEAR YOUR CHOSEN PEOPLE CALL,
    DEMANDING:

(*Protest signs appear quickly, and the crowd does a rally chant.*)

    WHAT DO WE WANT?
    —BIGGER DICKS!
    WHEN DO WE WANT EM?
    —NOW!!!

(*The protest signs vanish. The MAYOR is giving MOE and THE PROFESSOR their license in a public ceremony. Music continues under.*)

MAYOR. Professor, your invention has made quite a contribution to our community, and to life all around. Here are the keys to the city.

THE PROFESSOR. Thank you, Mayor Lucky.

MAYOR. And our city also congratulates our favorite health spa and its owner, Joe Hercules, for his contribution!

(*JOE HERCULES is forced to shake hands, but must at the same time fork over a wad from his profits, which the MAYOR pockets.*)

CHORUS. (*Sings.*)
GIVE US BIGGER DICKS FOR ALL,
WE ALL WANT BIGGER DICKS FOR ALL!

(*The festivities are interrupted by a guerilla protest by the Women Against Fur. The BABY SEAL is with them, wearing a drum major's hat as disguise. Music continues, under.*)

WOMEN. (*Sing.*)
NO MORE FUR!
NO MORE FUR!
NO MORE FUR!

(*O'FLAHRETY intervenes, grabs the WOMEN.*)

WOMEN. (*Assorted shouts.*) You monkey! You pig! You baboon! You dog!

MEN. You jackass! You bitch! You cow!

JOE HERCULES. Don't fight ladies: You'll be happier after you try one of our men who has tried our SX-70!

(*The WOMEN converge upon him, and beat him clear off the stage. MOE calms the crowd and resumes the song.*)

MOE. (*Sings.*)
IT'S A SHAME TO SEE IT HAPPEN,
BUT I TELL YA GUYS, DON'T SCOFF
EVEN I HAVE SOMETIMES HAD
AN UGLY WOMAN BEAT ME OFF!

BABY SEAL. Those women are hurting him! That's not nice!
BERTHA. Keep quiet! They'd do the same to you, and worse!

(*BERTHA and BABY SEAL exit.*)

THE PROFESSOR. I don't see Penny anywhere?
MOE. Why look for pennies? Look at the dollars!!

MOE. (*Sings.*)
OUR PERCENTAGE OF THESE MEMBERSHIPS
IS MANNA FROM ABOVE!

THE PROFESSOR. (*Sings.*)
IT'S THE END RESULT OF SUFFERING
FOR THE WOMAN THAT I LOVE
SOMEWHERE, OUT THERE, SHE'S GOT TO HEAR
MY TENDER MATING CALL

(*He's drowned out by a cacophony of shouts.*)

CHORUS. (*Sings.*)
GIMME! MINE! ME FIRST!
GET YOUR HANDS OFF MY—
BIGGER DICKS FOR ALL!!!
NOW THE FOUL-EST INVECTIVE
HOLDS A HAPPY NOTE OF CHEER:

(*People curse at each other, but smile through it.*)

PERSON. (*Sings.*)
YOU CAN SHOVE IT UP YOUR ASS!

RETORT. (*Sings.*)
YOU CAN BLOW IT OUT YOUR EAR!

CHORUS. (*Sings.*)
    WE WANT IT AND WE WANT IT NOW,
    HEAR YOUR PEOPLE CALL, DEMANDING
    BIGGER DICKS! BIGGER DICKS!
    BIGGER DICKS FOR ALL!
    GIVE US BIGGER DICKS FOR ALL,
    SWEET JESUS, BIGGER DICKS FOR ALL
    GIVE THE PEOPLE WHAT WOULD PLEASE US,
    WE WANT
    BIGGER DICKS FOR ALL!
    WE WANT IT AND WE GOT IT,
    AND WE'RE GONNA HAVE A BALL: YIPPEE!

THE PROFESSOR. Penny?
BABY SEAL. Mama?
MOE. Let 'em have it!

CHORUS. (*Sings.*)
    BIGGER DICKS FOR ALL!

<u>END ACT ONE</u>

ACT TWO

Scene 11 - On the Streets of the Town

THE WOMAN WHO WANTS... It's me again. Not that you want to see me. You just want to see all the people in town, strutting around in their overstuffed pants. Well, you can look around for yourself: do you think that will make everyone happy?

(*Back on the public streets— but this time, the spirit of the population has changed remarkably.*)

ASSORTED REMARKS. Whoops! Beg your pardon. So sorry. Have a nice day! After you. —No, after you. [etc.]
THE WOMAN WHO WANTS... What do you know! Now that everyone has big dicks, every person does have a happy life— Except for me! Waah!
BAG MAN. Fuzzy gloves for sale. Get your fuzzy gloves here. Help the homeless get a hot meal and two hours on a coin–operated cock machine.
MRS. CLIMSBY. Officer O'Flahrety? I would like to fill out a missing person's report. I haven't seen my husband Herman for nearly a week.
O'FLAHRETY. I'm sorry to tell you good Mrs. Climsby, but I've been getting reports like that filed from all over town. I'd suggest you check the membership rolls at Joe Hercules's place. A lot of men sign up there.
MRS. CLIMSBY. I tried, but the crowds are horrendous. I couldn't get near the place.
BUSINESSMAN #1. The gardener came yesterday morning, like he always does. And when I got home, he was still there— and my wife asked me for a divorce!

(*A pretty WOMAN catches the eye of BUSINESSMAN #2.*)

BUSINESSMAN #2. I'm sorry, I can't listen to your troubles right now. (*To the WOMAN.*) Want to take a ride in my sports car?
WOMAN. Maybe just as far as the back seat.

(*BARNEY approaches the BAG MAN.*)

BAG MAN. Fuzzy gloves for sale!
BARNEY. How much for the gloves?
BAG MAN. Four bucks.
BARNEY. That's cheap! (*Reads the tag.*) Antonovichovich? Where do you get this fine merchandise at such low prices?
BAG MAN. In the ash can behind that dyke–den. Those "Women Against Fur" throw out some great stuff.
BARNEY. For Delilah, my sweet. If I ever see her again.
BAG MAN. Just pay me and get lost, I wanna make a sale, not a friend.
THE WOMAN WHO WANTS... No one ever bought me gloves.
WANDA. Livonia Climsby, on the streets alone again, eh. Well, while the cat's away, there are plenty of mice to play with these days, don't you think?
MRS. CLIMSBY. I wouldn't know, Mrs. McGillicutty, I don't know a thing about it.
WANDA. You can play coy if you like, you're good at it. I mail–ordered one of those Cock Machines for my husband but until it shows up, we're S.O.L., since the Hercules Health Club's been packed to the rafters. I thought you might have a line on one, since everyone at the patent office knows your dear, wonderful husband is the top banana.
MRS. CLIMSBY. Wherever he is, I'm sure he wouldn't touch such a thing as an SX–70. We're not that kind of people.
WANDA. No, I'm sure you're not. All the same dear, if you find yourself with some free time while Mr. Climsby is away, I had a very interesting delivery this morning from the bag–boy at the Piggly–Wiggly. You might want to order a box of cereal or something.

(*Two other beautiful WOMEN in furs walk by.*)

WOMAN 1. (*Walking awkwardly, with a friend.*) It was fun at first, but I have trouble walking today.
WOMAN 2. Me too. But look at the size of my engagement ring!
WOMAN 1. Yes. And think how lucky we both are, to have these new Jaguar wraps.

WOMAN 2. I'm dropping hints for an ocelot hat I saw in the window at Marmonts. It has a wide feather brim adorned with artificial cherries.

WOMAN 1. I'm hoping for something more wintery, white, and soft.

WOMAN 2. Me too— if my poor body can hold up that long.

BABY SEAL. Pity me!

(BERTHA enters with a bucket of red paint and a five–inch brush.)

BERTHA. Fur is dead! *(She paints the women's backs.)*

WOMEN. EEEEEEEEEEEEEE ! Look what she's done!

WOMAN 1. Now I'll have to get Frankie to get me a new one!

WOMAN 2. Carlos will get me two, so I'll always have a spare.

(The WOMEN run off.)

THE WOMAN WHO WANTS... Well, maybe there are other people who see how hard a happy life is— big sex organs don't solve a thing! Waah!

(BARNEY passes by.)

WANDA. Barney. I haven't seen you in church for some time. Is that because you've been working out at the Jubilee? I could use an escort home.

BARNEY. My membership expired and it's going to stay that way! And as for church, well I won't go to that church ever again, not as long as Minister Barley is there. His hypocrisy has come between me and his daughter, and I haven't seen her for weeks!

WANDA. She's become a hospital volunteer, working with PWB's— People Without Big Dicks. It's the subsidized unit, for those who can't afford their own model. Maybe you could find her there.

(He exits, in hopeful search. MOE and THE PROFESSOR walk down the street, on the way to the lab. They are moved: the MEN cheer, the WOMEN beg. MOE enjoys the attention, THE PROFESSOR is annoyed.)

MOE. Thank you folks, make way. No phone numbers, no autographs, heh he!

THE PROFESSOR. Get away! Stop it! Leave me alone, get a life why don't you!

LADY JACQUELINE. Excuse me Hiram, I haven't heard back from you about my invitation—

THE PROFESSOR. I don't know anything about it, I'm busy!

LADY JACQUELINE. That's why I thought you'd enjoy a quiet soiree, away from the confusion that comes with fame.

THE PROFESSOR. Wouldn't everyone! Who are you now?

MOE. Professor! This is Lady Jacqueline, don't you remember? She lives across the street!

THE PROFESSOR. Oh! I'm so sorry!

LADY JACQUELINE. I must look like every face in the crowd.

THE PROFESSOR. Yes you do.

MOE. Professor! I'm sorry, Lady J., I——

LADY JACQUELINE. I can see you're under tremendous pressure. Forgive the interruption.

THE PROFESSOR. No, I'm sorry. Across the street you say? I'll come. When?

LADY JACQUELINE. The offer is withdrawn. I hope you find what you're looking for.

(*They go inside, MOE closes the door on the outer world.*)

Scene 12 - At the Professor's Laboratory

THE PROFESSOR. Close the door! What world am I living in?

MOE. I wonder the same thing myself.

THE PROFESSOR. What is that woman's problem anyway?

MOE. She's just got her heart set on someone who doesn't know she exists. You know what that's like.

THE PROFESSOR. Absolutely I do.

MOE. (*Observing CLIMSBY on the machine.*) Hey, look who's home. When're you going to get off that, Climsby?

CLIMSBY. Just a little more, please. Just a tiny bit more.

MOE. He's been here a week hasn't he?

THE PROFESSOR. What if he has? Why hasn't she called me?

MOE. She who? —Oh, don't say the name!

THE PROFESSOR. I thought certain that with the interviews, the local news and the magazine articles, she would have heard. She might have at least called to ask what's up.

MOE. Who knows, who cares. She's long gone. And you're stuck right where she left you, hanging on to one sore moment forever. Life is spinning by all around you, and you're missing out.

THE PROFESSOR. Eh. Let me check today's mail...

MOE. Speaking of spinning: Climsby!

THE PROFESSOR. Climsby, you have a wife. It's time for you to join her.

CLIMSBY. Now you mean?

THE PROFESSOR. I want to thank you for your contribution to my success. My research is complete. You are free to go.

CLIMSBY. Maybe I should just do a few more sets... I want to be sure that I can make her happy...

MOE. Come on, sport: Off.

(*CLIMSBY won't budge. MOE and THE PROFESSOR make a number of physical attempts to pull, push or knock him off the SX–70.*)

THE PROFESSOR. Here's a phenomenon my research did not uncover: Psychological dependence.

MOE. How's that?

THE PROFESSOR. Watch this, I'll demonstrate. (*He gets a club, and beats CLIMSBY in an unsuccessful effort to remove him.*) Do you see that? Regardless of the physical pain, he is obsessed with increasing the size of his penis.

CLIMSBY. What's wrong with that?

THE PROFESSOR. For whatever reason, Climsby simply wants more. Being in a state of "want" is different than demand–and–supply. For example, we get a demand for an SX–70. We supply one, and the need is met. Climsby however, is demanding not a specific quantity, like "four", which could be met and mastered. He wants the unspecified "more." Even though he definitely has achieved "more", it is an open–ended request: wanting more makes one only want more, regardless of what one has. More simply stated—

MOE. He's addicted!

(*He and THE PROFESSOR respond by beating the tar out of CLIMSBY before he is pried off the machine. Once freed, CLIMSBY stands panting, glaring, possessed, at his new member, approximately three feet long.*)

CLIMSBY. No one will laugh at me now.

(*He just stands there. MOE ushers him out.*)

MOE. There's the door. Outsky.

THE PROFESSOR. Isn't it your wife's birthday? Go home to her. She hasn't seen you in a week.

CLIMSBY. Last year I gave her a sweater.

(*He is kicked out the door.*)

MOE. An A to Z jerk, for crying out sideways.

THE PROFESSOR. If only I had a wife to go home to.

MOE. Don't start with that—!

THE PROFESSOR. I can't help but think, just a few summers ago, a delicate, mature woman, with flowers in—

MOE. Can it! Professor, I have something of high importance to teach you: you must never, never talk of the past.

THE PROFESSOR. Because it opens old wounds?

MOE. No, because it bores the crap outta me. (*He goes through the mail bag.*) Look at this professor: it's an invitation to the Petty Awards!

THE PROFESSOR. What are the Petty Awards?

MOE. I don't know, but they're being held at the Mean Cabaret! The classiest joint in town!

THE PROFESSOR. Wonderful! I'm rich. Successful. And now, I'll be honored. Accept the invitation, with my gratitude. Perhaps I will be seen there by someone special.

MOE. I'm sure you will, but could you see it if it happened, that's the question. And don't say that freakin' name!

THE PROFESSOR. Of course, Moe. A "Penny" for your thoughts.

MOE. What else is going on today: We gotta gas bill. Electric bill. Phone bill. Rent bill. Insurance bill.

THE PROFESSOR. We can pay them all!

MOE. It's like the answer to our prayers!

THE PROFESSOR. (*Snorts.*) If anyone answered my prayers, there would be——

(*There is a knock at the door. MOE goes to answer.*)

MOE. —Not a peep! Yeah?

LIMOUSINE DRIVER. Is this the home of a gentleman named Hiram, also known as "The Professor"? I have a mature lady in the car, with flowers in her hair. She would like to see him.

MOE. Prof? A lady to see you.

THE PROFESSOR. Did I really ask for this? I already have one case of heart–ache, thank you. That's more than enough.

MOE. No, I think you better take this one.

THE PROFESSOR. Yes?

LIMOUSINE DRIVER. I have a delicate, mature lady in the car who would like to see "The Professor".

THE PROFESSOR. In a car? She must have traveled a long way. Where is she from?

LIMOUSINE DRIVER. Niagara Falls.

THE PROFESSOR. (*Seizure again.*) Niagara Falls! Slowly, I turned down the sheets— and all I wanted was to smack someone! Kick 'em! Beat 'em!

(*The LIMOUSINE DRIVER is beaten off the stage. End of scene.*)

Scene 13 - At the Hospital

(*DELILAH, as nurse, cares for the men stricken by the need for physical improvement. Her fatigue hardly shows, through her brave mask of caring. One MAN finishes his round on the SX–70, and DELILAH helps the exhausted man onto a cot to rest, as ANOTHER PERSON mounts the machine. DELILAH applies gauze and salve to the suffering athlete.*)

DELILAH. There there. This will make you feel better.

PATIENT. Oh thank you. You're so kind to volunteer for we less–fortunate men.

DELILAH. It's nothing.

PATIENT. How did you get involved in this work, Nurse Barley?

DELILAH. I was a friend of Joe Hercules.

PATIENT. No kidding! Did you have sex with him?

DELILAH. Once. It was unforgettable.

PATIENT. Would you have sex with me? By the time I get out of here, I'll probably have eighteen inches.

DELILAH. Thanks, but—

PATIENT. I know. You probably have a special fella, don't you? The nice ones are always taken.

DELILAH. There is a boy who— I try not to talk about him. But I think of him always.

PATIENT. Does he have a big dick too?

DELILAH. (*Shakes her head.*) I love him for other reasons. I bought him a cock machine, back when this all started. He didn't understand. He was afraid. There was an argument, and since then—

PATIENT. That's a shame.

DELILAH. I keep hoping, some day, he might turn up as a patient here. I— I think I understand how he feels, and if he wants to use the SX–70, it's something I would like to help him with. Do you think I'm terrible?

PATIENT. I hope I find a girl who is as comprehensively understanding as you, Nurse Barley.

DELILAH. Call me Delilah.

PATIENT. Can I get back on the machine yet?

DELILAH. Your treatment is finished. We have to make room for a new patient.

PATIENT. What! I only have fourteen inches! I was supposed to get four more! I want more!

DELILAH. I'm sorry—

PATIENT. Sorry! Sorry doesn't help— Screw you! Bitch! Bitch!

(*DELILAH firmly, kindly leads him out, despite his protests. BARNEY enters, with flowers and gift box.*)

BARNEY. Delilah! I was told I could find you here.

DELILAH. I've been praying for the moment you'd walk in that door. (*They embrace tenderly.*) Have you been all right? Are you sleeping well?

BARNEY. Not well enough: I miss you Delilah. I want you, now more than ever.

DELILAH. After how I've hurt you?

BARNEY. Put it behind us. I'm going to take on extra shifts so I can buy you a little pink house, a stone's throw from here. And in the basement, our own SX–70, the home model.

DELILAH. I want two children: Diana and Pete.

BARNEY. Again I kneel before you. I offer you this ring, and this pair of fox–trimmed gloves: that is— if you will have me.

DELILAH. Is it finally going to happen? On Sunday, the 24th of July, will Miss Delilah Barley will become—

BARNEY. Mrs. Barney Terwhilligher? Say you will and make it true!

DELILAH. Of course I will! Do you want to use the SX–70! Just to get a head start?

BARNEY. Absolutely! And all for you, Delilah, for no one else but you.

(*She and BARNEY begin to eject the exercising patient when BERTHA and SONIA burst in, armed.*)

BERTHA. Freeze, fur killers!

DELILAH. Wait! Stop, this is my fiancé!

SONIA. Slaughter the fat–cocked butcher of the white seal clan.

BARNEY. What white seal clan? I'm here to use the cock machine!

BERTHA. No one's starting any more machines— Die! Die, that the animals might live! Come on honey, we'll save you from that awful man!

(*A bomb is thrown, and BERTHA and SONIA abduct DELILAH.*)

DELILAH. Barney!

Scene 14 - Headquarters, Women Against Fur

(*SONIA and BERTHA carry DELILAH in, and tie her hands. BERTHA's bicycle is propped against the wall.*)

BERTHA. Let's set her down over here. Tie her hands.

SONIA. We won't hurt you. Our mission is to build a society that does not discriminate against race or species. (*Notices gloves.*) Bertha look! Silver fox trim.

DELILAH. A gift from my fiancé.

BERTHA. We got her just in time. It might have been a hat next.

DELILAH. I'm sure he didn't mean to do wrong.

SONIA. But he did it all the same, didn't he? Men: mindless vandals. Now not a peep out of you. We have work to do.

BERTHA. We've got to decide on the picture for our next demonstration hand–out. I like the one with the head in the vice.

SONIA. We used it before, it's old. (*She is about to discard it, but first shows it to DELILAH.*) Those gloves you were wearing...? (*DELILAH recoils. SONIA returns to work.*) What about this one, with the skin peeled back and pinned to the electrodes?

BERTHA. (*Erupts in tears.*) Run off five thousand, and put the original in my scrapbook. When will it end, Sonia? When will the killing ever end?

SONIA. Not before we wipe men off the face of the earth, for starters.

(*The BABY SEAL enters, sniffing.*)

BABY SEAL. Mama? Is mama in here?

BERTHA. Why do you keep asking? Why don't you face the truth, little one?

BABY SEAL. I know I can find her. I know I can. And I got fifty dollars cash to pay back the hunters!

SONIA. (*Squeaks out tears.*) —My child!

BERTHA. You're giving no money to no hunters.

BABY SEAL. Um, Bertha? Sonia? Can I have fifty cents?

BERTHA. I thought you had fifty dollars.

BABY SEAL. I almost do. I did, but, you know, city living and all—

SONIA. You've been spending it on cigarettes, haven't you! What did we tell you about that?

BABY SEAL. Just a couple—

BERTHA. How much? How much, Baby Seal?

BABY SEAL. I'm short twelve dollars.

SONIA. Twelve dollars?!

BABY SEAL. ... and fifty cents. That's the part I was gonna borrow. I tried to get a job. Maybe I could earn money here. Doing windows or something.

BERTHA. You're getting no money from this organization! We need it for posters.

DELILAH. What an adorable creature! Baby Seal? Come over here and untie my hands. I want to pet you.

BABY SEAL. Really? (*To BERTHA.*) Can I let her? Please?

BERTHA. I guess it would be all right.

BABY SEAL. Oh Boy! (*Scampers to DELILAH, whispers innocently.*) You don't smoke, do you?

SONIA. I heard that!

DELILAH. Why this Baby Seal is the cutest thing! I could just hug you to death! (*BABY SEAL squirms in panic.*) —It's only an expression.

SONIA. Baby Seal's whole village was massacred by hunters.

DELILAH. How horrible!

BABY SEAL. Sometimes, I feel guilty about being the only one who lived, and sometimes I wish I had been killed too. Because I miss everyone so much and I want to be with them. But they've been pretty good to me here. Sometimes, being with Bertha and Sonia reminds me of my old home on the arctic shores.

BERTHA. (*Chuckles warmly.*) Good Gracious Sakes! How is that?

BABY SEAL. Because you look like a walrus.

SONIA. (*Absolutely appalled.*) Baby Seal!

BABY SEAL. Have you ever seen one of those things? Why I bet they weigh, oh! a hundred pounds at least!

BERTHA. (*Absolutely appalled.*) Baby Seal!

BABY SEAL. Well... maybe only a little bit like a walrus. Course, you don't have those big tusks... Some of them are kind of skinny, actually. Ummm... Maybe I wasn't thinking of a walrus, I was thinking of... a penguin or something. Maybe I don't feel like I'm at home at all...

BERTHA. Baby seal, you are hideous!
BABY SEAL. (*Starts crying.*) Mama! Mama!
SONIA. You better go read these pamphlets!

(*BABY SEAL exits.*)

SONIA. —And don't light up any ciggies, we can smell them!
DELILAH. I feel awful about what's happened to his village. I want to enlist as a member of your cause.
BERTHA. Great! What we really need is someone to infiltrate the fur killers.
DELILAH. I'll do it!
SONIA. I don't know: any of us would be spotted as a member of the Women Against Fur, because we are all womyn.
BERTHA. Maybe if we admitted one man as a member—
SONIA. Never! If only there was someone to work for us who wasn't a woman, but wasn't a man either. Wait! I just thought of a "certain individual", who I know is looking for work. Listen up, sisters: I have a plan...

(*LIGHTS FADE.*)

Scene 15 - A Sunny Afternoon in the Park

(*Accompanied by his wife, CLIMSBY walks awkwardly, with a baby carriage before him, which acts as a carriage for his huge endowment.*)

CLIMSBY. (*Not very happy.*) "...Happy Birthday, Dear Livonia, Happy Birthday to You..." You don't like your present?
MRS. CLIMSBY. Ignorant dunce. I'm mortified. All those years I wasted in church, shot to hell by one look at you.
CLIMSBY. (*Looks far across the park.*) Say, isn't that Harvey Angeltoon and his wife? And he's pushing a baby carriage too. Maybe I should go over and say hello.
MRS. CLIMSBY. (*Ice forms on her shoulders.*) Don't. You. Dare. My lord, here we are in broad daylight— And to make things worse, here comes that witch, Wanda McGillicutty, the town gossip.

WANDA. Livonia! Herman. Good afternoon. What a surprise to see the Climsbys in the park, with a carriage! I didn't know—

CLIMSBY. Uh– uh–

WANDA. May I see your baby?

MRS. CLIMSBY. No! We need to keep it covered up, the— the sun isn't good for the little squirt.

CLIMSBY. What do you mean, little?

WANDA. I didn't know you were even expecting. I saw you even last week, and you didn't show at all.

MRS. CLIMSBY. Uh. It's not mine, really.

WANDA. No? Then Whose?

MRS. CLIMSBY. A niece, who lives in a small town in another state. She— "Got into trouble."

WANDA. Got into trouble? What do you mean by that?

MRS. CLIMSBY. When you were a little girl, and you met a little boy, didn't you ever get "into trouble", and then your parents sent you to live in a far away town?

WANDA. Oh, so that's how it happened.

MRS. CLIMSBY. Yes.

WANDA. Where is the girl?

MRS. CLIMSBY. What girl.

WANDA. Your niece. If I can't see the child, I think I would enjoy meeting the parent.

MRS. CLIMSBY. Well, uh—— She uh... hung herself.

WANDA. Did she!

MRS. CLIMSBY. Yes. But wouldn't you? Rather than shame your family? The bright side is that her parents have forgiven her but she's with god now, so it hardly matters, but like I always say–

WANDA. Didn't I see a delivery van in front of your house a few days ago, from the Supercock Manufacturing Company?

MRS. CLIMSBY. No! No, you couldn't have. The Supercock Manufacturing Company— why— What is that? Why I have never even heard of the Supercock Manu— Have you heard of them Herman? (*He is admiring his endowment, doesn't hear her.*) Herman!!

WANDA. Perhaps I was mistaken. The Supercock Manufacturing Company would never come to a house like yours, I didn't mean to infer. Well, I think I will be on my way. Oh, and uh, Mr. Climsby: My husband has been wanting to see you, it would be so nice if you could pay him a visit. He is never home though, between the hours of eight thirty in the morning and three thirty in the afternoon; and those times I am home alone with so much to do, and I'm not sure if I could bear an intrusion. I hope you understand. So be sure not to come between eight thirty or three thirty, especially tomorrow. Good day.

(*She leaves. MRS. CLIMSBY wheels on her husband.*)

MRS. CLIMSBY. Oh you are intolerable! Disgrace! That's what you've brought me, disgrace, you damnable, bumbling big–dicked baboon. What are we supposed to DO with that now? And Wanda McGillicutty, did you hear what I had to tell her? The lies I'm forced to tell are worse than the truth— But at least the lies will keep me respectable! Do you see what havoc you've wrought on my personal moral fiber? My own sense of decency, instilled at childhood, is shit now, shit!

CLIMSBY. Come to the lake with me, dearest.

MRS. CLIMSBY. The lake? What for?

CLIMSBY. It's private. We can be alone.

MRS. CLIMSBY. What will people think if they see us? What are they thinking, seeing us now? You turd, you filth, you bum!

CLIMSBY. My dear. The approval of millions can be obliterated by the rejection of one. My greatest desire was to please you. Forgive me. The sin of pride will be unseen, no one will know if you lie with me.

MRS. CLIMSBY. Oh balls said the queen. I'd be king if I had to. I fear my goose is cooked. (*Sings.*)

TO DEFEND YOUR HONOR
TO PROTECT MY OWN,
I WILL LIE WITH YOU.

CLIMSBY. (*Sings.*)

TO SERVE YOUR SOFT AFFECTIONS
TO DEMONSTRATE MY OWN
I WILL LIE WITH YOU.

CLIMSBY & MRS. CLIMSBY. (*Sing.*)
  TO SUSTAIN THE HIGH OPINIONS
  OF PEOPLE WE DON'T KNOW
  TO UPHOLD THE PUBLIC VALUES
  AND ERADICATE MY OWN
  I WILL LIE WITH YOU
  I WILL LIE WITH YOU.

(*They go in the way of the lake. End of scene.*)

Scene 16 - At the Mean Cabaret

(*The Mean Cabaret is a very elegant nightclub. People sit at cafe tables with telephones. There is a huge moose head over the bar with a brassiere strung across the antlers.*)

THE WOMAN WHO WANTS... Here I am at the Mean Cabaret. It's overpriced and the waiters are rude, and it's the trendiest spot in town. A table for one, please.

(*WAITER seats her at a table.*)

THE WOMAN WHO WANTS... Waah! There is no one to talk to here!

(*Chit chat at various tables.*)

WAITER. (*To PATRON.*) We only serve beer at the Mean Cabaret.
PATRON. But I expressly asked for a creme de menthe frappe.

(*The person is escorted out. LADY A and GENTLEMEN B sulk at another table.*)

GENTLEMAN B. The romance has gone out of our marriage.
LADY A. But everything else refuses to die.

(*The man dials a number to the table phone. LADY B answers.*)

GENTLEMAN B. I'm laying in bed wearing nothing but a bowler hat and knee height stockings.

LADY B. I am shocked. I am absolutely shocked.

THE WOMAN WHO WANTS... I wish I could be like that couple: they've been married for years!

(*Our attention goes to a HUSBAND and WIFE staring angrily at each other across the table.*)

WIFE. You're stepping on my foot.

HUSBAND. I know.

WIFE. Then stop it.

HUSBAND. I was there first.

WIFE. Obviously you weren't.

HUSBAND. Move your foot.

WIFE. You move.

(*Neither moves.*)

THE WOMAN WHO WANTS... I hope the show starts before somebody notices me and finds out how sad I am.

GENTLEMAN B. Last night I broke into your house. Tonight, I will use your underwear for a teabag.

LADY B. I am shocked! I am absolutely shocked!

M.C. Good evening, distinguished citizens. Welcome to the Mean Cabaret. Before we get on with tonight's Petty Awards, we want to start with some entertainment:

(*NOTE: This is an open section for assorted personalities to entertain with short–and–funny off–color material: inappropriate jokes, dirty songs. If anyone sings, they only get a few bars into it before getting hooted off the stage, regardless of how good they are.*)

M.C. Just a quick reminder to all you SX–70 users: Next Thursday is our new wet zoot–suit contest— Ladies only! —except if you're entering, of course! Now, we'll take a short break before the awards ceremony.

(*JACQUELINE appears in the crowd, MOE calls her over to THE PROFESSOR's table.*)

MOE. Lady J! Over here!

LADY JACQUELINE. Good evening, Moe. Professor.

MOE. Nice to see you out tonight. We've been invited here special, it seems the Professor is receiving some sort of award. He's very excited.

LADY JACQUELINE. I guess you don't get out much, do you?

THE PROFESSOR. Well, you know me. Always working.

LADY JACQUELINE. No, I don't know you. Though I have tried.

THE PROFESSOR. I remember your invitation. I hope enough time has passed that you've forgiven my distraction.

MOE. You guys mind if I step away a minute?

(*MOE leaves the two of them together.*)

THE PROFESSOR. I've been involved in a passionate quest for some time. It's nice to come to the end of it— the success of my invention and all that. But all that work has created a somewhat lonely life.

LADY JACQUELINE. You mentioned some time back that your wife left you?

THE PROFESSOR. Oh. That. I can't stay mad with her. I knew she was the right person for me. Apparently she didn't understand that I was the right person for her, but since I've corrected that little problem, now there's no excuse. If there's anything I am, I am constant. She's the right one for me, so what's right is right and you can't change it. Once I decide on something, nothing, not elephants can change my mind.

LADY JACQUELINE. How interesting. So you both still get along?

THE PROFESSOR. I've never even seen her, I don't have any idea where she is. But I believe that love finds its calling, like a ship finding its light–house to the shore. I've always held a place for her.

LADY JACQUELINE. It's a very romantic notion. I've also held a place in my life for someone special.

THE PROFESSOR. At our age I would think you'd have found someone. You seem very kind.

LADY JACQUELINE. I'm very patient with people. But unlike yourself, I haven't found who I thought was "right."

THE PROFESSOR. I'm sure you've had plenty of attention.

LADY JACQUELINE. Yes. And in the process, years have passed.

THE PROFESSOR. And I'm sure you have many good years ahead of you! I know that I will be ready when I again meet my perfect mate.

LADY JACQUELINE. That is of course, if you ever actually see her.

M.C. Continuing on with our entertainment: a very special part of our evening ladies and gentlemen: This month's Petty Awards! For those who aren't familiar with the Pettys, let me explain. Of course, everyone knows about the Academy Awards, or the Tonys, or the Obies, or the VHI–Music Awards, the People's Choice for the Oscars, the TV–Guide Award, and on and on: There are more awards in this society than trinkets on a charm bracelet. But did anyone here ever get some recognition? So here at the Mean Cabaret, we give out awards for no reason at all, and people are still happy about it! This may be your night: to win the desperately–coveted Petty. The panel of judges, our kitchen staff and the hatcheck girl, have made their votes. And tonight, the winner of our first Petty Award is— You!

(*He points to a man in the audience, REGINALD, who runs to the stage, sort of.*)

M.C. Come on up and say hello to the folks. What's your name, sir?

REGINALD. Reginald Harkwater.

M.C. And tell the folks out there what you've done to deserve your Petty Award.

REGINALD. I never did anything important. But I've thought a lot about it. I have some really good ideas, if anyone cared. But they don't. Still, I sure am glad to be on stage, I like people looking at me. Could I have your job?

M.C. Fill out an application at the bar. (*REGINALD steps down.*)
And our Grand Prize Petty tonight goes to— You ma'am— The
Woman Who Wants A Happy Life!

(*She comes to the stage.*)

THE WOMAN WHO WANTS... Gee. That says it all. It's about
time something nice happened to me. Gosh thanks. You know,
earlier today, there was this man, in the market, and he stepped
on my foot, and he was really rude about it! But now I have
won the Petty Award. I wish he could see me now, he'd know
who he was dealing with. My parents never thought I'd come to
much. But Mrs. Kennedy, my kindergarten teacher, she would
be very proud. I owe part of this award to her. I bet she's not
here either. But thanks anyway. Bye–bye, everybody!

M.C. Ladies and Gentlemen, it has been brought to my attention
that we have a real celebrity among us, and we want to call him
up to express our thanks. A lot of us are enjoying the
enrichment and happiness given by, you all know what I'm
talking about, don't you— The SX–70. That machine has put
smiles on a lot of faces— well tonight, we want to give a special
Super–Petty Award to the man who invented the SX–70, a great
guy, and soon to be my closest friend, The Professor! Come up
here Professor, we want to give you an award!

THE PROFESSOR. I don't understand: is this serious or not?

M.C. Well Professor, check out my slacks: does this look serious to
you???

(*The room hoots and guffaws. THE PROFESSOR approaches the
stage. The audience has the cultivation of a pack of baboons,
undercutting everything he tries to say—*)

THE PROFESSOR. I'm honored to receive this recognition. I
think we all want to add something wonderful to the world we
live in— as difficult as it can be— in order to make life better
for—— those we care most about—

(*Uniformed police, including OFFICER and O'FLAHRETY,
charge the stage and arrest THE PROFESSOR and MOE.*)

OFFICER. You are under arrest!

MOE. What for, what for?

O'FLAHRETY. Murder.

THE PROFESSOR. Murder! That's preposterous! Of who?

OFFICER. Mrs. Climsby's remains were found by the lake— or pieces of her, we should say. Your machine caused the mutilation.

THE PROFESSOR. I'm innocent! I'm innocent!

O'FLAHRETY. Come quietly, people are watching

(The BABY SEAL, who has been selling cigarettes and cigars throughout the mean cabaret scene, is at a table, when his hat accidentally falls off.)

BABY SEAL. Yikes!

PATRON. It's a baby seal! Grab him!

(There is a riot in the cabaret. The BABY SEAL escapes, but MOE and THE PROFESSOR are hauled away.)

Entre Scene 17A

(The BABY SEAL runs to the WAF headquarters. No one is there, but BERTHA's bicycle is against the wall.)

BABY SEAL. Thank goodness for the Headquarters of the Women Against Fur: Don't let them get me— Hide me Bertha, Sonia— Where is everyone? Mama? *(He starts sniffing the air.)* Mama? I know it's you: Mama?

(The scent leads him to the bicycle seat, covered in soft white fur.)

BABY SEAL. Mama? *(He wails.)* Nooooo! Nooooo!

BERTHA. *(Who enters.)* What's wrong?

BABY SEAL. Nooooooo!

BERTHA. Oh my god— What have I done!! Baby—

(*She holds her arms out to embrace him in helpless shame— but in a rage, the BABY SEAL tears the cover from the bicycle seat, and bites her. Then he runs off.*)

BABY SEAL. Pity me!
BERTHA. I deserve it! I deserve worse! My life is a farce, a sham. I'd kill myself, but it wouldn't change a thing!

(*She exits, bleeding.*)

Scene 18 - The Waiting Room, Before the Trial

THE PROFESSOR. How can I be honored and disgraced for the same thing, at the same time? Moe, what does it all mean?
O'FLAHRETY. Nice ta see you there, Professor. And how might you be doing, Moe?
MOE. Wipe that grin off yer mug O'Flahrety. Get to the point.
STAFFER. Step against this line, please.
THE PROFESSOR. What world am I living in!
STAFFER. Strip search. Lower your pants.
MOE. With pleasure, ya cheese.

(*A delicate, prim woman enters— THE PROFESSOR's beloved PENNY.*)

PENNY. Goodness— is it really you, after all these years?
THE PROFESSOR. (*Horrified.*) Penny! (*Angry.*) Why do you come to me now? Because I'm successful? Well, this is it! You proud of me? What do you think of me now?
PENNY. So you really are the famous Professor I've been reading about...
THE PROFESSOR. Yes, that's me all right. Did you come here to— do you want to come back to me?
PENNY. No, I never expected to see you, I was just paying a parking ticket. I've remarried, you know.
THE PROFESSOR. I thought you would. When?
PENNY. The day after I left you. I know I was unkind. I hope you can forgive me. I was younger. I didn't understand life.
THE PROFESSOR. I did then. But now I can't figure it out!

PENNY. I'm sorry. Bilo's love is just as strong as ever. And thanks to your wonderful invention, our love is real, and true, and fresh. I suppose I should say "Thank you."

THE PROFESSOR. My heart! My heart is an echo chamber of pain, pain, pain! Get out of my life!

PENNY. The poor man. Well–hung and bitter: Success poisoned by the insanity that drove him to it. At least I can tell people, "I knew him when..."

THE PROFESSOR. Don't!

STAFFER. Your number is up. You may enter the courtroom.

(*PENNY leaves. They are escorted into the courtroom.*)

Scene 19 - The Court Room

JUDGE. Order in the court! Order in the court! In the case of the People versus the Professor and Moe, defendants in the death of a Mrs. Livonia Climsby. Professor, you are the inventor of the SX–70 penis enlarger, is that correct?

THE PROFESSOR. Everyone knows who I am.

JUDGE. You will now be sworn in. Please repeat after me: "I swear by Almighty God..."

THE PROFESSOR. "I swear by Almighty God."

JUDGE. "That the testimony that I give..."

THE PROFESSOR. That's right.

JUDGE. Repeat it.

THE PROFESSOR. What?

JUDGE. Repeat what I said.

THE PROFESSOR. What you said when?

JUDGE. "That the evidence that I give..."

THE PROFESSOR. "That the evidence that I give."

JUDGE. "Shall be the truth and..."

THE PROFESSOR. It will, and nothing but the truth!

JUDGE. Please, just repeat after me: "Shall be the truth and..."

THE PROFESSOR. What else would it be? I'm not going to make it up!

JUDGE. We can appreciate that. Just repeat after me: "Shall be the truth and..."

THE PROFESSOR. "Shall be the truth and."

JUDGE. Say: "Nothing...".
THE PROFESSOR. Okay. (*And he remains silent.*)
JUDGE. No! Don't say nothing. Say: "Nothing but the truth..."
THE PROFESSOR. Of course.

(*A PERSON comes running in.*)

PERSON. Doctor! Doctor!
JUDGE. There is no doctor here, this is a court of law.
PERSON. I have to see a doctor right away. I've just swallowed a roll of film.
JUDGE. Don't worry, nothing will develop. (*The PERSON runs out. Back to THE PROFESSOR.*) Now, I want you to say: "Nothing but the truth...".
THE PROFESSOR. We went over that.
JUDGE. Then say "Nothing but the truth..."
THE PROFESSOR. But I will!
JUDGE. I give up, that's close enough. Can I hear the complaints against the defendant?
BARNEY. His machine made me feel less. My engagement was ruined because of him.
JUDGE. (*To BARNEY.*) How is the Professor responsible for alienating your affection?
BARNEY. I proposed to my fiancé, Delilah Barley. The Minister's daughter. I wanted to make her: Mrs. Barney Terwhilliger. That is, if she would have me.
MINISTER BARLEY. I stopped that engagement! I don't want my daughter consorting with— you know.
JUDGE. And yet Minister Barley, everyone knows you're now holding confessions twice a day just to get people alone in the confessional. Case dismissed.
CLIMSBY. His machine made me want more. I became addicted, and harmed the one closest to me.
BERTHA. His machine was harmful to womyn, animals, and other living things.
JUDGE. Your proof?
BERTHA. It killed Mrs. Climsby for example.
CLIMSBY. I can't believe she's gone.
JUDGE. Bring in the coroner. You performed the autopsy?

CORONER. I felt an autopsy was unnecessary. Her brains were in a jar on the table.

JUDGE. Sounds convincing to me. Any other distinguishing marks?

CORONER. Big smile on her face.

JUDGE. How many autopsies have you performed on dead people?

CORONER. All of them.

MOE. Allow me to introduce my own evidence in this matter: the allegedly–deceased Mrs. Climsby!

CLIMSBY. Livonia!

MRS. CLIMSBY. Herman, darling!

CLIMSBY. But how—— he said your brains were in a jar on the table!

MOE. Everyone knows you don't need brains to live in this city.

MRS. CLIMSBY. —and I'm so much happier without them!

THE PROFESSOR. It appears that everyone here got what they wanted— except me.

MOE. Death be not proud.

MINISTER BARLEY. The early bird catches the worm.

BARNEY. Some of my best friends are Jewish.

DELILAH. Never mix, never worry.

O'FLAHRETY. Love thy neighbor as thyself.

MOE. Nothing ventured, nothing gained.

MRS. CLIMSBY. You get more flies with sugar than you do with vinegar.

CLIMSBY. Great minds think alike.

SOMEONE. Go ye forth and multiply.

RESPONSE. There's a sucker born every minute.

WWW. Treat your neighbors as you would have them treat you.

XXX. Bang the drum slowly.

YYY. Age before beauty.

ZZZ. Pearls before swine.

JUDGE. Case dismissed! Professor, you are free to go!

ALL. Hooray!

(In the jubilation, the BABY SEAL's hat is accidentally knocked off.)

BABY SEAL. Uh–oh...

MAYOR. It's the Baby Seal! Grab him!

(*There is a brief chase, and the BABY SEAL is caught. BABY SEAL is bludgeoned and his fur slashed and peeled from his head and body. PENNY appears, and sings a haunting serenade.*)

PENNY. (*Sings.*)
TREAT YOUR LOVE AS A DREAM;
A DELICATE VISION, FELT, NOT SEEN
AND TREAT YOUR DREAM AS A LOVE,
A BOLD DEVOTION.
WHEN EITHER BECOMES CRYSTAL–CLEAR,
THEY WILL MUTUALLY DISAPPEAR
AND YOU WILL FIND YOURSELF HERE.
A DREAM CAN DRIVE YOU HEAVENWARD,
WHENEVER YOU FEEL SAD...
OR IT CAN DRIVE YOU MAD.

(*She fades away. The rhythm continues. THE PROFESSOR, JACQUELINE behind him, voices his disappointment.*)

THE PROFESSOR. (*Sings.*)
ALL THAT I WANT WAS TO BE ALL I COULD BE;
WHATEVER IT TAKES SO THAT SHE'D WANT ME
ALONE I WORKED TO BUILD ALL MY CHARMS;
IN HOPES TO FOLD HER WITHIN MY ARMS...

LADY JACQUELINE. (*Sings.*)
ALL YOU DESIRE IS ALL AROUND,
OPEN YOUR EYES TO THE HERE AND NOW.

THE PROFESSOR. (*Sings.*)
WITH HOPES HELD HIGH, AND A HEART AGLOW,
I'M WORTHY NOW, BUT I'M ALL ALONE
WITH A HEART AS BROAD AS A STAR–FILLED SKY,
TO SEARCH FOR LOVE WITH A MILLION EYES...

LADY JACQUELINE. (*Sings.*)
ALL YOU DESIRE IS ALL AROUND,
OPEN YOUR EYES TO THE HERE AND NOW.

(Next to speak up are BARNEY and DELILAH: a reconciliation)

BARNEY. (*Sings.*)
MY DARLING DELILAH——

DELILAH. (*Sings.*)
MY BARNEY.

BARNEY & DELILAH. (*Sing together.*)
FORGIVE ME...

BARNEY. (*Sings.*)
ALL RESENTMENTS, RESIGNED.

DELILAH. (*Sings.*)
LET OUR LIVES BE ENTWINED WITH AFFECTION....

CLIMSBY. (*Sings.*)
I TREASURE YOU NOW MORE THAN EVER BEFORE

MRS. CLIMSBY. (*Sings.*)
YOU ARE ALL THAT I WANT

CLIMSBY. (*Sings.*)
BUT I WANT TO GIVE MORE

CLIMSBY / MRS. CLIMSBY / BARNEY / DELILAH. (*Sings.*)
ALL MY OLD INHIBITIONS
DISSOLVE IN THE VISION— OF LOVE....

JACQUELINE WITH CHORUS. (*Sings.*)
ALL YOU DESIRE IS ALL AROUND,
OPEN YOUR EYES TO THE HERE AND NOW

(JACQUELINE stands before THE PROFESSOR, and doesn't quite get it. He's envious of all the other couples uniting and feeling sorry for himself. BERTHA smacks him in the back of the head, as in "Pay Attention!!!" His eyes open, he and JACQUELINE unite as the chant changes to a faster, more excited

version of the same rhythm. All harmony breaks lose, with every company member happily uniting with their designated partner.)

ALL. (*Sing.*)
ALL YOU DESIRE IS ALL AROUND,
OPEN YOUR EYES TO THE HERE AND NOW
ALL YOU DESIRE IS ALL AROUND,
OPEN YOUR EYES TO THE HERE AND NOW
ALL YOU DESIRE IS ALL AROUND,
OPEN YOUR EYES TO THE HERE AND NOW
ALL YOU DESIRE IS ALL AROUND,
OPEN YOUR EYES TO THE HERE AND NOW!

(This chant continues through to the end. THE PROFESSOR and JACQUELINE prepare to be wed, at least visually. BABY SEAL remains dead, but rises to give his fur as a gift to THE PROFESSOR. As he does so, MAMA SEAL appears on a cloud in heaven, and he runs off to join her. THE PROFESSOR gives the fur to JACQUELINE, who is delighted.)

MOST PEOPLE. (*Sing.*)
NOW THE JOURNEY IS ENDED, THE VICTORY IS WON
YOU'VE FOUND YOUR TRUE LOVE,
NOW OUR STORY IS DONE
WE HAVE TAUGHT YOU A MORAL
BOTH SIMPLE AND BRIEF:
YOU ARE ALWAYS ENOUGH! (—OH YEAH?)
TRY TO BELIEVE IT!
IF TROUBLES BESIEGE YOU,
AND TORMENT YOU BLIND
YOU CAN LOSE EVERY ONE
IF YOU JUST LOSE YOUR MIND!
IT MAY NOT SEEM MUCH,
BUT SOME DAY YOU'LL WAKE UP:
NO LONGER ASLEEP,
YOU'LL FIND OUT YOU'VE BEEN LIVING
YOUR DREAM!

(CURTAIN.)

<u>END OF PLAY</u>

AN
IVAR
MEMOIR

(Previously titled "Follies of Grandeur")

TOP: Mary Louise Mooney. BOTTOM: Jennifer Dominguez, Daryl Brown and Kevin Kelleher in *Follies of Grandeur* (later titled *An Ivar Memoir*) at Theater for the New City, New York. (2006) Photo credit: Peter Madero

An Ivar Memoir (under the title *Follies of Grandeur*) was first performed at Theater for the New City, New York on February 2, 2006. Directed by Mark Finley; Assistant Director, Ric Gravenson; set design by Michael Muccio; lighting design by Igor Goldin; and costume design by Chris Weikel. The cast was as follows:

Melody...............	Jennifer Dominguez
Kenny.................	Brian Hoover
Rex....................	Daryl Brown
Stan...................	Kevin Kelleher
Barbie................	Jolie Meshbesher
Letanya..............	Bobbi Owens
Bonnie Lee...........	Mary Louise Mooney
Fawn.................	Melissa Center
Jerry/Leonard/Rolly.	McGregor Wright

SYNOPSIS

By the late 70s, the Ivar Theater in Hollywood had declined from a playhouse to a bottom-of-the-barrel strip joint. Both harsh and poignant, this is one man's recollection of the patrons, performers, and one girl who briefly stood out from the crowd.

CHARACTERS

MELODY   A drifter. 17 but looks older.

The men in her life, according to this viewing:

KENNY   Spotlight operator and janitor.

STAN   Owner and manager of the theater.

REX   A fixture of the audience.

The other girls at the Ivar:

BARBIE   Singer and M.C.

BONNIE LEE   Space-cadet.

LETANYA   Smooth, raunchy elegance.

FAWN   Just another plain face.

Plus **ASSORTED PATRONS, LEWD PERFORMERS, TRICKS,** and other **INNER-CITY HOLLYWOOD TYPES.** Everyone but MELODY and KENNY may double as audience members, and sometimes other girls if needed.

SETTING

The Ivar Theater, Hollywood, and surrounding environs.

SET

The set suggests the interior of the Ivar Theater. It is dominated by the runway, a structure approximately 3' wide and 12' long. Worn and broken theater seats to the downstage side of the runway. Far up right, a platform with mismatched chairs to serve as the dressing room, and make a space far down left to be defined as outside the theater when needed. Several panels to be used as shadow screens.

AN IVAR MEMOIR

By Ross MacLean

SCENE ONE

(*In the dark, spotlight finds LETANYA in mid-performance on the Ivar runway, three men in its audience. The fuzzy amplified music is noisy and energetic in contrast to the languid activity of the dancer and audience. At the same time, rock music from a small radio in the light booth adds to the audio confusion. When the music completes, dead air space, save for the rock radio in the background. Eventually the M.C., BARBIE, appears to make her announcement:*)

BARBIE. Letanya, ladies and gentlemen, that was Letanya. Let's hear it for Letanya.

(*Fatigued applause as LETANYA collects her tips.*)

LETANYA. (*Calls up to the booth.*) I can hear your radio! (*There is no change in the sound leak from the booth. She picks up two bucks from the runway, sees a jacket left on a chair.*) Thanks hon. Hey, you forget that?

BARBIE. Letanya, ladies and gentlemen. Now if you don't mind guys, I'm gonna say good night, I'm really tired but you've been a great audience... Mr. Tape Man, can you take over?

(*BARBIE exits, prepares to leave.*)

KENNY. That's it for our show at the Ivar Theater tonight, we're open again tomorrow at —

LETANYA. I'm still here, huh?

KENNY. Yeah, ok, now wave to the crowd... "Letanya, ladies and gentlemen, let's hear it for Letanya." (*As she's about to leave the stage, he reminds her.*) Say goodnight to the guys with the "Ivar Smile."

(*LETANYA, clothes collected, indifferently walks to the top of the runway, bends over and spreads her ass.*)

KENNY. OK guys, that's it for tonight, be sure to come back tomorrow, open at 11:00 with movies, live show starts at one. Thanks and good night.

(*Theater house lights on, and Ivar "exit music," KENNY's radio playing under. LETANYA dresses at the back of the stage as the audience clears out. Bits of trash all around, and a coat left on the floor. KENNY comes in, fiddles with his portable radio, if he needs to keep the noise going—throughout most of the play, noise never stops— then goes to his mop and bucket.*)

LETANYA. I could hear that thing all through my show.
KENNY. I didn't see it change much.
LETANYA. 'f you see Stan first, stop him. I'm gonna need a draw.
KENNY. (*Mostly to himself:*) Yeah, sure, go home.

(*He's trying on the jacket: it's stained and has footprints on the shoulder—but it fits, so he keeps it. LETANYA dresses and goes about her business, she'll return to the dressing room, wake another girl who will eventually pack up and leave. KENNY addresses the audience.*)

KENNY. In a few minutes, they'll be gone. Nothing I like better than having this all to myself— Emptiness! and possibility. But tonight: I want to share it with you. Tonight I want to show you a place, and some people, from a long time ago. I'm a lot older than I look right now, and a little nicer than I used to be. But I want to show you how I was then. I want to show you some people who, mostly, I didn't think much of at the time. But years later, I've learned to care about them quite a bit. This happens in downtown Hollywood, in the seventies... Let me describe the landscape some. You already know a lot about Hollywood, and Hollywood and Vine and all that. Well, behind the back alley of the world-famous corner of Hollywood and Vine runs a little street called Ivar Avenue. On that street is the Ivar Theater, a great little playhouse built in 1950, and brought a lot of culture to Hollywood and Los Angeles. In California, "theater" is called "culture." This is it! We're at the Ivar! At the Ivar they had alot of popular dramas and musicals: Edward Albee's *Tiny Alice* played here, so did *Dames at Sea*. Twenty-five-plus years of culture. *Godspell* was the last really big show, I saw it twice. Had a short run though: It's a small place, like 400 seats or so, and what with rising costs of as much as $7 a seat, even a sell-out like *Godspell* couldn't afford to play. That show closed, Jesus and all those other clowns went looking for work, and not long after it became a strip house. And I came to work here. They tore up the orchestra and built a runway seven rows into the audience. That runway was home to the most Beautiful Girls in the World, Live, Totally Nude, On Stage from 10 a.m. till 4 in the morning.

(*There is a loud pounding at the door.*)

KENNY. I'd been there as a kid, my grandmother took me to matinees here! I know what it had been. And I knew what it was. What I wanted it to be...? (*He knows, he senses it, but can't grasp it.*)

(*There is a loud pounding at the door.*)

KENNY. These are the follies of grandeur. This is the Ivar Theater. It is 3:30 in the morning, in 1978.

(*More pounding at the door.*)

JERRY. HEY! Hey, open up!
LETANYA. CLOSED!
KENNY. ...can't be cops.
JERRY. I know there's people in there.
KENNY. Maybe it's who left the coat.

(*KENNY goes to the door and cracks it open.*)

LETANYA. –What the hell you doing???
KENNY. What's the problem?
LETANYA. Fucking idiot!!

(*JERRY presses the door open a ways. All through the following exchange, we can hear the quiet sound of MELODY protesting, ad lib i.e: "No let's come back tomorrow, don't make me do it now, let's just keep going" etc.*)

JERRY. (*His tone is gentle and polite.*) Is the manager in? I got some business to discuss.

KENNY. (*Frightened, tries to close the door.*) Shit—

JERRY. I got a girl here, you need any girls?

LETANYA. We got amateur night tomorrow, have her come back around 7:30.

JERRY. (*Forcing the door.*) I thought he could see her now since we're here. Is that you?

LETANYA. (*Takes over.*) Try the peep show down Hollywood n' Western: Bye!

MELODY. Come on, it's freezing out here! Just for a minute—

(*JERRY forces his way in. A biker with heavy beard and leather jacket. He conducts himself, incongruently, as a considerate, soft-spoken gentlemen. At the end of his arm, a small plain drifter trails in: MELODY.*)

LETANYA. Holy crap—! —Get Out!!

JERRY. No, we're cool, we're cool. Not here for trouble. This is my girl. Say hi.

MELODY. Man I'm tired...

(*MELODY, exhausted, drifts over to the runway, tosses her bag on it and rests her head.*)

JERRY. My name's Jerry, I'm looking for a place for her to work.

KENNY. Best thing is come back tomorrow.

JERRY. Come on man, give the girl a break, it's cold out. We just got into town, if there's no chance of her working then we gotta keep moving.

KENNY. Letanya, wanna get Stan.

LETANYA. I'll be a minute.

KENNY. Nothing to worry about.

(*LETANYA goes.*)

JERRY. So that's not you.
KENNY. I'm not the manager, but I'm in charge. And do fix-up.
JERRY. I saw the jacket, I thought. Mind 'f I use the can?
KENNY. That way.

(*JERRY steps away. MELODY and KENNY alone staring at each other for a moment.*)

MELODY. Where is this place?
KENNY. The Ivar theater. You're in Hollywood.
MELODY. Why is it so cold then, I was always told it was all-year sunshine. Jeez. I thought they grew oranges here. (*Drowsy, wanting to be pleasant.*) I didn't plan on coming to California, it's just the rides I got. Always wanted to come to Hollywood. Everyone does, probably. Are there really movie stars here?
KENNY. Not this time o' night.
MELODY. Place looks big. I worked in lots little places, all over. But this is giant. Do they really fill up all these seats?
KENNY. Ones around the runway are pretty popular.
MELODY. Runway. I been on stubby little platforms, but this, I could get lost in all this space.
KENNY. I thought you said you were tired.
JERRY. (*Has returned.*) Somethin the matter? (*To MELODY.*) Don't mouth off to these people, we gotta get you something.

(*LETANYA returns with STAN, a rumpled man in his late 50s in a flimsy grey suit. They don't have to return just because JERRY finished his line. Let them all be stuck there for a bit.*)

STAN. (*He knows what it's about, this is just what he says.*) Hello, can I help you with something?
JERRY. Yes sir, my name's Jerry Marshall, this here is my girl, we're looking to find her a place to work.
STAN. It's kind of late.
MELODY. Uh huh. We've been riding a long way.
STAN. Any experience?
JERRY. She's pretty. Got real nice feet.
MELODY. I been in clubs mostly, but never in a real theater.
JERRY. Want to see her audition? She's real talented.
STAN. She over eighteen?

MELODY. Uh huh.

STAN. Do you have a tape? (*MELODY just looks at him.*) Music. Do you have your own music?

MELODY. I did, but it got lost. (*Digs in the bag anyway.*) I have a picture in here in my bag from one of the bars, but it got bent-up from the ride.

STAN. Kenny. Put on a tape for her.

MELODY. What for?

STAN. I want to see what you do.

KENNY. Now???

MELODY. But I'm just so tired. I don't have my costume on...

STAN. You don't need one.

JERRY. Go on baby, you'll do fine. Just for a couple minutes.

MELODY. Then can we get a find a place to stay?

STAN. Kenny, a tape?

KENNY. Shit! (*Throws down his mop and stamps off.*)

JERRY. Thank you sir, I really appreciate you giving us this opportunity.

STAN. Don't worry about it.

(*The music blasts on, Alice Cooper's "School's Out". The volume goes down, then up again. At the first blast, MELODY lurches, looks around like she's not sure if she should move— she does start moving, but each time the volume switches, she stops and starts over again.*)

STAN. Turn it down! Down!

(*Music goes off completely.*)

KENNY. What!

STAN. Down, not off!

(*Music comes back on, and continues as loudly as possible.*)

MELODY. I forgot to ask— Should I be on the stage?

(*MELODY crawls up onto the runway, and once standing upright responds to the music, her dance now a drifting, somnambulistic labor.*

KENNY returns to his clean-up work, knocking the bucket around and making all sorts of clatter. MELODY unzips her mechanic's overalls, but appears frightened about getting out of them. Throughout the following distractions, her apparently ignored audition proceeds.)

STAN. How long have you had her?

JERRY. Little bit, got her in Indiana. She's been good.

KENNY. Stan, you said you were going to get me a new mop. This is shot, look, there's dirt and shit caked in it, the strings are all tangled up.

STAN. Here: just, like this. Pull on 'em a little, they'll come undone.

KENNY. They're old and rotten, see?

STAN. It's three bucks for a mop head. You're washing the floor, not a dinner plate. (*When he's seen enough of MELODY.*) Go get the music.

MELODY. Should I keep going?

STAN. I thought you said you'd done this before. You shy about something?

MELODY. I didn't know you were paying attention— (*Music is plunked off. She steps out of the overalls, is wearing very plain bra and panties, and socks.*)

JERRY. Don't go any further. *(To STAN.)* So what do you think? You give her a job?

MELODY. Normally I had like yellow or green veils, scarves and stuff. Pro'lly hard to picture, like this.

STAN. You want to work here?

MELODY. Sure.

JERRY. Talk to me, I'll handle her business.

STAN. Who's this, your manager?

MELODY. (*He isn't.*) ...Yes.

JERRY. I'm just looking out for her.

MELODY. Can I put my clothes back on?

STAN. Letanya, can you wait a minute? Take the girl up to my office, I'll be right up after I talk to this gentleman.

JERRY. No, no, no, she's goin' nowhere until we work something out.

STAN. Of course, I just don't want to talk business in front of the girls. Oh: what's her name?

JERRY. She got a couple, you want her stage names or her real name?

MELODY. *Melody.*

(*MELODY and LETANYA leave.*)

STAN. You on run from the law?

JERRY. No sir. Just looking for honest work.

STAN. Drugs?

JERRY. No. Just no sleep. Came across three states, she can't really handle the road. You sign a contract here? Two or three weeks, what?

STAN. We don't do contracts, just in or out.

JERRY. Well I want to have some kind of advance. She's a good dancer and without something up front I'll take her someplace else.

STAN. I get a dozen girls a week, your choice. We'll be down in a few minutes.

(*STAN out. KENNY continues cleaning. JERRY eyes him constantly. Awkward. No rush to get this scene over with, but here's what they say.*)

JERRY. What are you here?

KENNY. I do the lights n music, show the porno in between. Little film editing when it breaks you know, good skill to have in this town. (*He is polishing the runway.*) And I do the announcing when the real M.C. goes home. I'm not the real manager, but I run things.

JERRY. Girls make good money here?

KENNY. Guess they do, I don't know.

JERRY. They need another light guy?

KENNY. Not right now but I could take your name.

JERRY. What's it pay?

KENNY. (*Proud.*) Three dollars an hour to start, but I get three fifty. (*Sets to task to demonstrate.*) But I'm worth it: see this gob, wet nail polish or something from some dumb twat rollin' around. Dust and stuff gets stuck to it, looks like hell if you leave it. I like to keep the place nice.

JERRY. S'there a place I can get a coffee nearby?

KENNY. Ranch Market's twenty-four hours. Over to Vine then down past Sunset on the left. You mind getting me one too, black, and half dozen donuts? Should come to about two and a quarter but all I got's a five.

JERRY. No problem. I'll be right back.

(*He goes out the door, it slams shut. KENNY looks after, mops for a bit.*)

KENNY. I lost five bucks.

SCENE TWO

(*In the theater.*)

KENNY. Amateur night, Tuesday. Let's speed things up a little, I mean, you know the girl didn't die, we could show you the amateur night, you could watch her win and pretend you're surprised, let's skip it. But how about some action, come to a play about the Ivar, you expect to see some talent, right?

(*The first of the "shadow scenes" sets up, while the show proceeds without pause*)

KENNY. Well amateur night didn't really have amateurs, girls from other clubs come in cuz it pays twenty-five bucks. Maybe half a dozen more or less like Melody. Well, there was one novelty, should give you an idea of the possibilities at the Ivar. Let me show you one of the losers: Winnie.

(*WINNIE performs behind the shadow screen, as described. Any audience members have no change in their interest level.*)

KENNY. Winnie musta been in her sixties, some ancient old bag who came by every couple weeks, me n' Barbie used to laugh our heads off when she came out. We called Winnie "the chicken lady", because, in a try to disguise her saggy breasts, she hiked her elbows up very high, and then trying to hide her flabby ass, she walked around taking really high steps. In real life, my own anyway, it was hysterical, you wonder why no one else laughed. But the audience at this place, as long as the clothes were off: enchantment. Beautiful, desperate or both, any woman's got a home here. For twenty minutes. (*Shrugs. Simply, not mean.*) Get her off. So even in her mechanic's overalls and socks, Melody came out a winner. Nothing like the glow of success.

SCENE THREE

(*In the Box Office, being paid after amateur night.*)

STAN. (*Explains to CUSTOMER.*) Ticket seller'll be back in a few minutes, we're on a break. (*To MELODY.*) Come on in. How'd you like it?
MELODY. I won the contest. Didn't you see me?
STAN. I had a look.
MELODY. Yeah, I was really blown away. I mean, bein' on stage in Hollywood, and winning on top of it! Is there any chance, uh I can come back?

(*STAN finishes counting out money, pays MELODY in singles.*)

MELODY. Thank you! I really, really appreciate this—oh—uh, is this right?
STAN. Yeah. What?
MELODY. It's twenty-five dollars.
STAN. Right.
MELODY. I won the contest.
STAN. Did you get the extra dance? OK, so how were your tips?
MELODY. Real good.
STAN. There's your prize money.
MELODY. Oh. All right.
STAN. Want a job? Come in tomorrow around 12, first show's at 1:00.
MELODY. Oh wow, are you kidding me?

STAN. You dance for 20 minutes, and everything's gotta be off by five. Last ten should be floor work, but most girls do more cuz it's better for tips.

MELODY. I will be really, really good, you'll see. How many can I do?

STAN. Well I don't know. You think you're good enough to be the star?

MELODY. You're kidding. Really??? (*Is flabbergasted.*) Oh Stan, this is fantastic! I don't know what I can do to thank you!

STAN. You've already done it. (*Flirtatious.*) But you could do it again.

MELODY. I'd like that.

(*She gives him a squeeze which turns affectionate. STAN proceeds unaffected, and she lets go.*)

STAN. I'm busy. Star is guaranteed three shows a day, with more if there's an empty spot.

MELODY. Wow, this is great, this is so fuckin great! Thank you!

(*She kisses him, but when she releases, he retains the embrace. Just a note: he's really a sweet man to the girls, there is nothing at all malicious or menacing in his conduct with them.*)

STAN. Is your manager still around?

MELODY. He wasn't really a manager.

STAN. I'd say not if he let you get away. But if you get a boyfriend he can buy a ticket if he wants to come in.

MELODY. Why would I get a boyfriend?

STAN. (*He takes a kiss.*) Wait for me out front.

MELODY. Sure. (*Treasuring her money, she folds it and puts it in her pocket.*) Thank you! Very, very much!

(*And she gives him a kiss. He leads her out of the office, and she proceeds to her hotel room on her own.*)

SCENE FOUR

(*Lights come up on MELODY's room at the Hotel Hastings. While a confusion of radios, creaking stairs and talking penetrates the wall, MELODY makes herself at home.*)

MELODY. Twenty-five dollars! Twenty-five dollars! Minus the hotel room, —not bad but it's all mine. What do I got: Nine dollars, great! –and these two, and the six I had. Star of the show, top that. Three shows guaranteed, seven dollars, twenty-one, plus tips, let's say thirty-three, I don't know, but if I'm the star, do I get more than seven? There has to be something extra for the star, maybe just a special dressing room, or there's gotta at least be five extra—Well, twelve would be an awful lot, thirty six a day, no, I don't want to be greedy, maybe ten a show. Three dollars extra isn't too much to expect, thirty dollars a day, and if I work every day, thirty times seven, more than 200 a week, eight hundred a month! No more damned bikini bars.

(*She's digging through her bag to see what she's got. Sometimes might pull out a weird object: maybe a toaster, or a record. She does find a small bottle of Bacardi, and a glass wrapped in cloth to drink it from.*)

MELODY. Gotta get some good costumes, wanna look pretty. Want stamps, send out postcards of the Hollywood Sign: see what they think now. Go to Las Vegas. Dance in movies. Jerry sees me on a billboard. Maybe advertising scotch or something. Sign autographs. God, thanks for bringing me to Hollywood. Jerry, thanks for leaving. Traveling, wandering so goddamn long. Now: I'm goin nowhere!

(*LIGHTS OUT on MELODY.*)

SCENE FIVE

(*KENNY cleans the theater.*)

KENNY. Once the lights are out in Hollywood, and I'm alone in here, I look at the stage and think of all that's gone on here before the walls went grimy. You know Judy Kaye? Her first part ever was here at the Ivar. *You're a Good Man Charlie Brown.* Watched her standing right there going "Dog lips, my lips touched dog lips!" Huh. How it was. Now dog lips in heels. I always wanted to work in theater. I put the new face on this runway, see this? So it would look good for the ladies. Before, it was all fucked up and hammered in sideways. But this is like, an altar or something, I don't care what kind of theater it is. Cut panels, measured 'em. You don't want to know what I swept out from under there. Wash bucket turned black, but it all ended up smelling like nice clean bleach.

(*Goes to a portion where a hole is kicked in the side and a paper cup with trash is poked into it.*)

KENNY. The men are a little harsh on the place.

(*He collects assorted trash from the floor, fast food bags, empty quart beer bottles a liquor bottle and wadded up Kleenex.*)

KENNY. You just wish they'd throw their old jack-wads into a bag or something. Yeah it's gross when they come in here and beat off into a Kleenex, but it's not half as bad as when they don't. I replace a lot of seats here. Tear up the balcony to do it. This one, (*Next to the runway.*) Broke so many times, hinge is gone, have to leave it empty. But every day, some idiot comes in, and up-ends the trashcan out of the men's room and sits here, fascinated. (*He hears pounding on the door*) And I play old music tapes from the shows that used to be here: kind of, "feed the theater." However.

(*Pounding on the door: He admits REX, neither acknowledges the other.*)

KENNY. At ten-thirty sharp every morning, every day of the year: Here's Rex, as usual. Still not dead. Watch this, watch what he's going to do.

(*REX shuffles in, an ancient cadaverous figure, chicken neck, bony ankles, no socks, and a black raincoat. He makes his way to his seat, carefully removes his raincoat and folds it in his lap.*)

KENNY. The theater house-cat, I have to let him in, something he worked out with Stan before I ever started, I don't know. "Mr. Ivar" the girls call him. Just live with it. Empty theater, nothing happening for another hour and a half, and he just sits there waiting, like the last act of "Our Town." Eventually, I leave and the theater comes to life.

(*The movie screen flickers a blurred porn movie, sound under, as the girls come into the dressing room for their next scene.*)

SCENE SIX

(*Thursday Afternoon at the Theater.*

Actors take their positions: REX in his seat, other audience MEN gather around the runway for the start of the show.

In the dressing room: Three stations. BONNIE LEE is talking to herself and sitting in any chair while she prattles on. BARBIE finishing brushing hair.)

BONNIE LEE. (*Mostly unintelligible, talking to herself: line doesn't need to complete.*) –then if it wasn't there, then how could I have—Oh, I was sitting here instead now it looks different. What's in my bag, did I remember to bring something to wear? Let me sit over here then, are you in here maybe...?
LETANYA. In my seat, sugar.
BONNIE LEE. (*Goes to BARBIE's chair, continues prattle quietly to herself.*) OK, sorry, I was just trying to see...
BARBIE. I'll be out of your way in just a minute—

(*STAN brings MELODY in, he pauses at the doorway before leading her in.*)

STAN. Knock-knock, everyone decent?
LETANYA. Dancers only, Stan.
STAN. Want to see my one-tassel dance? This is Melody, the new star.
LETANYA. C'mon in...
BONNIE LEE. Hey Stan, you want to try my pop rocks?
STAN. You want to try mine?

(*LETANYA laughs, MELODY worries if she should be jealous.*)

BARBIE. (*Over-apologizing, where there is no cause to apologize at all.*) Stan, I'm really sorry I'm late, but I was seeing an agent—
STAN. Doesn't matter, go on ahead.

(*BARBIE scurries out, brightens and taps MELODY on the shoulder as she passes.*)

BARBIE. Hey!
STAN. Everybody happy?
LETANYA. Out, Stan.
STAN. Letanya, you help her out OK?

(*STAN gives MELODY a squeeze, she gives him a coy kiss: not romantic, very father-daughter kind of thing.*)

LETANYA. Will do...
STAN. OK Melody, do good.

(*STAN leaves.*)

LETANYA. So, you Stan's new girl?
MELODY. I don't know about that. I won the contest last night, and suddenly I'm a "star", ha ha. (*She expects a response. They're not ignoring her, but there is none.*) Where should I go?
LETANYA. That chair's free.

MELODY. I thought maybe there was a separate dressing room for the star.

LETANYA. We got separate chairs, that'll have to do. One side, closer to the stage, other, closer to the toilet. Whatever's more important, star gets to choose.

MELODY. (*Takes the seat nearest the stage.*) The last place I was at, I had a private dressing room, and a driver, used to pick me up at the hotel and escort me right up to the stage door. (*Sets out her stuff on the table.*) There was always lots of fan mail and gifts, and flower arrangements, one in my contract, one from the music-players, you know, the band, and then, admirers, varied, sometimes roses, or sunflowers. Sometimes just candy.

(*BONNIE LEE and LETANYA are staring at her with fourteen eyes.*)

LETANYA. You're fulla shit, right?

MELODY. Ha Ha, fooled you! I'm Melody. I'm new around here, I came from a bunch of different places.

BONNIE LEE. Oh, like on a tour?

MELODY. Sort of. Little places for a couple weeks a shot. You probably did the same, nothing special, right?

BONNIE LEE. I only been here. I was always getting beat up a lot, I had to get a job.

LETANYA. I'll smack you myself if you— (*She snags something of hers back from BONNIE LEE.*)

BONNIE LEE. So you're traveling or are you staying put? I decided to stay here, most of the time. Sometimes I get sick.

MELODY. But not today, right?

BONNIE LEE. Today my Karma's working good. Bright and shiny.

MELODY. I know about Karma, guys in school always talked about it. Well I must've done something terrific, cuz I'm here.

BONNIE LEE. Your alternate might be having a bad day, I feel bad for mine when that happens.

MELODY. Who's this?

BONNIE LEE. You know: The alternate universe! It's just like this one, except backwards. Like, instead of if you're happy now, then in the other world you're sad, or if you're leaving a place somewhere then in the other universe you're just arriving.

LETANYA. In my alternate universe, I'm interested.
MELODY. Right now everything's pretty far-out!

(Phone buzzes.)

MELODY. Know what they used to say in high school? "Farm-Out."

(Phone buzzes. LETANYA answers.)

LETANYA. Dressing room Letanya. (*Listens, hangs up.*) Alternate universe called: Downstairs to start the show.

(BONNIE LEE collects herself and goes downstairs, stands near BARBIE.)

MELODY. I am just-so-psyched. You been here a long time?
LETANYA. I come and go. Here a couple weeks lately. Cash for the baby.
MELODY. You have a baby?
LETANYA. Jus' the guy I'm with. He big ol' baby.
MELODY. I had a boyfriend, he had to leave town though.
LETANYA. Shoulda stuck around to see the show.
KENNY. (*On mic from the light booth: a recitation devoid of enthusiasm.*) Good afternoon ladies and gentlemen, welcome to the Ivar Theater in Hollywood. We've got quite a show lined up for you this afternoon, but first, we got a couple rules before we can start: keep your hands and arms off the runway so you don't trip the girls up or get yourself stepped on, and please do not try and touch the dancers. And a special rule for some of you guys: the only people to expose themselves will be the dancers on stage. That said, let's have a warm hand for our M.C., let's bring her out: Barbie!
BARBIE. (*Not exactly devoid of enthusiasm, but you feel she's either done this for a thousand years, or that this is interrupting her TV soap operas.*) Thank you, thank you. Gosh it's really great to see you all today. Now if I can start things off with a little music, can I have my tape Mr. Tape Man?

(*While we hear KENNY fiddling with the cassette, sticking it in to the recorder, and the dead space while the tape gets into position, she copes with a pesky patron.*)

BARBIE. No, I'm not gonna take my clothes off, I'm gonna sing a song. No, I'll take them off in a little bit, would you rather hear a song first? (*Etc. She sings with manufactured cheer.*)
PLANT A RADISH.
GET A RADISH.
NEVER ANY DOUBT.
THAT'S WHY I LOVE VEGETABLES; YOU KNOW WHAT YOU'RE ABOUT!
PLANT A TURNIP.
GET A TURNIP.
MAYBE YOU'LL GET TWO.
THAT'S WHY I LOVE VEGETABLES;
YOU KNOW THAT THEY'LL COME THROUGH!

(*All the time she sings, MEN in the audience talk, smoke, ignore her in any way possible, walk away, changes seats, etc. When the stripping starts, they will pay closer attention.*)

BARBIE. (*Sings.*)
THEY'RE DEPENDABLE!
THEY'RE BEFRIENDABLE!
THEY ARE THE BEST PAL A PARENT'S EVER KNOWN!
WHILE WITH CHILDREN,
IT'S BEWILDERIN'.
YOU DON'T KNOW UNTIL THE SEED IS NEARLY GROWN JUST WHAT YOU'VE SOWN.
SO PLANT A CARROT,
GET A CARROT,
NOT A BRUSSELS SPROUT.
THAT'S WHY I LOVE VEGETABLES. YOU KNOW WHAT YOU'RE ABOUT!
LIFE IS MERRY,
IF IT'S VERY
VEGETARIAN!
A MAN WHO PLANTS A GARDEN IS A VERY HAPPY MAN!

Thank you. Now let's bring out another girl for you, she— (*Interrupted, answers a man in the audience.*) No, not now, my show is later, right now I was singing. I'll do that more later, too. But first let's have a round of applause and we'll bring out Bonnie Lee. Bonnie Lee, ladies and gentlemen, Bonnie Lee. This is Bonnie Lee.

(*Music: "That's Amore", Frank Sinatra. Teetering on her cork platforms and arms held a shoulder height, BONNIE LEE takes baby-steps to the end of the runway, turns, and walks back to the top. Repeat. At one end or the other, she'll remove sweatshirt, jeans, bra, panties, as artfully as anyone would while changing clothes in a locker room. She drops each item wherever she took it off. What she does has no connection to the music, she's not dancing in any way: just listening to her favorite song while scanning for tips.*

It might be reasonable to "freeze" BONNIE LEE during her performance to allow the following dialogue to continue. Should someone be able to stage it so that BONNIE LEE can continue without distracting from the dialogue, by all means, do it.)

MELODY. Wow, really pretty costume. I have some nice stuff too, but not like that. I usually make all my own. Most got lost on the road, but whatever I lose, I get back eventually. At this one place I had, I made some butterfly wings? Just out of material from scarves, you know?

LETANYA. A bug.

MELODY. Big wings though! Maybe here I could be a—a grasshopper then!

LETANYA. Don't tie up my mind with nonsense.

MELODY. I was just admiring. You look so... professional.

LETANYA. This stuff I got two boyfriends ago. That guy was rich.

MELODY. Really??

LETANYA. Worked in television, he told me. I rode in his car so I had to believe it. Liked to dress me up and show me off. Took a few trips with him too, Chicago and places. From back when I was living in Las Vegas.

MELODY. You worked Vegas?

LETANYA. World a big place, why not use it. Lotsa money, he had.

MELODY. If he was so rich and he liked you so much, why didn't you marry him or something.

LETANYA. Men like to change their jewelry same as I do. Whoever puts an arm through mine at least leaves a bracelet.

MELODY. I got that kinda chance, I'd think of somethin.

LETANYA. Uh huh. Next time think of somethin before he leaves town.

(*Phone buzzes.*)

LETANYA. Dressing room Letanya. Commodores. Tight spot on my pussy, pay attention this time. Uh huh. (*Hangs up.*) You do real nice. Maybe I see you in a few minutes.

(*LETANYA leaves to go down, as BONNIE LEE completes her performance onstage. At the end of her song, the tape is plunked off, and BARBIE comes out to announce her off. Dead air, smattered clapping while she collects her tips and clothes. Interminable pauses in BARBIE's announcing.*)

BARBIE. Bonnie Lee. Bonnie Lee, ladies and gentlemen. Let's have a nice round of applause for Bonnie Lee. And say goodbye with the Ivar Smile... That was Bonnie Lee. Let's have one last round of applause for Bonnie Lee. Bonnie Lee.

(*BONNIE LEE gives a fainter "Ivar Smile": clothes bundled in her arm, she faces upstage and spanks her butt lightly, and returns to dressing room.*)

BARBIE. Now let's have a round of applause and we'll bring out Letanya. Letanya, ladies and gentlemen, Letanya. This is Letanya.

(*Music: Commodores "Funky Situation." LETANYA begins her performance. MELODY fidgets, getting more nervous, preparing for her debut. Eventually BONNIE LEE makes it back to the dressing room. As before, whenever and however it can be done, following scene occurs.*)

MELODY. Do I look OK for a star?

BONNIE LEE. I was star once. Always had to stay til closing.

MELODY. Is there anything else I should know? Like, is it different from amateur night?

BONNIE LEE. Just we go twice as long and get seven dollars. Amateur night's better, sometimes they let you pretend you are one if enough girls don't show up. And then there's this guy you'll see, middle of the runway. Real old guy, he's here every day, "Mr. Ivar." Practice your Karma, give it to him, he'll give it to you. Not the best, but steady.

MELODY. (*She's buzzing the light booth, gets an idea.*) Maybe a costume where I'm a beauty contestant, make a banner says "Miss Ivar!" (*Takes a nip from a pint bottle of Bacardi in her bag.*) Just want to calm down the butterflies, do you still get 'em? Want some? I want to be really really good.

BONNIE LEE. Don't let anyone see that, you better put it away. Stan'd fire you, no drinking in the building. That's why I take pills. You want one?

MELODY. (*Declines.*) Are there lotsa people down there?

BONNIE LEE. Kinda slow this time of day. I don't worry, in the alternate universe I'm doing fine.

MELODY. Uh huh. I think you maybe should stay out of that place. It sounds goofy.

(*Phone buzzes, MELODY reaches for it, BONNIE LEE gets it.*)

BONNIE LEE. Showtime. Starburst.

MELODY. Fukkin-fabulous!

(*And she goes down, stands near BARBIE.*

SPLIT SCENE—PART ONE. As LETANYA's act becomes more graphic, a shadow screen is set up, and LETANYA does her "dollar-act", as described.)

KENNY. We don't have the same legal arrangement here the Ivar had, so in order to keep us from getting arrested, let me tell you what she's doing: this part here, she's about to lip-sync—with her pussy, picture it:

(*Music: "It's a Fwuuunky, it's a fwuuunky, it's a fwuuunky, it's a Funky Situation…"*)

KENNY. She asked me to make a tight pin spot on that—. (*Coaching her along, as LETANYA does what he implies.*) Now watch what she does next—

(*LETANYA makes a fan out of three singles, inserts them vaginally.*)

KENNY. Now wave to the people.

(*LETANYA flexes, and the fan moves up and down between her legs.*)

KENNY. Like I say, the first time I spotted her show, I was pretty shocked. But after being here a couple weeks and seeing how things are, I realized she was a pretty classy act.

(*SPLIT SCENE—PART TWO. This should play out simultaneously with the previous KENNY / LETANYA action and dialogue.*

MELODY goes backstage next to BARBIE. Their exchange should be done in regular "backstage voices", it's not necessary for the audience to hear what they're saying—the visual should do it.)

BARBIE. Hey, nice to see you, glad they asked you back!
MELODY. I'm really jazzed! Do I look OK?
BARBIE. I was hoping to see you again. Oh, you got—(*Picks some lint off her.*)

(*MELODY observes LETANYA doing her dollar act: is a little put-off by it. LETANYA's song finishes. END SPLIT SCENE.*)

BARBIE. What's your name, quick, what's your name??
MELODY. Melody.
BARBIE. No, your—
MELODY. Stardust. Lady Stardust, like the Bowie song?

BARBIE. (*Of course, her enthusiasm evaporates once she returns to work.*) Letanya, Ladies and Gentlemen, Letanya. Let's have another round of applause for Letanya. ...Letanya. One more round of applause for Letanya, Ladies and Gentlemen, Letanya. Now we have a newcomer to the Ivar stage, a very pretty young lady and also the star of our show, Stardust ladies and gentlemen, let's have a big welcome for Lady Stardust.

(*Routine applause from the AUDIENCE, and much genuine happiness from MELODY. She is no Gypsy Rose Lee, but she's definitely got more style than BONNIE LEE and less raucous than LETANYA. At some point, while she's entertaining REX, music cuts out for a moment, like stop-action, so KENNY can throw in his comment.*)

KENNY. I gotta tell you— Look, I don't know what you're thinking, but I know what *they're* thinking. Listen to this:
MELODY. They love me, I'm beautiful!
REX. ...Hot little piece, I'd like to blow a wad across her face.

(*Normal performance resumes. MELODY is of course, no Vegas talent, but in comparison to the other girls, a high artist for attempting a costume and moving in time to the music. She is alert and happy as she can be, in her own world. At completion of her act:*)

BARBIE. Lady Stardust, ladies and gentlemen, that was—Lady Stardust! Let's hear it for Lady Stardust. A wonderful new addition to our show: Lady Stardust!
MELODY. (*Exiting, waves happily.*) Thank you guys!
BARBIE. Let's hear it for Lady Stardust. Lady Stardust and a whole lot more will be back later today, but first we're going to have a little break and a movie for you guys. Don't go away, we got more girls straight through til four in the morning...

(*Intermission music starts. MELODY joins BARBIE at the side of the stage to re-dress. BARBIE's phone starts buzzing.*)

MELODY. Pretty good, huh?

(*Phone buzzes.*)

BARBIE. –Just a minute. Yeah? (*Separately, to MELODY*) Where you going on your break?
KENNY. (*Simultaneous with BARBIE's question.*) Where's she going on her break?
MELODY. Gonna see Stan.
KENNY. Tell her to wait for me a minute.

(*General restless activity as the intermission proceeds, nothing needs to be spoken. MELODY is assisted by BARBIE in dressing, and then makes her way towards the lobby.*)

KENNY. Melody—you got a minute? What are you doing between shows?
MELODY. You mean like later?

(*REX shuffles up.*)

REX. Hey. Very pretty girl. Cute, too.
MELODY. Thank you very much.
REX. You're new. I like you.
MELODY. Thank you.
KENNY. Come on Rex, move on out... We're talking. Go.

(*REX shuffles out.*)

KENNY. That fukkin turd's in here 12 hours a day, you wonder if he ever takes a bath.
MELODY. No reason to be mean to him. He's sweet.
KENNY. Take a whiff. –You want some gum? Freshen-up. Squirts in your mouth.
MELODY. You trying to tell me something?
KENNY. (*Sees that MELODY doesn't quite know who he is.*) We met before, night you got here? I'm Kenny, I do your lights and music.
MELODY. Oh, cool.
KENNY. So now you're "Lady Stardust?"
MELODY. Well, show business you know, glamorous name like the movie stars.

KENNY. You want to be in movies?

MELODY. (*Almost excited.*) Really???

STAN. Hey you, the famous one: Come on in for a minute...

REX. Pretty girl Stan. You gonna keep her, aren't ya?

STAN. She'll be around a lot, don't worry. (*To MELODY.*) C'mon in, I got something for you.

MELODY. (*To KENNY.*) Thanks for the bubble-gum. And my lights.

STAN. (*To KENNY.*) Where're you going?

KENNY. Air. Be right back.

STAN. Fifteen minutes.

(*STAN leads MELODY off. REX goes away.*)

SCENE SEVEN

(*KENNY goes outside, squints and shields eyes.*)

KENNY. Aaaach— sunlight.

(*In front of the theater, LEONARD passes by: a Hollywood Boulevard type: red plaid shirt, cut-offs, very gay hair; not sure he recognizes a former trick.*)

LEONARD. Kenny?

KENNY. Oh—Hi Leonard.

LEONARD. I'm was just goin' into the Gaslight. But hey, if you want to stop over man, rather take a sure thing than go fishin'.

KENNY. Can't, I'm just on a break, I gotta go back in.

LEONARD. You work here???

KENNY. I told you I worked at a theater.

LEONARD. Fukkin' beaver palace. You whore. Are you straight?

KENNY. I'm not anything, just go on. I gotta show a movie in ten minutes.

LEONARD. Come over my place a minute. Great mouth. Best on the boulevard I'd say.

(*REX goes hobbling past. The guy's postures and attitudes alter, trying to hide their existence from the fact of daylight. REX takes little if any notice of them. Just returns to his seat by the runway and waits.*)

LEONARD. They fixed the doors at the library men's room: Come on. Next door, right now. Got a load for you.
KENNY. I gotta get back to the booth.
LEONARD. I'll be quick.
KENNY. (*Looks both ways.*) Go into the stall, I'll be there in a minute.

SCENE EIGHT

(*STAN and MELODY, a private scene together in the box office. She's just finished blowing him. [If possible, another dancer performs simultaneously with this scene.]*)

STAN. Man, you're good.
MELODY. So're you. "Just Right." (*Fusses a little.*) I don't mind doing this, I want to. I like it, but um: Are you married, or anything?
STAN. Look, aren't you on in a couple minutes?
MELODY. (*Thinks he's kidding.*) Stan, you just SAW my show.
STAN. (*He says nothing, but face and gesture says he forgot all about that.*)
MELODY. —So you are married. She doesn't mind you having girlfriends?
STAN. Why you asking? You like three ways? Or maybe just you two and I'll watch?
MELODY. (*That's not at all what she had in mind, but she readjusts and rides the train.*) If that's what you want. (*Humble.*) If you'd like that.
STAN. HA. My wife's a regular catholic girl, a whore in the bedroom, which means anything I want I gotta pay for.
MELODY. I just meant, like, I like you. Older guys can be... real nice.

STAN. No, no: Felecia sees me with you, WHOOOH—- there goes half my house and everything I own, AND the theater.
MELODY. Well she's got to know that you play around, I mean, you're like Hugh Hefner here. Just... dirtier.
STAN. So're you. (*They both laugh.*) No, don't worry about messing things up. We'll keep things loose. Nice n' easy.
MELODY. Sure: Good. Good.

(*LIGHTS OUT on them, and KENNY comes forward.*)

KENNY. For a short period Stan wanted to clean up the place a little bit, I don't know why. Like all the guys jerking off, what else are they there for? It's showtime: Gentlemen, pitch your tents!" It was like seeing worms come out after a rain. So the deal was, in addition to the announcement you heard me make, I was supposed to shine the spot on a guy. You think that stopped them? — One stood up and turned around. And another time, the doorman, Marty, he took the tickets and was like a bouncer? Nice guy but small and skinny. He went with his flashlight and asked someone to put it away, and the guy pulled a gun on him. Marty disappeared out the side door, the other guy ran up the aisle, and the poor girl on stage broke into a panic. But she stayed on stage. Twenty minutes, seven bucks. That's the law.

SCENE NINE

(*MELODY as a Star.*)

KENNY. (*Over mic.*) All right guys, it's quarter to four and someone's probably got to work tomorrow, but before we close the Tuesday midnight show, hold on for the Star of the Show, let's have a round of applause for a heavenly body: Lady Stardust, guys: Lady Stardust.

(*MELODY performs very nicely. Way short of classic elegance. However, she is so concentrated within her private personal vision, she lives out for us the rich, abundant glory that appears in her mind. At some point during her strip.*)

MELODY. Hey everyone: guess what? I just found out it's Rex's birthday! Yaaay!

(*She reveals that she's wearing a black t-shirt with "MR. IVAR" in white iron-on letters. She massages the shirt between her hands and breasts before pulling the shirt off and pulling it over REX's face. Now that REX is essentially hooded and blindfolded, MELODY wraps her legs around his head or squeezes her breasts in his face or both. Big party time. Once the fun is over, she reclaims her grace and completes her performance.*)

KENNY. I tell you something about that shirt, when the girls made that for him— they all made it for him, Melody's just the one who gave it to him— that old geezer never took it off. Never. Same shirt always. The girls liked him, I don't know why. Maybe cuz they wore perfume, some of them, they couldn't notice, but to me he always smelled like he was wearing a diaper. Anyway. Let's jump ahead a few days for another special event every week: Camera night.

Brian Hoover in *Follies of Grandeur* (later titled *An Ivar Memoir*) at Theater for the New City, New York. (2006) Photo credit: Peter Madero

SCENE TEN

(*Camera Night.*)

KENNY. (*On mic.*) That's it for the movie-time, but it's Wednesday night, Camera Night is coming up next, so gents, don't go away.

(*Intermission music on. In the Dressing Room: MELODY is drawing on a paper fan with a colored marker. BONNIE LEE wanders in.*)

BONNIE LEE. What're you making?
MELODY. I used to have a butterfly costume but I saw a picture at the library of this old dancer from the forties dressed like a bird? All in feathers, and these giant fans. I thought that would be really neat.
BONNIE LEE. I never seen that kind of stuff.
MELODY. Well, in the past things were really fancier. So I'm gonna make one. But I could only find little fans to start. So I'm gonna be Chinese. It will be fun for the camera show.
BONNIE LEE. I hate camera night. I don't like knowing people have pictures of me. Sometimes I check the magazine stand to make sure they're not making money off me. I'd do that.

(*Phone buzzes. MELODY picks it up.*)

MELODY. Dressing room, Melody. Yeah?
KENNY. Hey, Kenny here. Stan wants to talk to you, he's backstage with Barbie.
MELODY. Sure. Should I go down?
KENNY. Is that an offer?
MELODY. (*Pissed off.*) Fuck, man—!
KENNY. Sorry. Hey, Melody, would you be up for like going to a movie or a play with me after Camera Night? I'm off in a half hour and you're not back til the midnight show.
MELODY. I don't know, maybe. I don't like to mix business with, whatever, social life at least.
KENNY. It's not social, it's just friendly.
MELODY. I'll let you know, I got to go downstairs.

(*MELODY goes downstairs to STAN. BARBIE retreats to her reading. Happy and flirtatious, MELODY shows STAN her paper fan.*)

MELODY. Stan look, it's part of a new idea, you like it? I figure since I'm the star I should keep doing new things, what do you think?

STAN. Nice. Oh, Melody, I gotta tell ya: I have a new girl coming in, she's gonna be the new star.

MELODY. (*Would have a line here if she knew what to say.*)

STAN. I just gotta make a change, no big deal

MELODY. Why, what's wrong: I thought I was OK, did I do something?

STAN. No, you're fine. You've had, what: six, seven weeks?

MELODY. Five.

STAN. So it's time to make a change, she'll be next, we'll make room for you after.

MELODY. But *starting*, why does anyone have to start in my place? I thought you were gonna—uh— Do I still have a job here?

STAN. Nothing's changed. Only difference is your schedule.

MELODY. There's a schedule?

STAN. Now you're going to come in around eleven or twelve the days you want to work, you call the booth, whoever's up there will tell you what they got. Depends on how many girls come in, but you'll always get at least one show a day, that I promise.

MELODY. But Stan— couldn't you make it that way? So I can have at least even two? I mean, one show a day, that's only forty-nine dollars a week.

STAN. Look, I know you need a little help: Now, I got a friend called this morning, a performer, he's in a tight spot, needs an assistant right away. Like to be a magician's assistant?

MELODY. Those girls are usually real beautiful...

STAN. You're good enough. I'll give him a call, you go see him, eh?

MELODY. Can I still keep my job here?

(*STAN leaves MELODY alone. During the following, he'll retrieve FAWN, and lead her to the dressing room exactly as he did with MELODY.*)

BARBIE. What's the matter?

MELODY. Stan got another girl. Some "Girl" took my place—I'm supposed to be the star. I am. I should quit. I'm just going to get my stuff and walk out of here.

BARBIE. Just go up to the dressing room. Relax.

MELODY. How am I going to pay for my room? —I don't want to go into the dressing room, I'm gonna look so stupid. I thought I had three more shows tonight.

BARBIE. Hey, I'm done after this, you want to go with me and get coffee?

MELODY. Maybe. Stan said he'd introduce me to a friend about another job. But I want to stay here!

BARBIE. Doing what?

MELODY. I don't know: a magician's assistant. But what does a magician's assistant DO, I mean, would I have to go to magic school or something? How am I gonna keep my hotel room.

BARBIE. You know, sometimes girls here share a room. I don't know if you'd be interested, but I got a nice place, and, I like you. Well, NO I mean, you... I—I mean... you're very pretty.

MELODY. Aren't you upstairs o' me?

BARBIE. It's a little more expensive, but cheaper to share. We could, you know, hang out. It'd be fun. C'mon, I'm out after the camera show—or no, I'll say I don't feel good, Kenny'll cover for me.

MELODY. I'd like that.

(*MELODY goes upstairs, passes STAN. He makes no unkind notice of her.*)

BARBIE. (*Interior thought.*) "We could save money, share expenses. We could wake up together, I'd fix her orange juice and cranberry muffins and when my career gets going she could come see me at the night clubs: I'd get it together a lot faster if I had someone to take care of..."

(*In the dressing room, FAWN is making herself at home with the other girls—and sitting in MELODY's chair. MELODY says little or nothing, moves gingerly around FAWN to collect her things and leave.*)

FAWN. Not what I'm used to, but I'm just doing this for fun. I was Prima Ballerina with the San Francisco ballet. Now that my career's ended, I thought I'd test the waters in Hollywood.

LETANYA. Really. Name a ballet.

FAWN. (*Thinks a bit.*) Swan Lake.

BONNIE LEE. Oooo, pretty! What part?

FAWN. The title role. I'd still be there if it wasn't for that robbery. The gun. The window. That horrible fall. I can't go on-point ever since.

(*Intermission ends; BARBIE returns to reality.*)

KENNY. That's our intermission; now let's continue our Camera Night, let's have a round of applause, let's bring out Barbie again, ladies and gentlemen: Barbie.

BARBIE. Welcome back, ladies and gentlemen, let's keep our Camera Night going, hope you changed your film rolls so you'll have more of us to take home. Next up, we have a newcomer to the Ivar stage, a very pretty lady and Star of the show, let's have a good hand and bring out Fawn, ladies and gentlemen: Fawn…

(*FAWN begins her performance. As she proceeds, MELODY pauses on her way out to watch her, taking a seat in the audience. At the conclusion of FAWN's performance, a crackling of flashbulbs, and a couple stray ones as she collects her clothes to leave.*)

BARBIE. Fawn, ladies and gentlemen: the Star of our show, Fawn …and now say goodnight with the Ivar smile…

(*FAWN doesn't know what that is, so she continues without pause, smiles and waves goodbye, and goes off.*)

SCENE ELEVEN

(*Outside, in front of the theater, after Camera Night.*

BARBIE collects MELODY from the audience and they go out together.)

KENNY. Melody— You leaving? I'm off as soon as Al shows up. Think you'd like to do something?
MELODY. Oh, I can't tonight. I gotta do some stuff with Barbie.

(*REX shuffles up.*)

REX. Oh. Hey. Hey. Got some good ones. Good pictures of your show.
MELODY. But I'm not in it.
REX. From last week, silly.
MELODY. Oh. Yeah.
KENNY. Rex, you're missing the show.
REX. It's intermission, don't bother me. (*To BARBIE.*) When're you gonna do those new songs you promised me, Barbie?
BARBIE. Any day Rex. I'm working on them really hard.
REX. Now they got a new star, huh? You're not leaving us are you?
MELODY. (*Sweet, assures him.*) I'm not going anywhere.
REX. Don't try it, I'll just come get you and bring you back. And thanks again for the shirt last week. You really made me feel special.
MELODY. You do the same for all of us.
KENNY. Rex, we're talking here—
REX. I'll show you those pictures I got, you'll see 'em. –and don't forget my new songs!

(*REX shuffles away.*)

MELODY. He's so sweet.
KENNY. Sweet, he's a one-man monster movie.
MELODY. You can be fukkin nasty sometimes, you know?
KENNY. Sorry.

MELODY. I liked having my picture out front. Huh. You think Stan's gonna take my picture out from the show window?

(*The Scene transforms, without pause: at home with BARBIE and MELODY, in BARBIE's hotel room.*)

SCENE TWELVE

(*In BARBIE's hotel room.*)

BARBIE. Well, not for a year or two, according to the one you replaced. Do you have everything put away?

MELODY. It's nice you made space for me so fast.

BARBIE. Well, I don't have much to start with so it wasn't hard.

MELODY. Thanks for letting me stay with you. It's just temporary?

BARBIE. Why should it be temporary? We're "room-mates," helping each other out. With our careers.

MELODY. Huh. I never thought of it as a career.

BARBIE. Start. That's why I told Stan I wouldn't dance anymore, just be MC and do my singing.

MELODY. You still strip.

BARBIE. Not a real strip. The little bit I do doesn't interfere with my professional integrity.

MELODY. We're from different worlds.

BARBIE. I've been in Hollywood long enough to know how things work.

MELODY. I'm just grateful for some money and a place to stay.

BARBIE. All I need from you now, darling, is ten dollars for tonight, that'll be enough, OK?

MELODY. Mine was fourteen.

BARBIE. I was in one of those but we're in a good room now. So your half's ten.

MELODY. OK. I thought we'd be saving some money.

BARBIE. We are. (*Shows a window.*) And you get to be two floors higher: look what's out the window: Capitol Records! It's perfect, man. Regular gig, and Capitol Records like, right there! We're just so close to the center of everything. When I had my picture out front a guy came in from a recording studio. This is Hollywood, things can happen.

MELODY. Did anything come outta that? When the recording guy saw your picture?

BARBIE. No, but it was really exciting for a couple days. He was talking about the Hollywood Bowl, and record contracts. I bought a dress. I still got it, so when my break comes, I'm ready.

MELODY. I got my break. Maybe my new name, instead o' Lady Stardust: "Dusty"

BARBIE. Jeez, drama. Knock it off. You know Melody: at the Ivar, no one cares about the star. I know it means more to you, but, since that changed... you've been a lot nicer.

MELODY. Just time to come to earth and meet the humans, I guess.

BARBIE. (*Shyly embraces MELODY, who relaxes into it.*) Welcome home.

MELODY. Thank you.

BARBIE. I liked you from when I first saw you. Could you tell?

MELODY. Well you must see everyone, so I guess that's a compliment. Where can I put this?

BARBIE. I'll clear a drawer for you tomorrow, for now just leave things in your bag.

MELODY. Sure, I don't want to be in the way. Stan called a guy, so I can see someone tomorrow about a job. If it works out, maybe we could get an even bigger room!

BARBIE. Yeah, yeah: maybe I could pick up a few extra gigs—we could even get a house together.

MELODY. A whole house... wow.

BARBIE. But if that job works out, are you going to leave the theater?

MELODY. No! I'd never want to be so famous I give up the theater. I'm happy there. Maybe I could talk to Stan, he could get you something too.

BARBIE. (*Reluctant.*) He did before...

MELODY. He knows lots of people. Heck, someone told me he owns the Pantages, is that true?

BARBIE. I heard that but it's hard to believe, so I'm not sure.

MELODY. I'll ask him for you. Yeah, I do want to talk to him, he still likes me. Maybe set up a nightclub thing for you. And I could be your introducer!

BARBIE. Truth about Stan is he's a small-potato guy: what I really need is talk to Stigwood or someone. Stigwood could get me seen by a lot of people, give me a chance to, reach way out there, I could really tell people my music, what I'm all about.

MELODY. Maybe Stan knows him.

BARBIE. I never thought of that. Could you find out for me?

MELODY. Sure. (*Snuggles into Barbie's arms.*)

BARBIE. You know what scares me... what if I don't get famous? What if this is all there is?

MELODY. You ever been anywhere better? So hold on to it. Want to sing for me?

BARBIE. Not right now, I got to save my voice. And I want to reach millions of people!

(*LIGHTS OUT on this scene.*)

SCENE THIRTEEN

(*Shadow Scene.*

KENNY comes forward to introduce the next shadow scene.)

KENNY. You don't need to watch them act out this part, you know what that's like. Let me tell you about this other girl came through for a couple weeks: She called herself "Peaches" from guess-where: Georgia. Peaches the Georgia Peach. Clever, huh? She wasn't very pretty, had straight, kind of flat-red color hair, and bad teeth. Real ugly smile, but she smiled a lot. I watched this girl, butt-ass naked, walking on her knees down the runway—and I think she'd had a baby and her tits were huge, or swollen— And she could squeeze them and hit guys in the face with her milk.

(*In shadow we see the men lean forward, stretching their necks with their tongues out, wagging, to get even the tiniest taste.*)

KENNY. I watched this guy tilt his head back, to let his whole face be covered in this fine, milky spray. Boy, did they go for that.

(*Shadow scene dissolves.*)

SCENE FOURTEEN

(*KENNY's apartment.*

KENNY brings MELODY in to his apartment; there's a shirt for him to change into, and some soft- porn magazines, like Blueboy or Mandate underneath it.)

KENNY. Come on in. So here's where I live.

MELODY. Nice. You just move here?

KENNY. About a year ago.

MELODY. Then what are the boxes for?

KENNY. I figure why unpack, I'll move again eventually. I still get stuff when I need it.

MELODY. Oh, smart.

KENNY. I just want to change shirts before the movie, just be a minute.

MELODY. Not just a trick to get me into your apartment.

KENNY. It about takes that. I've been wanting to get together with you since you started. But you've been a little more open lately. Or is this just a trick to make me give you more spots on the schedule?

MELODY. Well in fact, I was on an interview today. Thinking of, you know, developing more of my career and trying things.

KENNY. Oh? As what?

MELODY. Stan set me up with this guy. I'm not going to take it though. He says he does a magic act at some place, the "Magic Castle." Sounds like a part of a miniature golf course.

KENNY. The Magic Castle was Houdini's house. It's up on Franklin, it's a very exclusive club.

MELODY. Oh? All it was was to carry out a bunch of sticks and trays and stuff.

KENNY. I guess the interview didn't go so good.

MELODY. I was so nervous, I started feeling like an idiot. It's not something I'd want to do. Besides, I spoke with Stan, and because I asked he set up an appointment for Barbie to sing at a high-class restaurant. I was thinking maybe of trying that out, you know, if she'd let me. I was thinking we could sing a duet.

KENNY. Guess you're better off where you are. (*Sees magazines, smoothly turns them face down.*) I didn't have a chance to clean up, sorry. You want to wait for a minute—

(*He turns his back to change shirts. While he's doing this, MELODY turns one of the magazines face up, then puts it back like it was. He does not see her do either of these things.*)

MELODY. Are you gay?

KENNY. Sometimes. Is that a problem? There's a Playboy in there too.

MELODY. No, it's just that, I don't know why you brought me here then.

KENNY. I'm not gonna be gay with you. I like you. —So I thought we could go this movie over at La Brea, two-dollar movie shows old classics, I think there's *His Girl Friday*. Sounds good?

(*MELODY is confused, doesn't respond. KENNY sits next to her.*)

KENNY. Or if there's something else you'd like more recent that'd be OK too. There's *Pretty Baby* or *Deerhunter*'s supposed to be good. You OK?

MELODY. You don't act gay.

KENNY. What's your point.

MELODY. I guess I don't have one.

KENNY. I think you're pretty, OK? I seen all kinda crap in that place for the time I been there, When I threw the spot down on you... I saw a little piece of it shine back.

(*She takes his hand, this initiates an intensifying make-out session.*)

KENNY. —Hold on: let me turn the lights off.

(Passion resumes, and which will fade out once it's obvious that they're going to be late for the eight o'clock show. LIGHTS OFF, and we only see shadow or faint candlelight: he's trying to enter her but getting no place.)

KENNY. uhh— What's the problem—?
MELODY. No, nothing's wrong—
KENNY. Damn.
MELODY. Just wait a minute—
KENNY. I had as much trouble openin' oysters.
MELODY. Don't make fun of me. I just need to relax.
KENNY. About what?
MELODY. Sometimes I get nervous with younger guys. Try using your tongue first.
KENNY. Really? I've never done that.
MELODY. If you do that for a while, that will make me relax.
KENNY. Really? Why?
MELODY. It's something my dad used to do.
KENNY. Did you like that?
MELODY. I got used to it. Now I like it.
KENNY. OK. *(He hesitates.)*
MELODY. I did it for you.
KENNY. Can I use poppers?
MELODY. Sure.

(LIGHTS FADE OUT on this portion.)

SCENE FIFTEEN

(Back at the theater.

BARBIE would be finishing a rousing song, if she weren't so restless, impatient and bored. She sings "That's Entertainment," but forgets the words. [NOTE: "That's Entertainment" requires a separate licensing agreement with Chappell & Co., Inc. (ASCAP) if used in production.]) She stops singing but the recorded tape continues.)

BARBIE. Mr. Tape Man, I don't think I'm going to finish this song, OK? Mr. Tape Man? Hey!

MAN'S VOICE. (*From back of the house.*) What?

BARBIE. Stop the song, please.

(*Tape is punched off. Buzz of silence.*)

BARBIE. My voice is a little strained, you guys would rather see me strip anyway, right? Mr. Tape Man, can I have my dance music please?

(*A tape is plunked in, and started midway into the song. BARBIE's Strip: Music starts. She takes off her sweatshirt, folds it up and places it on the floor. Puts her arms up, like a "What do you think?" pose. Turns front and back, side a, side b. She sits on the floor and takes off her boots. She stands up and takes off her jeans, has to sit to finish them completely, folds and places them on top of her sweatshirt. Again, the "What do you think?" pose. Turns front and back, side a, side b, and when she's done, picks up her clothes and waves towards the light booth. Music plunked off.*)

BARBIE. OK, guys that's it, we're going to take an intermission— What? You really want me to sing another song? (*She is extremely complimented.*)

SCENE SIXTEEN

(*Post sex discussion.*)

MELODY. You seem quiet.

KENNY. Quiet is ok.

MELODY. That was nice. I was surprised. For being, you know.

KENNY. Hell Melody, it's sex, not a trapeze act. Anyone can do it.

MELODY. Not "anyone."

KENNY. Apparently.

MELODY. Oh.

KENNY. About this other stuff, you know the, uh.

MELODY. What?

KENNY. Your dad. What's that about?

MELODY. I don't know. There's really nothing to tell. Just from when I was a little girl in a little bed. I used to had a yellow like flannel blanket? with little toys printed all over? And I'd be asleep all cozy but I'd start and go cold, cuz I'd know: Wait a minute. A crack o' light. And the shadow in the doorway. There's no more to it than that. Head rocking against the headboard. No background music. No violence. I learned about that, no big deal. Smell of drunk sweat. Mostly quiet, I learned that pretty fast too, not to make any sound. Sometimes I'd be asleep when it started, but I got to where I could mostly stay asleep or at least act like it til it was over. And I learned when it hurt how to think of something else and later on it didn't even hurt and I didn't have to think at all, just go completely blank, a little boat on the waves, rocking against the headboard. He had this shirt sometimes that had little twinkles on it, and red and black sort of tic-tac-toes. I just kept still and patient until he finished. Don't know why he stopped though. A little after my 11th birthday, and he just kind of... stopped. It was normal by that time, and by that age, you know, it was feeling pretty good, so I thought I did something wrong. Eventually I found out not every girl in fourth grade was banging their dad. I felt pretty stupid about that. Real stupid. It's over. Like I say, there's nothing to say.

KENNY. Let go of my hand.

MELODY. Hurt?

KENNY. Just wet. (*Gives her his other hand.*)

(*Music intro for the next scene comes up under...*)

MELODY. (*All new topic, all new energy. *that doesn't necessarily mean light-hearted.*) I'm making more costumes. Maybe like a Spanish type. And then I saw this one in a book, a bird.

KENNY. Bird? Buncha feathers making a mess? That's a stupid idea.

MELODY. Oh. Well. Oh.

SCENE SEVENTEEN

STAN. In case any of you came in to see "Gypsy", by now you can tell I don't run that kind of show. I remember the old days, I like what I got now. What Letanya does in my place is fine with me. But she was just old enough to come in at the tail-end of that era. Let's go back about twenty years, to the kind of act she used to do when she was a kid in Detroit.

(*LETANYA performs an exquisite, elegant classic strip tease. As it nears its completion, it's overtaken by present-day performance of the Ivar girls in their much less refined manner. As MELODY leaves the theater, she takes a look back at both, and exits out onto the street.*)

SCENE EIGHTEEN

REX. Melody—
MELODY. Not tonight Rex, I'm really tired.
REX. I got something for you. Something to show you.

(*This catches her interest, and she waits.*)

REX.   See what I took on camera night? Here's Alexa... That's Bonnie Lee. This one look familiar?
MELODY. (*Her head jerks back.*) That's horrible...
REX. 'ts you. Real pretty, furry little muff, eh?
MELODY. My legs are fat, tits all flopped to the side, I don't even have a head, this is just parts.
REX. Nice parts though, I thought you'd like it.
MELODY. No, no I don't. Give it to me, you can take another one.
REX. At my place?
MELODY. No way.
REX. (*Endearing, not lecherous.*) Aw sweetie, give an old man a break. I know how I look. There was a time girls went for me, had all I wanted. 'f you knew me then you'd eat out of my hand. Now you're on your side, I'm on my side. I'm just looking at you through the years.

MELODY. There's no years, I'm right in front of you.

REX. There's nothing wrong with pictures, they just keep you nice as you are now. Your little titties. Cute little pussy on you, mmmm, taste it.

MELODY. You know Rex, everybody wants to be liked, I want to be liked, I want to like you, but you make yourself so gahdam disgusting. Just gimme the pictures and I'll get out of here, Jeezis.

REX. (*Gives them to her.*) Why you so uppity all of a sudden? This is your job: You're a cute little girl, you won't stay that way forever. Picture helps hold it still, give you something to remember. I'll remember you all my life.

MELODY. Which is what: five years or something.

REX. Might be. Might be. Once I'm gone, you'll still have me in your head, every day, all you want. Rest of your life too. Thanks, Melody. I'll see you tomorrow.

SCENE NINETEEN

(*BARBIE and MELODY waking up at home.*)

MELODY. Barbie – Wake up

BARBIE. Hmm… why?

MELODY. Eight o'clock. Coffee's ready. Got you juice.

BARBIE. What're you doing all this for man? I did four shows yesterday…

MELODY. (*Reminding.*) Spaghetti Factory? Ten A.M.?

BARBIE. The audition—shit. I… I can't go there, my voice is tired. I have to wait.

MELODY. You can wait til ten, then you sing. In the meantime, get ready. What are you going to wear?

BARBIE. What're you buggin me for, huh? I don't want this shit. Maybe later it'd be nice, but I worked hard.

MELODY. If you're going to be famous, you're going to work harder. Might as well get used to it, build up your performance muscles.

(*MELODY tries to snuggle in, and is shoved away.*)

BARBIE. Knock it off. What is this crap anyway?

MELODY. Cranberry muffins. I went down to the Ranch Market.

BARBIE. All that way? You could've just stayed at the counter, let me sleep.

MELODY. I wanted to share it with you.

BARBIE. (*Takes a bite.*) Mmmm. uh-uh. You have the rest, I don't like this.

MELODY. I thought you liked those.

BARBIE. They always looked good, but I never had one. Didn't want to spend the money. They don't taste like they look. I think they got a lot of cyclamates in 'em anyway. Might give me cancer.

MELODY. There's no cyclamates in cranberries.

BARBIE. Something then. Something's not safe about them. I better just not go to that audition. I got more shows today, I can't bruise my vocal chords. I could develop the flu or something, can't afford to miss the work.

MELODY. At least call.

BARBIE. What are you whining about, it's my career. If I call, they'll think I'm unreliable. I'll just not go, show up some time tomorrow and act like they told me the wrong time, get all indignant, and gracious about it, and we'll set up something else later, when I feel like it. When I'm ready.

MELODY. You'd be ready if you wanted.

BARBIE. Not with these crumbs in my throat. I know you wanted to do something nice, but next time, ask me first. This might really fuck up my performance. Where'd you get the idea I liked cranberry muffins, for cripes sake?

MELODY. (*Snuggles in.*) You said you used to look at 'em.

BARBIE. Not to you.

MELODY. How's your coffee.

BARBIE. Now I won't be able to get back to sleep. This is gonna make me have a hard day, I'm singing at 11:30, 2:00, 5:30 and 9:00, that's 12 songs. I'm gonna need treatment when this day's over.

MELODY. Twelve songs in twelve hours, well sorry. I didn't realize you were going to be dragging an anvil down the runway with your vocal chords, I would have been more considerate.

BARBIE. That's just what I mean, you don't understand how hard it is for me, how much I put into it for what I get back. Try and poke fun at me, well you try and sing and see who gives you two dollars. Not everyone can do what I do.

MELODY. Or what I do.

BARBIE. Everyone does. (*Continues eating the muffin.*) Well this is the last time I'll ever think about eating a cranberry muffin. You know what I've always wanted? Corn muffin. That would have been really good.

MELODY. Wouldn't it.

SCENE TWENTY

(*KENNY comes in to relate another shadow scene: TIFFANY.*)

KENNY. We had this other girl—you know how in the seventies, the look for a lot of girls was straight brown hair, parted down the middle, they all looked like Joni Mitchell? Well Tiffany was like that, a really pretty girl, like from out of a cornfield. Saddest girl I ever met. She was about five- foot four, and seven months pregnant. And I'm in the light booth and the phone buzzes, I say "Light booth" and she says "I don't want to live." And I'd say "Hello Tiffany, you're on in five minutes" and she'd say "I want to kill myself." So she'd come out on stage, walking so careful down the runway, one arm protecting her belly, one held out straight ahead, like she's afraid she would fall. —When I did the announcing, I always introduced her as "Two Girls in One" but when Barbie did it, all she said was "Tiffany ladies and gentlemen: Tiffany." And she'd do her floorwork, she'd get down on the runway and open her legs, and it was incredible how intensely the men looked up her. Straining, trying to see, what? Life? One even used a flashlight so he could see what? Deeper? What were they looking for, what did they think they were going to see? It's right in front of them. So much life, all those "Humans"—separated, women here, men there. And between them: Void.

SCENE TWENTY-ONE

(*The scene transforms, without pause, to MELODY's arrival as a resident in KENNY's apartment.*)

KENNY. Do you have everything put away?

MELODY. It's nice you made space for me so fast.

KENNY. Well, you don't have much to start with so it isn't hard.

MELODY. Thanks for letting me stay with you. It's just temporary?

KENNY. Don't worry about it, you're here as long as you need. Not permanent but as long as you need. I've never lived with anyone, this'll be a good experiment.

MELODY. And I'm like a crayfish or something?

KENNY. You are such a child. Big switch from what you do at the theater.

MELODY. What can I tell you, I'm an actress. So like, should I do housework or something? You sure you don't want money?

KENNY. Yeah, it would help if you could keep the place neat. I will too, it's not like you're the hired girl.

MELODY. I'm good at cooking when I have a stove. Do you like to eat?

KENNY. I do it once in a while. Now just because you're with me doesn't mean we have to sleep together.

MELODY. (*Suppressed alarm, frightened for her security.*) But I want to.

KENNY. OK. OK, that can work.

MELODY. Do I get my own key?

KENNY. You don't really need one. We both work at the same place, and I'll be here and there at most all the same times you are.

MELODY. Well still, to make it easier on you—

KENNY. Sometimes I have people over. It wouldn't be nice of me.

MELODY. OK. Ok, that can work. You wouldn't want to do a three-way?

KENNY. The girl always gets left out.

MELODY. You like being with me don't you?

KENNY. Oh yeah. It's neat.

(*MELODY drapes some fabric across the bed.*)

MELODY. Do you think this is pretty?

KENNY. Yeah but I don't like that there. Here's a question: why do all the police know your name?

MELODY. Common sense: I want to know where the help is.

KENNY. Do you ever, uh, get together with any of them?

MELODY. I do not, but if I do, I promise to invite you so you can have your "three-way."

(They laugh and goof— it looks like we might be in for another sex scene.)

KENNY. You wearing perfume?

MELODY. No, just some powder maybe, but that was this morning.

KENNY. Why don't you go shower off, I'll put your stuff away. *(In narration mode.)* You meet a guy, nice looks, hot sex, next morning he starts talking about his crazy family and I'm glad he goes, I give him a fake phone number. Get another one. Girl comes up, talks about her old boyfriends and how I'm so much nicer and I try and find out why, soon as I can, I fix that and she's gone. Free for another one. Most people, all they leave is a phone number and maybe a sheet to wash. Now it's bits of glitter and sequins in the carpet. Now any time I want to go home, guess what? There's someone else there, and I brought her: why don't I like that? I asked her how things were going with Barbie, or if she had any other friends around... neither of us said it out loud, but she understood, she understands a lot about people. I like it like the way it is at the theater: girl comes out, OK, great, had enough of you, who's next? You know, variety. Keep em moving. From up in the light booth, I'm so far away, up in the ceiling and looking down over it all. On the other side of the spotlight. I see it all and no one sees me.

SCENE TWENTY-ONE

(*MELODY is on the runway, she pauses before a patron.*)

ROLLY. Hey—hey—

(*MELODY smiles, pauses. Tips divert her attention and she moves away. MELODY does floor work for a patron opposite him; while she's leaning back, he whispers, adventurous, urgent:*)

ROLLY. Come out with me! Come out with me!

(*She flirtatiously ignores him, continues her performance. He pulls a gift from his bag and sets it on the runway: She leans back to retrieve it, and opens it: a feather boa: she grandly extracts it from the box and wraps herself in its luxury, all within context of the performance.*)

ROLLY. Out front? When you're done? Side door, near the bar. So pretty. So pretty.

(*Other girls watch her perform, speak her thoughts: but they've been through it, now they're bored. Not derisive, they've already lived through the excitement and they're tired:*)

ALL DANCERS. (*Randomly.*) Does he have a nice car? Maybe he's an agent and I'll be discovered! He'll take me to Musso and Franks! The Brown Derby! "I'll never be hungry again." Someone to buy me clothes! Get married. House in the hills, and beautiful cars. Swimming naked together.... Someone to sleep with, someone to wake up with. Someone to hold me, someone to hold. Someone to care.

KENNY. (*As announcer.*) Melody, ladies and gentlemen: that's was Melody.

(*She gathers her tips in hand, and waves as she exits, a "secret nod" to her suitor.*)

MELODY. Love you guys. Love you!

(She races to the dressing room, the girls continue reciting they're wisps of hope. Downstairs, LETANYA takes the stage, and the spirit is old and dim. She reaches a point where the scene holds in tableaux, while MELODY dresses with excitement: again, the vocalization continues throughout, FAWN is in the dressing room.)

FAWN. Candyman's a nice guy, I went out with him before.

MELODY. Does he go out with everyone?

FAWN. Not particularly. Not usually. I went out with him. We went to a mansion in Beverly Hills. I swam naked for him and he served us dinner at the poolside.

MELODY. You're making it up.

FAWN. How would you know? You'll know if I was making it up when you get there. Then you'll see. There were fireflies in the palm trees.

MELODY. Fireflies don't go up that high. –I just want a clean bed and a shower that works. Who knows, who knows. Meet the right man, and I might even get a house. Come here every day in a taxi. *(Buzzes the booth.)* Kenny? I'm not doing my next show, you got a space at the end?

KENNY. Now you can watch them both: look at it, you can see it but neither of them can. She sees—what: "Jane Mansfield" coming down the stairs to meet "Sam Elliot." He's a trawler, reeling in another fish. And I see a lot of energy spinning out to no real purpose, and one little girl I've got to take care of.

ALL DANCERS. *(Continuing, randomly.)* Jewelry! Perfume! White-wall tires. Academy awards. Jet to Europe. Las Vegas: I'll go to Las Vegas and star in a revue! A family, children, Ocean Voyage to London. Movie premieres. Cocktail parties. Autograph signings. "How does it feel to be the wife of a famous man? How does it feel to be married to the most famous star in the world? Is it true you got your start at the Ivar Theater? "It's something I did when I was starting out: I'm not ashamed of it, and I'll always be grateful for my days at the Ivar Theater..."

(MELODY, trying to appear humble despite the overwhelming feeling of being chosen, meets ROLLY, projecting some concocted version of manners and sophistication. They go off together.)

SCENE TWENTY-TWO

(*At a motel room.*)

ROLLY. Can I drive you back to the theater?

MELODY. No, I'll walk, thanks.

ROLLY. It's no trouble.

MELODY. It's better if you don't. We're not supposed to go out with the guys from the audience.

ROLLY. And you believe that? Sheesh, I been with just about every one I wanted that I had time for.

MELODY. Oh?

ROLLY. Hey, don't play modest. You had lotsa guys up there I bet you that.

MELODY. Well, some.

ROLLY. Some, hell. You fuck like a piece o' machinery, you're good. You had lotsa guys up there. What are you gettin' so bashful about?

MELODY. Nothing. It's just was... doing this with you. It's different all the time.

ROLLY. "All the time" she says, I was right. Different, I doubt it. Tits are a different color or a different shapes, some move less than others, but the event's all: BANG! haha, you know? BANG!!!

MELODY. (*Trying to move on to another subject.*) I appreciate the boa. I was starting a bird costume, but I want to change it now. I got some nice jewels and things, rubies and diamonds and a rhinestone pin? They're not real rubies: they're fake.

ROLLY. No shit.

MELODY. I'll beat Letanya now with this stuff.

ROLLY. Well that's just great Melody, but don't knock yourself out. The show doesn't really start till that crap hits the floor, you know what I mean? BOING!!!

MELODY. God you're an idiot.

ROLLY. Aw hell, I'm just stating the facts. You dance, you get naked, you turn guys on. There's nothing more to it than that.

MELODY. I don't know what world you live in.

ROLLY. This one: there's two people in the world: Men and Women, and— (*He sees she's hurt, and just lets it drop.*) Here, you said you had a late show, why don't you go and try it out. Don't wait to be beautiful, it'll look good now. Lemme give you my card, I wrote in the hotel number. I'm here for a couple more days.

(*MELODY looks at it, is greatly conflicted.*)

ROLLY. Cab fare. Since I can't drive you.
MELODY. This is two hundred dollars.
ROLLY. To help with your costume. What, don't you need it?
MELODY. (*Bewildered, she needs it but doesn't want to take it.*) This isn't— I'm an entertainer.
ROLLY. I'll say!
MELODY. Hey: I starred in that show a couple weeks ago, you realize that?? I'm an entertainer, not a prostitute! None of us are, I don't want any "help." You can't help me, keep your lousy boa! I'll make my own way, and my own costumes, and— and I am taking the boa!
ROLLY. Jeeps, girlie—!

(*She stuffs the boa in her bag and stamps out. She's still holding on to his card: on the street, she tears it up and throws it. End of scene.*)

SCENE TWENTY-THREE

(*Back at the Theater [continuous].*

In the dressing room: FAWN, LETANYA.)

FAWN. You know what? Too many people know who I am, I'm going to change my name.
LETANYA. Just don't change it to mine.
FAWN. Something more exotic. Something taller. "Duchess." Sound good?
LETANYA. I had a dog named Duchess.

FAWN. Katrina. Maybe I'm German.

LETANYA. That was that T-S in here last month, what're you thinking.

FAWN. Fawn is tired, I didn't like the ballet. I think, I'm a showgirl this time, from Paris. The Follies what's-it-called. Extraordinaire.

LETANYA. Bergere.

FAWN. (*Exaggerated accent.*) "Follies Bergere". I am from Paree! and my name is Gigi.

LETANYA. Well that's settled. OK, that's it for me tonight—

(*MELODY returns to the dressing room.*)

LETANYA. Why are you here?

MELODY. I said I'd be back. Just sooner than I thought.

LETANYA. So how was your date with Candyman?

MELODY. Well, you probably know— Like Fawn said before, I mean—

FAWN. Fawn is dead, she no longer exeeest. She re-incarnate as the famous showgirl, Gigi, with no knowledge of her past.

LETANYA. So how was Candyman? Go swimming like you thought? Had dinner yet?

MELODY. How dead is Fawn?

FAWN. (*Not French.*) She died in a fire.

MELODY. I had a wonderful time. Dinner at Musso and Franks, very expensive. He offered me more, but I refused.

FAWN. Is this beautiful boa a gift from your lover? Can I wear it in my show?

MELODY. No, it's mine.

(*MELODY buzzes the light booth.*)

MELODY. Why's it so busy tonight?

FAWN. Full moon.

LETANYA. Tour bus I think.

MELODY. They bring a tour bus here?

LETANYA. Foreigners. They don't have titties in Japan.

FAWN. Candyman gave me a box of dildos once.

MELODY. A box?

LETANYA. I got gloves.

FAWN. An assortment, you know, different sizes, do different things, batteries... One had a crank on it so it would do a hula in your pussy.

MELODY. Hey, what happened to Gigi?

FAWN. Being French is too much work.

MELODY. Kenny? Melody.

KENNY. What do you want, I thought you were gone for the night. I saw you leave with the Candyman.

MELODY. (*Hushed.*) Was it that obvious? Was Stan around?

KENNY. Nah, nah. No problem.

MELODY. Are you mad at me or anything?

KENNY. No: I saw you leave, you missed your show and I gave away your last one.

MELODY. What if Stan says? Is he here?

KENNY. I don't know. Tell Fawn to go downstairs. (*Hangs up.*)

FAWN. Hey Melody, the boa is really neat. Can I wear it for my show?

MELODY. No. You're on.

FAWN. I'll give you four dollars if you let me.

MELODY. You're not even dressed, you gotta get downstairs now!

FAWN. I'm ready: this is it.

MELODY. Then whaddya wanna look good for?

FAWN. It's pretty! Seven bucks for the show, here, I'll give it to you now. Everyone's making tons o' tips tonight.

MELODY. Don't ruin it.

FAWN. I'll look like I'm floating on a cloud!

(*Phone buzzes.*)

KENNY. She's on!

FAWN. I'm going!

KENNY. Bonnie Lee, ladies and gentlemen, Bonnie Lee. Bonnie will be back later tonight if you're staying with us, as well as more than twenty-five of the most beautiful girls in Hollywood, here on the Ivar stage. Next up is Fawn. Let's have a round of applause for Fawn, ladies, and gentlemen: Fawn... (*Intercom buzzes, just a beat, then.*) Gigi.

(Music starts up and FAWN, giggly and delighted to be wrapped in the boa, has all the elegance of a six year old boy with a plastic snake: She goofs with it, wags it around stupidly, the idea that she could be "classy" or "elegant" is a joke to her. During her set she even forgets about it occasionally, kicking it around or losing it while she does floor work in her panties.)

KENNY. After I closed up that night, I went out front. I looked around a bit, but I didn't see her. Things were pretty cool for a couple weeks, and I avoided going home.

(He goes outside the theater and waits. A MAN [DAVE] and KENNY see each other. KENNY takes a few steps. The MAN walks past him, both his comment and KENNY's response are muttered as if they might not really have said what they said: similar to how drug dealers communicate what they're selling.)

DAVE. Want to make a hundred dollars?
KENNY. Fuck off.

(The cruising dance begins: the continued walk, the backward glance, the not seeing, the change in direction and the "accidental" meeting.)

DAVE. You a cop?
KENNY. Don't waste my time, what do you want.
DAVE. Fool around?
KENNY. Could.
DAVE. Car's this way, just over to the Roosevelt.

(They trail off not quite together, KENNY kind of following.)

SCENE TWENTY-FOUR

(*Outside the theater.*)

MELODY. Hey, Rex.

REX. Uh? Wha?

MELODY. You're leaving early?

REX. Sometimes I do, sometimes I do. But don't worry, I'll be here in the morning. You done for the night?

MELODY. Yeah! Feel like doing anything?

REX. You should have asked me that a few minutes ago. I'm just going to go on home.

MELODY. Which way is that?

REX. Well! You're asking some pretty personal questions!

MELODY. We see each other all the time.

REX. That's true, least I've seen plenty of you!

MELODY. Be nice.

REX. I'm just over at the Mark Twain on Wilcox.

MELODY. I'll walk you there. I've been staying at a friend's place, but I might go back to the Hastings. Can't make up my mind where I'd like to be best.

REX. Don't know the Hastings.

MELODY. Just up on the Boulevard.

REX. Oh yeah, seen it across from the Frolic Room. Well, I'm here. Guess we should say good night.

MELODY. Don'tcha want to ask me in?

REX. You kiddin' me?

MELODY. You could give me the pictures!

REX. Oh sure. Pictures.

(*They arrive at REX's room at the Mark Twain hotel.*)

REX. s'this about like yours? Nice here, I like it. Been here 55 years. Not me, the hotel. I been here 23 years. I was still with the studios then.

MELODY. Like television?

REX. Film. First I was a developer, went into editing, you know: cutting out whatever I didn't like, make the clips look exciting.

MELODY. For real movies?!

REX. Nah, newsreels, n' stuff. Crap work, was a good job to start in. I did what I did. I'm still here. Not always this room though, this room eight. I don't need so much space any more, good savings week to week. What do you pay at the Hastings?

MELODY. Sometimes it varies. I wouldn't mind living in this place, this is a nice room. What do they charge?

REX. There's not too much turnover here, mostly long-term residents. Stable. Want to sit down? C'mere. Sit down with me.

MELODY. Isn't there a chair?

REX. If you want to move all those newspapers. Too much for my back, I won't hurt you.

(*MELODY sits.*)

REX. Every couple days I take a few down, but every day I bring back another one. Makes kind of an active history of my days here. I bet some of those paper's are collectors' items. Got all the Strangler articles from the Examiner in that stack.

MELODY. Can we open a window or something?

REX. Naw. Paint. Same problem with the toilet in the hall, you gotta use a hook.

MELODY. My place was like that, Bonnie Lee gave me incense, you ever try it? That could make it nice in here. I could.

REX. Eh. Smoke. Bad for pictures, turns the walls brown.

MELODY. It's fun though, to try something different. Where I am now, you know, sometimes you like a person but, the guy I'm with —

REX. Kenny? I know what he is, I don't know what he's doing with you.

MELODY. He's nice.

REX. Where's he got you?

MELODY. Just down on Melrose, near Fairfax.

REX. That's a long walk.

MELODY. There's a bus comes right here.

REX. Nice to see a star out of the spotlight and up close. Dream of my life to have you here Melody. You look different in here. In my bed.

MELODY. I'm not in really in your bed, I'm just sitting here. How about if you get me those pictures?

REX. You could stay here if you want. We could look at pictures all night.

MELODY. You got that many?

REX. I usually fold out the couch, but I could leave it up, there'd be floor space and I got a clean blanket. I'd take the floor of course.

MELODY. Aren't you sweet. Let's just start with my pictures.

(REX goes for them but hands her a different photo instead.)

REX. Oh. Here's me. What I used to look like.

MELODY. *(Impressed.)* Wow. *(Looks at him in the present-day, her face screws up.)*

REX. "What happened," right? Happens to everyone. When I worked at the studio every little secretary and want-to-be'd follow me to any burger stand I went. That's what life does to you. Hasn't done anything to you yet, thank goodness.

MELODY. Who are these people, does no one at the theater have a face?

REX. That's how it looks from where I sit.

MELODY. Which one is me? Which ones in the pile are me?

(The pictures are starting to cover the bed.)

REX. Now settle down, you'll mess them all up. *(Hands her a separate envelope.)* Here's you.

MELODY. *(Looks at a couple.)* These are awful.

REX. I said I was an editor, not a photographer.

MELODY. Couple legs or tits, you have any objection to my whole body?

REX. None at all. Here's nice one o' you: a moment of glory. Nice, huh?

MELODY. *(Puzzled.)* I don't look like that.

REX. Evidence says you do.

MELODY. I look like some kind of goblin. What was I doing, I must have been making a turn or something...

REX. You see why I don't care for it either.

MELODY. When I perform I'm like... *(Puzzled, she strikes the pose.)* doing beautiful things. I do beautiful things, and magic.

(*Puzzled, she again strikes the pose, and REX, holding the photo, REX melts into her pose. They the create a beautiful embrace.*)

REX. You look much better up close.

(*They initiate an honestly affectionate session.*)

MELODY. Out of all those people and pieces...

(*Soon he lays her back on the bed before the mounting. As he does so, she begins thrashing, spilling envelopes and knocking over boxes of pictures.*)

REX. What the hell is wrong with you, you here to play or not?
MELODY. Play???

(*She kicks or swipes at the photos.*)

REX. You're a loony bird, that's what you are, stop tearing up my home!
MELODY. Here: Here's your home: (*Knocks a pile on the floor and mixes them up.*)
REX. You crazy bitch, you're fucking them all up, now I won't know who I'm looking at!
MELODY. Maybe it would help if anyone had a head or a face!
REX. Crazy fukkin nut, think you're too good.
MELODY. Now this is my time, I was the star, you want what I got.
REX. Tits n butts n cunts, that's what I want, now I got one with a mouth on it! What, are you some jungle bing-bong thinks taking your picture you lose part of your soul?
MELODY. Don't give me soul-shit, I could twist my soul inside out and you wouldn't know what you're looking at.
REX. (*Simultaneous with MELODY's next lines.*) I DON'T NEED TO KNOW WHAT I'M LOOKING AT, WHAT GOES ON IN MY HOME AND IN MY HEAD IS NONE OF YOUR GODDAM BUSINESS. YOU WILL BE WHATEVER I WANT YOU TO BE, BUT ONCE YOU OPEN YOUR MOUTH YOU RUIN EVERYTHING. ALL I WANT IS TO LOVE YOU DAMMIT, NOT THAT I WOULD ACTUALLY

BE SEEN WITH ANYONE LIKE YOU, YOU BITCH YOU
SLUT YOU WHORE! YOU DON'T DESERVE ANYONE
BEING NICE TO YOU, YOU DON'T BELONG HERE! YOU
DON'T BELONG HERE!

MELODY. (*Simultaneous with REX's lines.*) WHAT AM I
SUPPOSED TO BE? WHAT DO I HAVE LEFT? THIS IS IT
YOU BASTARD, I'M STANDING RIGHT HERE AND YOU
JUST CAN'T SEE IT. YOUR IMAGINATION IS DEAD,
YOUR EYES ARE DEAD, YOU TURN EVERYTHING I
COULD EVER BE INTO PICTURES! AND I'M RIGHT
HERE! I AM WHAT YOU WANT AND I AM WHAT YOU
WILL NEVER HAVE, YOU OR ANYONE ELSE, YOU
SCUM, YOU DIRTBAG, FUCKER FUCKER FUCKER! I'M
RIGHT HERE! I'M RIGHT HERE, I'M RIGHT HERE!!!

(*REX leaves the scene. MELODY in the pile of photographs.*)

KENNY. Man or woman. One looks at the other. What is it. Any
combination of either. One looks at the other and wonders what
it is. A crowded street or my apartment hall, sometimes one
comes into focus for a while, and gets replaced by another.
There's just too many to hold on to.

SCENE TWENTY-FIVE

(*At the theater, one after the other down the runway is LETANYA,
BONNIE LEE and FAWN, each returning to the dressing room.*)

KENNY. Like I said a while back, I've seen hundreds of girls
come and go while I've been here. I don't think all girls are the
same: they just start looking that way. What was different about
Melody? She never left. I quit the place eventually, I mean, the
excitement wears off after a while. One night though I met this
guy, we were talkin and laughin and so I brought him in, just for
a joke. Even being gone just a few weeks, familiar as I was with
it, the place looked wrong. Unfortunates dancing for seniors and
dishwashers. This girl came out, never seen her, Rochelle, I
think her name was, stuck a book of matches in a notch on the

runway, lit it, pulls her knees back and— Not exactly a "blow out your candles Laura" moment. The guy I brought in left. I guess everyone didn't find it as funny as I did at the time. And then, who's next out on stage, but Melody.

(MELODY begins her walk down the runway. None of her earlier joy is apparent, she's as plain as anyone else had been.)

KENNY. A flicker of a person. A vision to shuttle through my mind for the next thirty years.

MELODY. My new room at the hotel is bigger, and I painted one wall orange. I got this neat candleholder from a shop on the boulevard, and some artificial flowers: they're pretty, and they'll stay that way. Bonnie Lee's always goin' on about reincarnation. I know all about it, I been dying from the inside out all my life. That feeling's gone away, lately. If a person really does go on from one lifetime to the next, then this has to be one of them: This one's mine. Another spec of dust has landed on the runway.

REX. Huh, she's not so much. Now that girl Fawn... heh heh baby. Pretty little butt, pretty little tits, oh yeah. That's something to look forward to...

(Still performing, MELODY takes her collection of snapshots, and lays them out on the runway, assembling them like a puzzle. Don't mistake this to mean she has all the pictures and everything turns out fine: she's just tenderly doing what she can to put the pieces together.)

MELODY. An hour from now I'll be alone, asleep, and I will know absolutely nothing. Magical. Sleep. But for now: I'm the one they wish they could have. All around me. Every once in a while, I look up, and they all disappear. I'm probably the only one who can see the dust sparkle in the light. I like that.

(MELODY continues what she's doing, while every woman present on stage, whatever they are doing, "expands" their position, transforming into a moment of beauty.)

KENNY. I know how it really was, but all the same. I always remember it as something beautiful.

(*The scene retracts to what it was, and KENNY signals to turn the spotlight out.*)

END OF PLAY

The Advent and Art of the One–Line Play

By Ross MacLean

Each time the federal budget gets examined, budget for art and culture falls under attack. For ongoing decades we've had to mourn the loss of funding to the arts. At this time, rather than outcry, perhaps we should take time to re–evaluate the art of Theatre and its place in today's culture, and move toward meeting the needs of its present audience. History easily shows a shrinkage of the drama, from the full–day Greek and Roman tragedies, through the five and six act plays of Shakespeare and Moliere, to the common two and one–act plays of today. In explanation: civilization has been in place for several thousand years, we already know much about life. One need not or cannot spend much time focused on any one subject. In recent years, the newer, more efficient 10–minute play has gained popularity among small theater companies. Extremely short, they are valuable for the excitement of seeing an adept writer rapidly make a point (or in negative cases, valuable for the relief of knowing that dullness will not last long.) Still, our familiarity with existence makes us demand shorter, faster work. I suggest, rather than enduring a slow and painful shrinkage of art, theater professionals rocket forward to the newest form which an audience will appreciate: The One–Line Play.

One line plays have their roots in the old Vaudeville tradition of the Posing Act, a series of staged tableaux commonly built around beautiful women in romanticized settings. For example, the pose "Justice" might show a blindfolded woman in a flowing gown, bearing balanced scales and both breasts. Similar tableaux carried titles such as "Virtue" "Liberty" or "The Shame of Eve."

Another incarnation of the One–Line play is the advertising slogan. In a slogan, one phrase forges a powerful link between a product and the mind of the buyer. Some classics have been: "If I've only one life, let me live it as a blonde!" and "Just Do It." Politicians also make use of slogans, which we could consider as one line plays. Indeed, the country is traditionally run by the one who gives the most convincing performance of the line "I will cut taxes!". Combine the splendor of the posing act with the brevity of the advertising world, and we witness the most modern theatrical form in all its wonder and glory.

A good one–line play delivers considerable impact. In a one–line play, the subjects and pronouns are the cast of characters. The verb indicates all dramatic action, before and after the play itself occurs:

How My Marriage Ended
By Taylor Godfried

(*A man in suit pants, loosened tie and shirt tails out, is shoved onto second–floor landing. Door slam. He races down stairs to street.*)

DOMINIC. She hates me!

(*An electric iron is thrown from the apartment. Door slam.*)

Curtain.

~~~~~~

One line plays are generally all- encompassing, declarative statements, such as "The operation was a success!" [from "Out Damn Spot", Henny Kaplan] or "You are free!" [Ketcham's "The Civil War".] One–line plays almost never contain simultaneous statement and action (exceptions, for example, are M. Brightman's excellent murder mystery, "Ill–Bread Manor", where hero halts crime in progress with the shout "So you *are* the butler!", and Keltorn's chilling "Guignol", whose mad knifer finishes both play and victim, crying, "Take *that*, and *that* and *that*!")

One line plays compress a person and situation into their purest essence. The playwright must exercise great care in selecting the words to convey his story. When we see a swimmer sink into a whirlpool, "Help, help!" is all we need to hear; the tragedy is full-told; in another example, that same swimmer would need only say "Goodbye, cruel world!" and *presto*: a complete comedy. And here I will caution eager novices: do not make the mistake of thinking any speakable line will make an exciting night in the theatre. Painful flops in recent years were "Grandmother's Sewing Box" at The Women's Project ("Where is that darned yellow thread?"), and Pegasus Theater Company's offensive production of a work entitled "Full Pants", whose obscene one line I will not quote here.

However, like longer works, a one-line play can be improved with the proper help and nurturing of an experienced dramatist. For example, let's take a look at a work by one young lady which, with my guidance, became a stirring event.

Show and Tell
By Cindy Evans

SALLY. Here are my cats and their kittens!

The End.

~~~~~~

This is a very bad one-line play. There are no interesting characters, there is no action, and it is void of conflict. And I can never emphasize enough, do not depend on sets or costumes to vivify your script. Example: Curtain raises on the Mayflower. Goodey Newton, happy brown-haired daughter of Prior Walter, skips along the deck in black skirt, white cap, apron and buckled clogs. She points beneath a tarpaulin and exclaims: "****". Obviously, no production values will enhance this story, even if it were set in outer space *[Curtain rises on flying saucer, etc., young Martian flies across room, etc, points, says, here's kittens, etc.]*. The key, then, is to focus on structure, character, those elements which create *drama*. What does the author want to say, what does the playwright want to impart to the audience? An intense interview with our young scribe revealed the wish to illustrate her delight in the simplicity of life. I advised her that while life may be happy, there may also be rough patches along the way (Conflict = Action = Drama). With my help, Cindy rewrote this little play, better demonstrating life's delights and complexities:

My Favorite Pets
By Cindy Evans (with the aid of Ross MacLean)

(*Curtain rises on a suburban garage with car parked in the driveway. Little Sally, in pink skirt, skips on stage, jumping rope. She notices a single paw extending from beneath one of the tires. She stops, looks under the car, and exclaims in horror:*)

SALLY. Here are my cats, and their kittens!

Curtain.

~~~~~~~

The premiere production was a huge success, due in part to the stunning set by Jonathan Wagner, which featured a turntable stage and remote–controlled garage door. Lest any should accuse me of self–contradiction regarding the value of attractive sets: with no loss of impact, in the touring production, the car and garage were scaled down to simply a bucket of water.

I hope this essay points the way for theater artists who may be feeling despair. As the One-Line Play comes into its own, it is a happy guarantee that producers will be able to mount affordable seasons that will satisfy the national passion for theater. The minimized risk and high reward will give birth to a multitude of playwrights both traditional and controversial, and a huge population of working actors, however briefly employed. And if we keep our sights geared ever toward the future, perhaps our society will spawn another Aeschylus, another Euripides, another great soul who may lead us on to new vistas. Perhaps, if our culture can absorb it: maybe the two–line play?

ABOUT THE PLAYWRIGHT

The playwright, circa 1978...
(Photo credit: Paul C. Babin)

... and today.
(Photo credit: Lester Blum)

Ross MacLean was first produced at La Mama Hollywood, the West Coast branch of the New York company. He was the house playwright at Smitty's Deja Vu Coffeehouse in Hollywood for five years, and a member of Los Angeles Actor's Theater's Playwrights Unit. Regionally his plays have been produced at Denver's Changing Scene and at the Actor's Theater of Louisville. In New York he's worked with Theater for the New City, Ensemble Studio Theater, the 4th E Company, and Manhattan Theater Club. He lives in New York City.

ALSO AVAILABLE

B-MOVIE NIGHT:

EIGHT PLAYS OF PURE EXPLOITATION!

LARVA! by Sean Abley

BIRDS IN A CAGE by Kelly Goodman

COLD WAR by Greg Machlin

WORSTEST MOVIE EVER by Nathan Wellman

RAISE YOUR HAND... FROM THE DEAD! by Natalie Nicole Dressel

HOW TO BE ATTRACTIVE by Amy Seeley

SLAVES OF THE BEAN by Adam Hahn

LADY KILLERS by Megan Gogerty

SkyPilot Theatre Company in Los Angeles asked their Playwright's Wing to create a series of B-movie plays to be presented live on stage for a benefit performance. The result: Nuclear maggots, women in prison, murderous snowmen, disembodied body parts, and more filled the stage for their wildly popular "Night of the Living Fundraiser." And now Plays to Order is proud to present this collection of cinematic stageplays, ripe for exploitation by your own theater company, preferably on some dark and stormy night...

PLAYS TO ORDER

www.playstoorder.com

ALSO AVAILABLE